BETWEEN FORBEARANCE AND AUDACITY

When international courts are given sweeping powers, why would they ever refuse to use them? The book explains how and when courts employ strategies for institutional survival and resilience: forbearance and audacity, which help them adjust their sovereignty costs to pre-empt and mitigate backlash and political pushback. By systematically analysing almost 2,300 judgements from the European Court of Human Rights from 1967 to 2016, Ezgi Yildiz traces how these strategies shaped the norm against torture and inhumane or degrading treatment. With expert interviews and a nuanced combination of social science and legal methods, Yildiz innovatively demonstrates what the norm entails and when and how its contents changed over time. Exploring issues central to public international law and international relations, this interdisciplinary study makes a timely intervention in the debate on international courts, international norms, and legal change. This book is available as Open Access on Cambridge Core.

EZGI YILDIZ is an Assistant Professor at California State University, Long Beach, and a Research Associate at the Geneva Graduate Institute. She is a member of the Expert Group for the EU's Anti-Torture Regulation (2019/125) and the Coordinating Committee of ESIL's Interest Group on Social Sciences and International Law.

ENDORSEMENTS

"*Between Forbearance and Audacity* meticulously explains how and why the European Court of Human Rights has expanded the prohibition on torture from a narrow negative interpretation that bans government agents from using torture during interrogations to a broader understanding that includes positive government obligations to prevent torture and protect victims in multiple contexts, such as domestic abuse and medical settings. However, the Court has not always followed an expansive approach. Using in-depth interviews and a systematic content analysis, Yildiz demonstrates that pushback from Western European governments has at times curtailed the Court, such as on cases involving refugees. Deeply rooted in both law and political science, this is a masterful book that should be of interest to those interested in human rights, international courts, and the development of international legal norms."

Erik Voeten, Peter F. Krogh Professor of Geopolitics and Justice in World Affairs, Edmund E. Walsh School of Foreign Service and Government Department, Georgetown University

"Ezgi Yildiz's carefully researched book is the crucial text on changing norms against torture and inhumane and degrading treatment. But it also offers the most impressive evidence to date of how human rights can evolve through the audacious interpretations of a court."

Kathryn Sikkink, Ryan Family Professor, Kennedy School of Government, Harvard University

"*Between Forbearance and Audacity* tells the story of how the European Court of Human Rights has developed the norm against torture over the past five decades. It shows how courts are always situated in history and that the development of the law necessarily has to be tailored to the constraints that courts face at given moments of time. This is neither an optimistic nor pessimistic account of the European Court of Human Rights; it is a realistic account that considers all the complexity of making torture illegal in Europe."

Mikael Rask Madsen, Professor and Director of iCourts, Faculty of Law, University of Copenhagen

"*Between Forbearance and Audacity* is an insightful and ambitious analysis of how the European Court of Human Rights has transformed the norm against torture and renegotiated its own position in the process. This book brings together rich empirical analyses and a novel conceptual framework to advance the current thinking about how human rights courts work and how they respond to pressure from member states and beyond. This is a must-read for anyone interested in understanding how international human rights courts shape, and are shaped by, evolving human rights norms."

Courtney Hillebrecht, Hitchcock Family Chair in Human Rights and Humanitarian Affairs and Professor of Political Science, University of Nebraska-Lincoln

"In *Between Forbearance and Audacity*, Ezgi Yildiz chronicles and explains an international legal revolution, in which the European Court of Human Rights expanded the meaning of torture and the responsibility of states to prevent it. Drawing on a range of quantitative, qualitative, and interpretive methods, Yildiz provides the definitive account of the transformation of the law against torture in Europe. Essential reading for political scientists, lawyers, and anyone who wants to understand the conditions for the protection of human rights around the world."

Mark Pollack, Jean Monnet Chair and Professor of Political Science and Law, Temple University

STUDIES ON INTERNATIONAL COURTS AND TRIBUNALS

General Editors
Andreas Føllesdal, University of Oslo
Geir Ulfstein, University of Oslo

Studies on International Courts and Tribunals contains theoretical and interdisciplinary scholarship on legal aspects as well as the legitimacy and effectiveness of international courts and tribunals.

Other books in the series

Mads Andenas and Eirik Bjorge (eds.) *A Farewell to Fragmentation: Reassertion and Convergence in International Law*

Cecilia M. Bailliet and Nobuo Hayashi (eds.) *The Legitimacy of International Criminal Tribunals*

Amrei Müller with Hege Elisabeth Kjos (eds.) *Judicial Dialogue and Human Rights*

Nienke Grossman, Harlan Grant Cohen, Andreas Follesdal and Geir Ulfstein (eds.) *Legitimacy and International Courts*

Theresa Squatrito, Oran R. Young, Andreas Føllesdal, Geir Ulfstein (eds.) *The Performance of International Courts and Tribunals*

Robert Howse, Hélène Ruiz-Fabri, Geir Ulfstein and Michelle Q. Zang (eds.) *The Legitimacy of International Trade Courts and Tribunals*

Marlene Wind (ed.) *International Courts and Domestic Politics*

Christina Voigt (ed.) *International Judicial Practice on the Environment: Questions of Legitimacy*

Martin Scheinin (ed.) *Human Rights Norms in 'Other' International Courts*

Freya Baetens (ed.) *Legitimacy of Unseen Actors in International Adjudication*

Shai Dothan *International Judicial Review: When Should International Courts Intervene?*

Silje Langvatn, Mattias Kumm, Wojciech Sadurski (eds.) *Public Reason and Courts*

Daniel Behn, Szilárd Gáspár-Szilágyi, Malcolm Langford (eds.) *Adjudicating Trade and Investment Disputes: Convergence or Divergence?*

Sondre Torp Helmersen *The Application of Teachings by the International Court of Justice*

Daniel Behn, Ole Kristian Fauchald, Malcolm Langford (eds.) *The Legitimacy of Investment Arbitration: Empirical Perspectives*

Eric De Brabandere *International Procedure in Interstate Litigation and Arbitration: A Comparative Approach*

Chiara Giorgetti and Mark Pollack (eds.) *Beyond Fragmentation: Cross-Fertilization, Cooperation and Competition among International Courts and Tribunals*

Stavros Brekoulakis and Georgios Dimitropoulos (eds.) *International Commercial Courts: The Future of Transnational Adjudication*

Mark Gillett *Prosecuting Environmental Harm before the International Criminal Court*

Sassan Gholiagha *The Humanization of Global Politics: International Criminal Law, the Responsibility to Protect, and Drones*

BETWEEN FORBEARANCE AND AUDACITY

The European Court of Human Rights and the Norm against Torture

EZGI YILDIZ
California State University, Long Beach

CAMBRIDGE
UNIVERSITY PRESS

CAMBRIDGE
UNIVERSITY PRESS

Shaftesbury Road, Cambridge CB2 8EA, United Kingdom

One Liberty Plaza, 20th Floor, New York, NY 10006, USA

477 Williamstown Road, Port Melbourne, VIC 3207, Australia

314–321, 3rd Floor, Plot 3, Splendor Forum, Jasola District Centre, New Delhi – 110025, India

103 Penang Road, #05–06/07, Visioncrest Commercial, Singapore 238467

Cambridge University Press is part of Cambridge University Press & Assessment, a department of the University of Cambridge.

We share the University's mission to contribute to society through the pursuit of education, learning and research at the highest international levels of excellence.

www.cambridge.org
Information on this title: www.cambridge.org/9781009100045

DOI: 10.1017/9781009103862

When citing this work, please include a reference to the DOI 10.1017/9781009103862

First published 2024

A catalogue record for this publication is available from the British Library

A Cataloging-in-Publication data record for this book is available from the Library of Congress

ISBN 978-1-009-10004-5 Hardback

Additional resources for this publication at www.cambridge.org/9781009100045

To my grandparents,
Naciye and Ali Dede Yıldız

CONTENTS

An online annex for this publication is available at www.cambridge.org/9781009100045

FIGURES

TABLES

FOREWORD

The European Convention of Human Rights is a short document, and its text is often vague and somewhat open-ended. But today, it is widely seen as a quasi-constitutional instrument for Europe, with precise prescriptions on issues ranging from voting rights to environmental protection, the treatment of refugees, and the status of transsexuals. When the Convention was drawn up in 1950, few observers could have imagined (or did, in fact, foresee) that the Convention could gain such breadth and depth, nor that it would exert the influence it has today on national courts and legislatures of the 46 states that form the Council of Europe today.

How did this transformation happen? For a long time, neither international lawyers nor international relations scholars had convincing answers to this question – legal scholars were less interested in the political dynamics behind legal change than in the interpretation of the law itself, and students of international politics found law and courts not sufficiently relevant to their pursuits. This has changed over the past twenty years, with much more engagement at the boundary of the two disciplines and a significantly deeper understanding of many of the processes around international law, especially around international courts.

Ezgi Yildiz's book takes this line of research into a new and fresh direction, and she advances a bold account of how the European Court of Human Rights – the "Strasbourg Court" – has reshaped the European Convention over time, how it has expanded its requirements to cover many of the most controversial issues in European politics. It does so especially by focusing on the way in which judges approach the cases before them – with audacity or forbearance – and on the changes in this approach over time. The book takes us through more than a half-century of development, structured through three crucial phases, punctuated by the creation of the Court, the radical shift to a permanent Court in the late 1990s, and the rise of fundamental contestation of the Court by several important member states around 2010.

Dr. Yildiz's interest is in understanding how the strategies of judges have changed through these phases and how we can account for those changes. She does so by focusing on a particular – and particularly important – set of cases, those around Article 3 of the European Convention on Human Rights, the prohibition on torture. This prohibition has given rise to a significant reinterpretation over time through which the Court has developed a range of different aspects related to torture, including positive obligations to protect persons from threats. Focusing on this set of cases allows Yildiz to not only take into view an important subset of the jurisprudence, but also to inquire into them with significant attention to detail and granularity. As a result, she manages to achieve what few scholars of either international law or relations have achieved, namely, to marry a deep understanding of the substance and arguments of the cases with a bird's eye view, underpinned by statistical analysis, of trends in these cases over time.

This allows her to trace, with substantial evidence, the major shift in jurisprudential approach that occurred with the turn to a permanent Court from the late 1990s onward. Two main factors can help us account for the more expansive, "audacious" stance of the new Court, she claims: a wide discretionary space created by the new institutional underpinning, and a (relative) absence of negative feedback from states at the time. This set judges free to establish broader obligations for states in a way the more "forbearing" court of the previous period – much more similar to other international courts – could hardly contemplate. On the other hand, Dr. Yildiz shows a more cautious attitude returns after 2010 in response to the backlash from countries such as the UK, Switzerland, but also Russia. This does not lead to "forbearance" across the board, though. Instead, the book shows how selective forbearance operates in that period, with continuity or even expansion on a number of issues, such as police brutality, but a significantly less strict reading of the implications of Article 3 for the refoulement of refugees. The Court seems thus much more responsive to challenges from Western European countries – for whom refugee issues were one of the central bones of contention – than from others.

Dr. Yildiz's account opens up many avenues for further research, with respect to the Strasbourg Court just as well as other international courts and the development of international law in general. It makes us think about the role and positioning of judges in the making of transnational adjudication and about the role of states. For many international lawyers just as well as scholars of international relations, states stand at the center of the field, dictating how it operates and changes. In Yildiz's story, states are important, but over time they move to a background role. Having created and sustained a powerful court for long, they now find it difficult to regain control over it – even if the Court is somewhat responsive to challenges, it continues on its audacious path in many areas despite significant backlash. This points to a broader picture in which states remain in secondary roles while change is propelled on paths no longer controlled by them – an issue Dr. Yildiz and I have worked on for several years as part of our PATHS project. This picture varies, of course, across issue areas and institutional contexts, but it signals a significant reorientation and flexibilisation of the international legal order well beyond the realm of courts.

The European Court of Human Rights sits on one end of the spectrum of this order, and Dr. Yildiz's book presents us with a strong account of how it came to occupy and fill the central role it has now. With its focus on judicial strategies, it also reminds us that the story of the Court's transformation is not only one of the external conditions and formal institutional development, but that it is, to a significant extent, the result of choices made by individuals (and by judges as a collective). This is important well beyond the realm of specialists in European human rights law. It is a reminder that, and how, individual agency matters in international politics – and that there is often a choice between audacity and forbearance that can determine the course of international norms and law.

Nico Krisch
The Geneva Graduate Institute,
November 2022

ACKNOWLEDGMENTS

Writing this book was like an archaeological dig, not only through the history of the European Court of Human Rights and its anti-torture jurisprudence but also a dig through my own drafts that took shape over years and years of work. While the initial idea behind this book was my doctoral dissertation that I wrote at the Geneva Graduate Institute, to my chagrin, I ended up writing an entirely new manuscript – one that truly reflected the maturation of my knowledge of the Court and the norm against torture and inhuman or degrading treatment. My analysis and findings were shaped in different sites of research with the support of several co-conspirators. I am particularly indebted to my interviewees, including the judges and the Registry lawyers at the European Court of Human Rights, as well as human rights experts and members of civil society organisations. My understanding of the issue got sharpened in the course of our conversations. I am also grateful for the financial support from the Swiss National Science Foundation (grant agreement no. 149034), which allowed me to spend some time at the Court and undertake these interviews, and complete my dissertation research.

I began thinking about the book and the main argument during my research stay at the iCourts at the University of Copenhagen under the supervision of Mikael Rask Madsen. Later, in 2016, I spent a semester at the Institut für die Wissenschaften vom Menschen (Institute for Human Sciences) (IWM) in Vienna, where I presented an early idea and received excellent feedback from my colleague and friend Aspen Brinton. Then, I moved to the Carr Center for Human Rights at the Harvard Kennedy School, again with the generous support of the Swiss National Science Foundation (grant agreement no. 168282). I had several opportunities to discuss my book with Douglas Johnson, Alberto Mora, and Avery Schmidt in the context of their Costs and Consequences of Torture project and with the Center's directors, Sushma Raman and Matthias Risse. I am particularly indebted to Kathryn Sikkink, who took the time to read and comment on the earlier versions and helped me navigate the book publication process. I also benefited from discussions with other Carr Center fellows, such as Judge Mark Wolf, Leonardo Castilho, and Isabela Garbin Ramanzini, with whom I shared a passion for studying international courts and human rights. While at Harvard, I also spent some time at the Center for European Studies, where I presented my early findings at the Visiting Fellows' seminar. I received feedback and support from my cohort, particularly from Başak Bilecen, Tom Chevalier, Philipp Dybowski, Ivana Isailovic, and Regine Paul.

In 2018, I returned to the Geneva Graduate Institute to take up a postdoctoral researcher position at the Global Governance Center as a member of the Paths of International Law: Stability and Change in International Legal Order, financed by the European Research Council under the European Union's Horizon 2020 research and innovation program (grant agreement no. 740634). My ideas around change processes and how they manifest themselves within the European human rights regime matured in the context of this project and my close collaboration with Nico Krisch. Nico offered invaluable mentorship throughout the publication process. The final draft also benefitted from a book workshop I organised with Mark Pollack, Stephanie Hoffmann, Thomas Biersteker, Nina Reiners, and Erna Burai. Their thoughtful feedback and constructive criticism were crucial for the book and the main argument presented therein.

It certainly took a village to bring this book to completion. Various colleagues from the Global Governance Center, including Velibor Jakovleski, Ueli Staeger, Moritz Neubert, Aurel Niederberger, Farzan Sabet, Monique Beerli, Zuzana Hudakova, Oana Ichim, and Roxana Radu lent me their supportive ears whenever I needed them. I also benefitted from discussing the book and the book publication process with Natasa Mavronicola, Moritz Baumgärtel, Kyle McNabb, Kujtese Bejtullahu, Ioana Tuta, Amalie Thystrup, Ioana Puscas, Franka Bosman, Merih Angin, Emily Wiseman, and Kathryn Chelminski. Finally, I am grateful for the support from my International Law sisters Başak Bağlayan, Anil Yilmaz, Gamze Erdem Türkelli, Aysel Küçüksu, and Başak Etkin, as well as my coach Alma.

Working with a good editor is the key to successfully bringing a book project to completion. I was lucky to have support from great editors. Tom Randall and Marianne Nield carefully guided the review and publication process at Cambridge University Press. I am also grateful to the series editors Andreas Føllesdal and Geir Ulfstein for supporting the publication of my manuscript as part of Cambridge Studies on International Courts and Tribunals. Before working with Tom Randall at Cambridge University Press, I received initial encouragement from Peter Agree at the University of Pennsylvania Press and Mary Murrell, who reviewed and commented on an early version of the manuscript.

There are a few individuals whose constant support was crucial to me. I am thankful to my friend and colleague Umut Yüksel for reading and commenting on multiple chapters and versions of the book and to Farrah Hawana for skillfully editing and proofreading the entire book. She is the best language editor one can hope for. Finally, I am grateful for the emotional support from my dear family, in particular my sister Yağmur Yıldız and my partner Peter Stevens, whose unwavering encouragement was essential in bringing this book to the finish line. Peter has been a true ally, and I am lucky and grateful to have him in my life.

FUNDING STATEMENT

This book is part of The Paths of International Law: Stability and Change in the International Legal Order project that has received funding from the *European Union's Horizon 2020 research and innovation programme* under grant agreement no. 740634.

Funded by the European Union. Views and opinions expressed are however those of the author only and do not necessarily reflect those of the European Union or the European Research Council Executive Agency. Neither the European Union nor the granting authority can be held responsible for them.

erc

European Research Council
Established by the European Commission

ABBREVIATIONS

Abbreviation	Definition
APT	Association for the Prevention of Torture
CAT	Convention against Torture and Other Cruel, Inhuman or Degrading Treatment or Punishment
CEDAW	Convention on the Elimination of All Forms of Discrimination against Women
CIA	Central Intelligence Agency
CPT	European Committee for the Prevention of Torture and Inhuman or Degrading Treatment or Punishment
DHRA	Diyarbakir Human Rights Association
ECHR	European Convention on Human Rights
ECtHR	European Court of Human Rights
EHRAC	European Human Rights Advocacy Centre
ERRC	European Roma Rights Centre
ETA	Basque Country and Freedom
IACtHR	Inter-American Court of Human Rights
IRA	Provisional Irish Republican Army
KHPR	Kurdish Human Rights Project
NGO	Non-governmental Organisation
OHCHR	Office of the High Commissioner for Human Rights
OSJI	Open Society Justice Initiative
PKK	Kurdistan Workers' Party
RAF	Red Army Faction
Romani CRISS	Roma Center for Social Intervention and Studies
UDHR	Universal Declaration of Human Rights
UN	United Nations
VCLT	Vienna Convention on the Law of Treaties

Introduction: The Court Redefines Torture in Europe

Nahide, a mother of three, was born in Diyarbakır in southeast Turkey. Like many women in this region, she had a tragic life. Although violence against women is pervasive throughout Turkey, women in the east and southeast lead particularly difficult lives as many may lack access to education and employment opportunities, health services, and means of redress for injustices suffered.[1] Nahide's case was no different. She started living with Hüseyin Opuz in 1990, and they married five years later.[2] Hüseyin already had a pattern of abuse, but the violence grew worse after their marriage. In April 1995, he savagely beat both Nahide and her mother. They were covered with evidence of their abuse, which was confirmed by a medical report that described them as unfit to work for five days due to their injuries. Brushing aside the pain and the shame of being victims of domestic abuse, the women approached the public prosecutors and filed a complaint against Hüseyin. Afterward, they grew doubtful and withdrew their complaint. The local court discontinued their case due to a lack of evidence and the complaint's withdrawal. No protective measures were taken.

A year later, almost to the day, on April 11, 1996, Hüseyin and Nahide had another fight during which Nahide was again brutally beaten. According to the medical report, she was left with life-threatening injuries to her right eye, right ear, left shoulder, and back. Hüseyin was remanded, but, at a hearing on May 14, 1996, the public prosecutor requested that Hüseyin be released pending trial due to the nature of the offence and Nahide's quick recovery. When Hüseyin was released, Nahide withdrew her complaint, and the case was discontinued.

Almost two years later, on March 4, 1998, Hüseyin rammed into Nahide and her mother with his car, nearly killing Nahide's mother. The following

1 Yakin Ertürk, Report of the Special Rapporteur on Violence against Women, Its Causes and Consequences, Mission to Turkey, *A/HRC/4/34/Add.2* (January 5, 2007), 2.

2 The information provided in this story is taken from a court case: *Opuz* v. *Turkey*, application no. 33401/02, ECHR (June 9, 2009).

day, Hüseyin was taken into custody again. Two weeks later, on March 20, 1998, Nahide initiated divorce proceedings after suffering Hüseyin's abuse for years. Nahide and her mother also filed a petition specifically requesting protective measures from the local authorities. Hüseyin had been threatening to kill them both if Nahide would not return to live with him. Nahide, who had been living with her mother for about a month at the time, had no intention of doing so. The authorities ignored their petition, and the local court decided to drop their case due to lack of evidence. Fearing her husband's death threats, Nahide also dropped the divorce case. She could find neither remedy nor protection in the Turkish justice system. On November 14 of that same year, Nahide reported that Hüseyin threatened to kill her again; once more, her complaint was dismissed due to lack of evidence. Five days later, her mother filed another complaint, warning of death threats that grew more and more terrifying by the day. This complaint was not taken seriously, either, and their pleas for protection were ignored. This cycle of violent attacks, court proceedings, and discontinued cases repeated over the next few years.

In the face of the Turkish government's inaction, Nahide and her mother realised that escaping their fate meant leaving their hometown, their family, and their lifelong friends. What they needed was a fresh start. With this in mind, they planned in secret to move to Izmir on the west coast of Turkey. When Hüseyin found out, he was enraged and once again threatened to kill them. The two women, however, were determined. They picked a morning in early March 2002 to leave Diyarbakır, their home, and everything else behind. Nahide's mother made arrangements with a transport company. She loaded up their few belongings onto a truck with the driver's help and sat beside the truck driver. Had she known that Hüseyin was aware of their plans, would she have chosen to take the bus instead? Would it have made a difference? After all, Hüseyin had pledged that "wherever [they] go, [he] will find and kill [them]!"[3] As they set off on their journey, a taxi pulled in front of the truck and stopped. Hüseyin got out, opened the truck door, and shot Nahide's mother dead.

On March 13, 2002, the Diyarbakır Public Prosecutor filed an indictment accusing Hüseyin of murder. In 2008, Hüseyin was finally convicted of murder and illegal possession of a gun and sentenced to life imprisonment. However, due to Hüseyin's good conduct during the trial, the local criminal trial court reduced his sentence to fifteen years and ten months plus a fine. This decision was based on the conclusion that Hüseyin had

[3] *Opuz* v. *Turkey*, §54.

been provoked by the victim because the crime had been committed in the name of *family honor*. In many regions of the world, these two words are shockingly effective in reducing a sentence or letting the perpetrators of gender-based violence entirely off the hook. They would help Hüseyin, too. Hüseyin was released from prison because the criminal trial court counted the time he spent in pretrial detention and considered the fact that his case was pending appellate review before a higher court. Immediately following his April 2008 release, Hüseyin went right back to pursuing Nahide and issuing death threats. Nahide once again requested protection from the government, but to no avail.

In June 2008, Nahide brought her case before the European Court of Human Rights (the Court). In 2009, the Court found Turkey in violation of the European Convention of Human Rights (the Convention) for not protecting a domestic violence victim. In so doing, the Court broke new ground in European human rights law. It examined Nahide's complaint against the backdrop of "the vulnerable situation of women in south-east Turkey"[4] and the "common values emerging from the practices of European States."[5] The Court referenced relevant legal instruments such as the Convention on the Elimination of Discrimination against Women (CEDAW) and the Belém do Pará Convention (the Inter-American Convention on the Prevention, Punishment, and Eradication of Violence against Women).[6] The former prohibits gender-based discrimination, and the latter sets out specific state obligations to eradicate gender-based violence. Interights, a London-based nongovernmental organization (NGO), had intervened in the proceedings to argue that states are required to be vigilant about domestic violence complaints because women are often too afraid to report abuse to the relevant authorities.[7] The Court further relied on reports provided by leading civil society organizations such as the Diyarbakır Bar Association and Amnesty International, as well as the CEDAW Committee's Concluding Comments on Turkey. Providing a detailed description of the systemic nature of discrimination against women in Turkey and state authorities' passivity toward domestic violence victims, these reports reinforced Nahide's story.[8]

In light of the evidence brought by Nahide and the abovementioned reports, the Court decided that the Turkish government had failed to

[4] Ibid., §160.
[5] Ibid., §164.
[6] Ibid.
[7] Ibid., §157.
[8] Ibid., §192–93.

take protective measures that could have deterred Hüseyin from violating Nahide's personal integrity. It also ruled that the Turkish government bore responsibility for the abuse that Nahide had endured and that it had violated Article 3 (prohibition of torture) of the Convention. Even further, the Court found the Turkish authorities had discriminated against Nahide based on her gender, arguing that "judicial passivity in Turkey, albeit unintentional, mainly affected women."[9] Finally, it identified the episodes of violence against Nahide and her mother specifically as gender-based violence – a form of discrimination against women.[10]

The Court's judgment offered some compensation for the harm done to Nahide, but did not ask for Hüseyin's retrial or re-incarceration. Nonetheless, it became a landmark decision that opened the way for others to bring domestic violence complaints before the Court under Article 3 and inspired the 2014 Istanbul Convention on Violence against Women.[11] When the Court recognised the victimhood of Nahide and others like her, it fundamentally changed the meaning of the prohibition of torture and inhuman or degrading treatment. The decision also strengthened the principle that states may bear responsibility for acts perpetrated by private actors should they fail to protect the victims or punish the perpetrators.[12] The precedent set in this case would come to influence the lives of many domestic violence victims by allowing them to seek justice under this *expanded* meaning of the prohibition.

Indeed, treating domestic violence cases as torture or ill-treatment was not what the founders of the European human rights regime had in mind when they drafted Article 3 in 1950. The foundational premise of the prohibition against torture and inhuman or degrading treatment is to protect individuals against the acts of state authorities, not against family members or private individuals. Built on the conceptual divide between public and private spheres, the norm against torture was crafted as a protective shield against the excesses of state authorities acting in their official

[9] Ibid., §200.

[10] Article 14 (prohibition of discrimination) reads as follows: "The enjoyment of the rights and freedoms set forth in [the] Convention shall be secured without discrimination on any ground such as sex, race, colour, language, religion, political or other opinion, national or social origin, association with a national minority, property, birth or other status." This means that Article 14 can only be invoked in conjunction with other articles in the European Convention.

[11] Selver B. Sahin, "Combatting Violence against Women in Turkey: Structural Obstacles," *Contemporary Politics* (2021): 1–21.

[12] The origins of this obligation in relation to Article 3 go back to earlier case law such as *A. v. the United Kingdom*, application no. 100/1997/884/1096 (September 23, 1998).

capacities. It did not initially mean to cover abuses committed by an individual (in their personal capacity) within the private sphere.

To understand the degree to which the meaning of the prohibition of torture has shifted over time, let us look closely at the original definition under Article 3, which reads: "No one shall be subjected to torture or to inhuman or degrading treatment or punishment." Alastair Mowbray explains that, like most other rights under the Convention, Article 3 is formulated as a *negative obligation*; that is, an obligation to refrain from violating a right.[13] Negative obligations are derived from the classical liberal idea of curbing state interference in people's lives.[14] At its core, the prohibition holds that states must refrain from subjecting their citizens to torture and inhuman or degrading treatment. The Court's ruling in Nahide's case represents a new type of obligation – a *positive obligation* to protect and guarantee the fulfilment of individual rights.[15] States incur such obligations when they possess concrete knowledge of the risk of harm.[16] They are then required to take proactive measures to ensure that individuals facing such risks may enjoy their rights.[17] This may sometimes imply that states have to mobilise their resources to protect vulnerable groups, such as domestic violence victims, minors, or refugees,[18] or offer adequate medical treatment or minimally acceptable conditions to individuals under their control, such as detainees or prisoners.[19] Compared to negative obligations,

[13] Alastair Mowbray, *The Development of Positive Obligations under the European Convention on Human Rights by the European Court of Human Rights* (Oxford and Portland: Hart Publishing, 2004), 5.

[14] Dimitris Xenos, *The Positive Obligations of the State under the European Convention of Human Rights* (London and New York: Routledge, 2012), 2.

[15] For a comprehensive assessment on the relation between positive and negative obligations, see Laurens Lavrysen, *Human Rights in a Positive State: Rethinking the Relationship between Positive and Negative Obligations under the European Convention on Human Rights* (Cambridge, England; Antwerp and Portland: Intersentia, 2016).

[16] Vladislava Stoyanova, "Fault, Knowledge and Risk within the Framework of Positive Obligations under the European Convention on Human Rights," *Leiden Journal of International Law* 33, no. 3 (2020): 603.

[17] Xenos, *The Positive Obligations of the State under the European Convention of Human Rights*, 2.

[18] Moritz Baumgärtel, "Facing the Challenge of Migratory Vulnerability in the European Court of Human Rights," *Netherlands Quarterly of Human Rights* 38, no. 1 (2020): 12–29; Moritz Baumgärtel, *Demanding Rights: Europe's Supranational Courts and the Dilemma of Migrant Vulnerability* (Cambridge University Press, 2019).

[19] For a great overview on how criminal law can be mobilised to fulfill such positive duties see, Laurens Lavrysen and Natasa Mavronicola, *Coercive Human Rights: Positive Duties to Mobilise the Criminal Law under the ECHR* (Oxford and New York: Hart Publishing, 2020).

positive obligations are, therefore, more resource-intensive in nature and have a clear socioeconomic dimension.[20]

It is also interesting to note that such resource-intensive new obligations were not added to the European Convention through an official amendment procedure or by means of an additional protocol. Instead, it was the European Court itself that introduced these new obligations under the prohibition of torture and inhuman or degrading treatment in the 1990s and the early 2000s.[21] In so doing, the Court expanded the definition of what constitutes torture or ill-treatment in that period. This was a *prima facie* judicial innovation with which the Court significantly expanded the scope of individual protections under this prohibition and began prescribing more demanding obligations. It effectively took *thou shalt not torture* and made it *thou shalt prevent torture.*[22]

However, this is not to say that the Court is the protagonist in this story of change. While courts play an important role in processing and pronouncing legal change through their judgments, the origins of such change episodes are the *victims*. Victims are the real protagonists. Nahide's case is a good illustration of how real experiences of suffering and injustice come to be translated into legal language and then distilled as standards in the course of court proceedings. Their stories are where it all begins, and through their complaints, the law is refined to reflect and shape moral progress.[23] The Court's jurisprudence weaves individual experiences and the law together. They are the warp and the weft in the Court's brocade. From them, the Court derives abstract standards for appropriate behaviour.

[20] Natasa Mavronicola, *Torture, Inhumanity and Degradation under Article 3 of the ECHR: Absolute Rights and Absolute Wrongs* (Oxford and New York: Hart Publishing, 2021), 128.

[21] This is not the only example where the Court took the lead by engaging in a judicial innovation. The Court played a similar role in the introduction of the pilot judgment procedure. For more, see Ezgi Yildiz, "Judicial Creativity in the Making: The Pilot Judgment Procedure a Decade after Its Inception," *Interdisciplinary Journal of Human Rights Law* 8 (2015): 81–102.

[22] Although there are also scholars who argue that there is no clear-cut ideational separation between positive and negative obligations, there are differences when it comes to the time of their introduction, the frequency of their use, as well as the Court's reasons for not finding a violation of them, as this book makes it clear. See also, for example, Sandra Fredman FBA, *Human Rights Transformed: Positive Rights and Positive Duties* (Oxford: Oxford University Press, 2008).

[23] Michael Goldhaber provides a brilliant account of how individual stories shape European human rights law. For more, see Michael Goldhaber, *A People's History of the European Court of Human Rights:* (New Brunswick: Rutgers University Press, 2008).

Even if the Court effectuates legal change through its judgments and decisions, the true driving force behind this change is the victims.

Case Selection: Positive Obligations under Article 3 and the European Human Rights System

The emergence of positive obligations under the prohibition of torture and inhuman or degrading treatment within the European human rights system is an ideal case to glean information about the conditions of *progressive legal change* – the main focus of this book. I define progressive change as expanding the range of protections afforded to victims and the correlative obligations states must comply with, and I investigate when we can expect to observe such foundational changes. The introduction of positive obligations is an unequivocal episode of progressive legal change undertaken by a court that is not unequivocally progressive.[24] Rather, it is known to have conservative origins and practices.[25] Unlike other courts and institutions, such as the Inter-American Court of Human Rights or the United Nations (UN) Treaty Bodies, which have more or less consistently followed a progressive line,[26] the European Court's record is mixed.[27] The European Court has not been as progressive compared to

[24] Alexander Orakhelashvili, "Restrictive Interpretation of Human Rights Treaties in the Recent Jurisprudence of the European Court of Human Rights," *European Journal of International Law* 14, no. 3 (2003): 529–68; Ezgi Yildiz, "Enduring Practices in Changing Circumstances: A Comparison of the European Court of Human Rights and the Inter-American Court of Human Rights," *Temple International and Comparative Law Journal* 34, no. 2 (2020): 309–38.

[25] Marco Duranti, *The Conservative Human Rights Revolution: European Identity, Transnational Politics, and the Origins of the European Convention* (Oxford and New York: Oxford University Press, 2017); Orakhelashvili, "Restrictive Interpretation of Human Rights Treaties in the Recent Jurisprudence of the European Court of Human Rights,"529–68; Ezgi Yildiz, "Extraterritoriality Reconsidered: Functional Boundaries as Repositories of Jurisdiction," in *The Extraterritoriality of Law: History, Theory, Politics*, ed. Daniel S. Margolies et al. (Routledge, 2019), 215–27.

[26] A good comparison is the Inter-American Court, which is known to predominantly engage in progressive interpretation. For more, see Lucas Lixinski, "The Consensus Method of Interpretation by the Inter-American Court of Human Rights," *Canadian Journal of Comparative and Contemporary Law* 3 (2017): 65.

[27] See, for example the state obligation to inform the families of disappeared persons. Eduardo Ferrer Mac-Gregor, "The Right to the Truth as an Autonomous Right under the Inter-American Human Rights System," *Mexican Law Review* 9, no. 1 (2016): 121–39. M. T. Kamminga, "The Thematic Procedures of the UN Commission on Human Rights," *Netherlands International Law Review* 34, no. 3 (1987): 299–323; David Weissbrodt, "The

other human rights courts and tribunals and stands out as a deviant case.[28] The European Court has been rights-expansive at certain times and for certain obligations.[29] Notably, it has oscillated between the audacity of its ruling in Nahide's case and its more forbearing attitude and deference to member states in other cases. The legal change explored here is shaped by these two opposing attitudes.

The book explains why the Court needs to oscillate between forbearance and audacity, and how this oscillation has shaped the norm against torture and inhuman or degrading treatment. This explanation sheds light on a broader question: what are the conditions under which we can expect international courts to be progressive?

Focusing on the European Court's recognition of new state obligations under Article 3, this book seeks to understand what it takes for the Court to be unambiguously progressive.[30] Analyzing change in environments that are not constantly progressive presents us with richer insights into the conditions under which progressive change is more or less likely to occur.[31] The Court is a compelling case to uncover the dynamics of change – especially in the context of the prohibition of torture and inhuman or degrading treatment – for at least three other reasons.

Role of the Human Rights Committee in Interpreting and Developing Humanitarian Law," *University of Pennsylvania Journal of International Law*, no. 4 (2010 2009): 1185–1238.

[28] Deviant cases are atypical cases that stand out. They are ideal for explanatory studies that look into underspecified explanations, as is the case here. For more, see Jason Seawright and John Gerring, "Case Selection Techniques in Case Study Research: A Menu of Qualitative and Quantitative Options," *Political Research Quarterly* 61, no. 2 (2008): 302.

[29] See for example, Giovanna Gismondi, "Denial of Justice: The Latest Indigenous Land Disputes before the European Court of Human Rights and the Need for an Expansive Interpretation of Protocol 1," *Yale Human Rights and Development Law Journal* 18 (2016): 1. See also, Christine Byron, "A Blurring of the Boundaries: The Application of International Humanitarian Law by Human Rights Bodies," *Virginia Journal of International Law*, no. 4 (2007 2006): 839–96.

[30] Mikael Rask Madsen, Pola Cebulak, and Micha Wiebusch, "Backlash against International Courts: Explaining the Forms and Patterns of Resistance to International Courts," *International Journal of Law in Context* 14, no. 2 (2018): 197–220; Ximena Soley and Silvia Steininger, "Parting Ways or Lashing Back? Withdrawals, Backlash and the Inter-American Court of Human Rights," *International Journal of Law in Context* 14, no. 2 (2018): 237–57; Malcolm Langford and Daniel Behn, "Managing Backlash: The Evolving Investment Treaty Arbitrator?," *European Journal of International Law* 29, no. 2 (2018): 551–80. Erik Voeten, "Populism and Backlashes against International Courts," *Perspectives on Politics* (2019), 1–16.

[31] For a different assessment of conditions of change, see Nico Krisch and Ezgi Yildiz, "The Many Paths of Change in International Law: A Frame," in *The Many Paths of Change in International Law* (Oxford and New York: Oxford University Press, 2023).

First, beyond Europe, the Court is relevant on a global scale as a crucial source of authority in shaping the nature and the content of fundamental human rights.[32] With particular respect to the norm against torture and inhuman or degrading treatment, European jurisprudence has shaped the definitions currently in use.[33] For example, the UN Convention against Torture (CAT) adopted its definition of torture and inhuman or degrading treatment based on the one developed by the European Commission of Human Rights in the 1969 *Greek Case* decision.[34] Similarly, the well-known "minimum level of severity" criterion was first established in a European Court judgment.[35] In its 1978 *Ireland* v. *the United Kingdom* judgment, the Court pronounced that the alleged ill-treatment "must attain a minimum level of severity" to be considered under the prohibition of torture and inhuman or degrading treatment. The Court specified that the assessment of this minimum level should be relative, depending on the case's specific circumstances, including "the duration of the treatment, its physical or mental effects and, in some cases, the sex, age and state of health of the victim."[36]

Second, in more recent history, the Court played an important role in debates around the redefinition of torture in the aftermath of the 9/11 attacks. The European Court's initial involvement was rather controversial and involuntary. The United States (US) government attempted to revise the legal definition of the norm against torture during its War on Terror that began in 2001. Former President George W. Bush's legal team meticulously distinguished torture from other forms of ill-treatment in an August 2002 Department of Justice memo (part of a series of memoranda known as Torture Memos).[37] This document limited the definition of torture to acts

[32] Helen Keller and Alec Stone Sweet, "Introduction: The Reception of the ECHR in National Legal Order," in *A Europe of Rights: The Impact of the ECHR on National Legal Systems* (Oxford and New York: Oxford University Press, 2008), 15.

[33] John T. Parry, *Understanding Torture: Law, Violence, and Political Identity* (Ann Arbor: University of Michigan Press, 2010), 44.

[34] Magdalena Forowicz, *The Reception of International Law in the European Court of Human Rights*, International Courts and Tribunals Series (Oxford and New York: Oxford University Press, 2010), 195.

[35] Association for the Prevention of Torture, "The Definition of Torture: Proceedings of an Expert Seminar" (Geneva, November 10, 2001); Aisling Reidy, "The Prohibition of Torture: A Guide to the Implementation of Article 3 of the European Convention on Human Rights," Human Rights Handbooks, No. 6 (Strasbourg: Council of Europe, 2003).

[36] *Ireland* v. *the United Kingdom*, application no. 5310/71, ECHR (January 18, 1978) §162.

[37] A set of legal memoranda drafted by John Yoo, then Deputy Assistant Attorney General, and signed in by Jay S. Bybee, then the head of the Office of Legal Counsel of the Department of Justice.

causing extremely severe pain, equivalent to what one would feel when experiencing organ failure or death.[38] In so doing, the Torture Memos effectively permitted other coercive and cruel interrogation methods falling short of this specific definition as lawful instruments under the euphemism "enhanced interrogation methods."[39] When crafting this circumscribed definition, the Torture Memos relied on the European Court's reasoning in the 1978 *Ireland* v. *the United Kingdom* judgment, where the Court indeed invoked a restricted definition of torture. However, as we will see in Chapter 4, this 1978 judgment was issued in a specific political context in which the Court had limited discretionary space. In subsequent rulings, the European Court changed its position and expanded the definition of acts that could be characterised as torture.[40] Yet, the abovementioned memos disregarded these more recent developments and referred only to *Ireland* v. *the United Kingdom.*

The European Court's direct involvement in this debate was different. The Court had a chance to weigh in on the legality of this distinction and of American interrogation practices. It did so by reviewing cases concerning European countries that aided and abetted the US extraordinary rendition program and associated interrogation practices.[41] The European Court was the first international court to characterise the US government's use of enhanced interrogation techniques as torture in *El-Masri* v. *The Former Yugoslav Republic of Macedonia.*[42] The Court was also the first international court to cite and use parts of the Senate Intelligence Committee's

[38] For more, see Karen J. Greenberg, ed., *The Torture Debate in America* (Cambridge and New York: Cambridge University Press, 2006), 362; See also, Lisa Hajjar, *Torture: A Sociology of Violence and Human Rights* (New York; London: Routledge, 2013).

[39] Karen J. Greenberg and Joshua L. Dratel, eds., *The Torture Papers: The Road to Abu Ghraib*, 1st edition (New York: Cambridge University Press, 2005).

[40] *Selmouni* v. *France*, application no. 25803/94, ECHR (July 28, 1999).

[41] Extraordinary rendition is a War on Terror method whereby suspected individuals would be apprehended, detained, transferred, and interrogated without due process, often in secret locations with the consent or support of foreign governments. For more on extraordinary renditions, see Jane Mayer, "Outsourcing Torture: The Secret History of America's 'Extraordinary Rendition' Program," in *The United States and Torture: Interrogation, Incarceration, and Abuse* (New York and London: New York University Press, 2011).

[42] These cases are *El-Masri* v. *The Former Yugoslav Republic of Macedonia*, application no. 39630/09, ECHR[GC] (December 13, 2012); *Al-Nashiri* v. *Poland*, application no. 28761/11, ECHR (July 24, 2014); *Husayn (Abu Zubaydah)* v. *Poland*, application no. 7511/13, ECHR (February 16, 2015); *Nasr and Ghali* v. *Italy*, application no. 44883/09, ECHR (February 23, 2016); *Al-Nashiri* v. *Romania*, application no. 33234/12, ECHR (May 31, 2018); *Abu Zubaydah* v. *Lithuania*, application no. 46454/11, ECHR (May 31, 2018).

report investigating the CIA's treatment of detainees during the War on Terror between 2001 and 2006.[43]

Third, the European Court's rich jurisprudence allows one to observe the full extent of the prohibition of torture and inhuman or degrading treatment.[44] This diverse jurisprudence has been formed in light of political events ranging from counterterrorism operations in Northern Ireland, Turkey, and Chechnya, to Europe's recent migration crisis. More recently, the Court has also issued judgments establishing states' positive obligations to investigate racially motivated police violence or to protect victims of domestic abuse from their perpetrators. However, the expansion of the norm's meaning has not always been a smooth process. The European Court has been intermittently challenged by different waves of political pushback since its inception. As a result, the Court often felt the need to (re-)negotiate its role and the scope of its functions with member states. The following chapters present an empirically rich analysis of how these instances of negotiations and tactical balancing have left their mark on the way the norm against torture developed. They also evaluate the repercussions of formally or informally controlling courts and the normative consequences of pushback, backlash, and resistance against international courts.

Charting the Transformation of the Norm against Torture and Inhuman or Degrading Treatment

Between Forbearance and Audacity maps out how the scope of the norm against torture has transformed through the Court's jurisprudence over nearly five decades. My analysis of the case law shows that this expansion was a result of two developments. First, beginning in the late 1970s, the Court started lowering the thresholds of severity required to establish a violation under Article 3. The criteria used to assess complaints became

[43] Senate Select Committee on Intelligence and Dianne Feinstein, *The Senate Intelligence Committee Report on Torture: Committee Study of the Central Intelligence Agency's Detention and Interrogation Program* (Brooklyn: Melville House, 2014).

[44] For doctrinal analyses on the extent of this prohibition, see for example, Mavronicola, *Torture, Inhumanity and Degradation under Article 3 of the ECHR*; Elaine Webster, *Dignity, Degrading Treatment and Torture in Human Rights Law: The Ends of Article 3 of the European Convention on Human Rights* (London: Routledge, 2018); Eva Brems and Janneke Gerards, eds., *Shaping Rights in the ECHR: The Role of the European Court of Human Rights in Determining the Scope of Human Rights* (Cambridge: Cambridge University Press, 2014).

even more inclusive in the late 1990s. Second, the Court imposed new state obligations in the late 1990s. These new obligations, also known as positive obligations, had not traditionally been associated with the prohibition of torture or inhuman or degrading treatment. The case of Nahide is an example of this foundational change.

This norm's transformation has generated practical effects for the victims (i.e., the rights holders) and states (i.e., the duty bearers). It has revolutionised how we understand what states are responsible for and who can claim to be protected under this prohibition. The introduction of positive obligations means that states are now legally obliged to take a variety of resource-intensive progressive measures. They are expected to take steps to *prevent* violations before they occur and to *rectify* the harm done to the victims afterward. This includes passing legislation to protect domestic violence victims and offering them appropriate remedies, improving the conditions of detention facilities, and training law enforcement officers.

New victim groups have benefited from this foundational change in the norm. Traditionally, the norm covered victims of interrogative torture or ill-treatment, such as prisoners or terrorist suspects. The norm's transformation opened avenues to justice for new victim groups, such as the relatives of disappeared persons or detained migrants who spend long stretches of time in government-run detention facilities. Moreover, this expansion helped turn the spotlight on other victims needing protection from private actors, such as domestic violence survivors like Nahide, or disabled persons in privately run institutions. Indeed, more and more victim groups began seeking protection under this strong prohibition, whose violation has long been considered a source of embarrassment for states.[45] *Between Forbearance and Audacity* explains how we got here and what was at stake in generating this foundational legal change in Europe.

The book examines torture *together* with other forms of inhuman or degrading treatment. It, therefore, differs from most contemporary accounts of torture that primarily focus on torture under interrogation, particularly as a part of War on Terror policies.[46] In most of these

[45] Interview 28.

[46] Alfred W. McCoy, *Torture and Impunity: The U.S. Doctrine of Coercive Interrogation* (Madison, Wisconsin: The University of Wisconsin Press, 2012); Douglas A. Johnson, Alberto Mora, and Averell Schmidt, "The Strategic Costs of Torture," *Foreign Affairs* (2017); Andrea Liese, "Exceptional Necessity – How Liberal Democracies Contest the Prohibition of Torture and Ill-Treatment When Countering Terrorism Special Issue – Contested Norms in International Relations," *Journal of International Law and International Relations*, no. 1 (2009): 17–48.

accounts, torture is seen as an extraordinary act incompatible with democratic governance and so is treated "as a separate, universally prohibited, egregious form of conduct."[47] There is a special stigma attached to torture as it reminds us of "the violent images from the premodern past," such as "the crucifixion by the Romans, the Inquisition [or] the Salem witch trials."[48] Nevertheless, there is a discontinuity between such torturous practices and the way torture is employed today. Torture is now more "clean" and much closer to other methods of ill-treatment.[49] Therefore, torture is not an isolated incident reserved only for extraordinary circumstances.[50] It is a classic tool in "the continuum of violent state practices" and has a natural link to other forms of inhuman or degrading treatment.[51]

In order to fully understand torture as a phenomenon with more varied implications, it is more appropriate to examine it together with other types of ill-treatment, some of which are newly acknowledged in cases like Nahide's. The debate on torture should therefore be broader.[52] It should include, for example, non-interrogative forms of torture and ill-treatment as well as states' obligations to prevent torture and to provide legal remedies. In a similar vein, the debate should also cover new victim groups recognised under this norm, such as minors, domestic violence victims, relatives of disappeared individuals, or irregular immigrants at detention centres.

This is how several of the UN Special Rapporteurs on Torture and the UN Committee against Torture have approached the topic. For example, former Special Rapporteur Sir Nigel Rodley maintained in his 2001 report that "the question of racism and related intolerance, which he believes

[47] Parry, *Understanding Torture*, 12.

[48] Robert M. Pallitto, *Torture and State Violence in the United States: A Short Documentary History*, 1st edition (Baltimore: Johns Hopkins University Press, 2011), 6.

[49] Darius Rejali, *Torture and Democracy* (Princeton: Princeton University Press, 2009); Paul W. Kahn, *Sacred Violence: Torture, Terror, and Sovereignty* (Ann Arbor: University of Michigan Press, 2009).

[50] Rebecca Gordon, *Mainstreaming Torture: Ethical Approaches in the Post-9/11 United States* (Oxford and New York: Oxford University Press, 2014); Parry, *Understanding Torture*; Tobias Kelly, *This Side of Silence: Human Rights, Torture, and the Recognition of Cruelty* (Philadelphia: University of Pennsylvania Press, 2012).

[51] Parry, *Understanding Torture*, 12.

[52] This rich debate includes several important works on interrogative torture such as Shane O'Mara, *Why Torture Doesn't Work: The Neuroscience of Interrogation* (Cambridge, MA: Harvard University Press, 2015); Paul Lauritzen, *The Ethics of Interrogation: Professional Responsibility in an Age of Terror* (Washington, DC: Georgetown University Press, 2013); McCoy, *Torture and Impunity*; Johnson, Mora, and Schmidt, "The Strategic Costs of Torture"; Liese, "Exceptional Necessity"; John W. Schiemann, *Does Torture Work?* (Oxford and New York: Oxford University Press, 2018).

is all too relevant to issues falling within his mandate."[53] Former Special Rapporteur Manfred Nowak emphasised in his 2010 report that "among detainees, certain groups are subject to double discrimination and vulnerability, including aliens and members of minorities, women, children, the elderly, the sick, persons with disabilities, drug addicts, and gay, lesbian and transgender persons."[54] This point was also raised in the Committee against Torture's General Comment No.2. The Committee highlighted that "being female intersects with other identifying characteristics or status of the person such as race, nationality, religion, sexual orientation, age, immigrant status, etc., to determine the ways that women and girls are subject to or at risk of torture or ill-treatment."[55]

Former Special Rapporteur Juan Méndez, an Argentinian lawyer who was a victim of torture during Argentina's military dictatorship,[56] called for recognizing "abuses in healthcare settings as torture and ill-treatment."[57] In his 2013 report, he stressed that abuses in healthcare facilities should be examined through the lens of the prohibition of torture and inhuman or degrading treatment since this would help better understand these violations and identify relevant state obligations.[58] Former Special Rapporteur Nils Melzer has adopted a similar approach to domestic violence.[59] He underlined that domestic violence is a form of inhuman or degrading treatment that amounts to torture when it involves "the intentional and purposeful or discriminatory infliction of severe pain or suffering on a powerless person."[60]

This call for a broader approach, endorsed by international authorities alongside the European Court, is not to trivialise or normalise torture. Rather, it is to point out that concentrating *only* on interrogative torture

53 Sir Nigel Rodley, Report of the Special Rapporteur on the Question of Torture and Other Cruel, Inhuman or Degrading Treatment or Punishment, *A/56/156* (July 3, 2001).

54 Manfred Nowak, Report of the Special Rapporteur on the Question of Torture and Other Cruel, Inhuman, or Degrading Treatment or Punishment, A/HRC/13/39 (February 9, 2010).

55 UN Committee against Torture, General Comment No. 2, *CAT/C/GC/2* (January 24, 2008)

56 For an account of Mendez's personal experience and work for progressing human rights, see Juan E. Méndez and Marjory Wentworth, *Taking a Stand: The Evolution of Human Rights* (New York: Palgrave Macmillan, 2011).

57 Juan E. Méndez, Report of the Special Rapporteur on the Question of Torture and Other Cruel, Inhuman, or Degrading Treatment or Punishment, *A/HRC/22/53* (February 1, 2013).

58 Ibid.

59 Nils Melzer, "Relevance of the Prohibition of Torture and Other Cruel, Inhuman or Degrading Treatment or Punishment to the Context of Domestic Violence," *A/74/148* (July 12, 2019).

60 Ibid., p. 19 §62.

implies that other forms of ill-treatment are somehow less problematic and, at times, even acceptable. Focusing on the exceptional makes us lose sight of the mundane. As this book will show, there are a host of other issues that deserve to be discussed in the context of the prohibition of torture and inhuman or degrading treatment.[61] In addition, as this book shows, the types of punishment considered inhuman or degrading treatment by today's standards could very well fall under the category of torture in the future. As Tobias Kelly explains, torture is not a neutral term; rather, it is a "historically contingent" category reproduced by legal and medical professionals and bureaucrats.[62] *Between Forbearance and Audacity* examines the transformation of torture and inhuman or degrading treatment as historically contingent legal categories within the European human rights regime.

Toward a Theory of Court-Effectuated Legal Change

Methodological Approach

In order to analyze what this norm is made of, and when and how much it changed over time, I have studied its transformation using a mixed-method approach that combines social science methods and legal analysis. To trace how the norm's coverage expanded, I have relied on content analysis of all Article 3 judgments issued between 1967 and 2016 – amounting to 2,294 judgments.[63] When carrying out this analysis, I read and analyzed every decision regardless of its importance. This approach differs from traditional legal analysis, whereby a few landmark decisions are duly analyzed. Instead of treating the prohibition of torture and inhuman or degrading treatment as a single unit of analysis, I recorded the different obligations that each judgment concerned. That is, I have disaggregated the norm into its constituent obligations and analyzed change by taking obligations as a reference. What is novel about this approach is that it shows not only what a specific norm is made of, but also how much it has changed.

[61] Having said this, important works exist that explore interrogative torture and why it does not work. Schiemann, *Does Torture Work?*; O'Mara, *Why Torture Doesn't Work.*

[62] Kelly, *This Side of Silence*, 14.

[63] I have only looked at the final rulings, in order to avoid overrepresenting certain claims in the dataset. For example, if there was an appeal to a ruling, then I only looked at the appeal. Similarly, I focused on the European Court rulings over the decisions of the European Commission except in instances where the cases were never referred to the Court. Of the cases analyzed, the European Court issued 2,270 rulings. In addition, I analyzed 24 decisions that were issued by the European Commission and not reviewed by the Court.

Employing content analysis, I carefully documented all the distinct obligations falling under the norm and determined when they appeared on the scene. I then used the information I gathered through content analysis to create an original dataset on the Court's Article 3 jurisprudence. Running analyses with this dataset, I could isolate each obligation and trace their developmental tracks separately. This has revealed when, how fast, and how much the norm changed. I have also used this analysis to assess the directionality of the change and whether the Court is uniformly or selectively progressive about obligations falling under the same norm.

I supported the insights I gathered from this large-N analysis with an in-depth reading of select judicial decisions and elite interviews. First, the legal analysis helped me refine this general account by zooming into specific and important judgments. Second, the insights gathered from expert interviews contributed to creating a framework of analysis that explains what motivated the Court to issue audacious rulings or adopt a forbearing attitude to accommodate member states' interests. In 2014 and 2015, I conducted thirty-six semi-structured interviews with experts in and around the Court. I adopted a purposive sampling approach to ensure that the insights from all the relevant experts were included in my analysis.[64] My interviewees consisted of current and former judges, law clerks working for the Court's Registry, representatives of civil society groups, and lawyers who brought cases before the Court. While the majority of interviews took place in Strasbourg, France, I also spoke with experts in Geneva and Bern, Switzerland; London and Essex, the United Kingdom; Copenhagen, Denmark; and İstanbul, Turkey.

The Framework of Analysis

Although international courts may appear neutral bodies, they often have multiple motivations and divergent concerns. These range from ensuring compliance with rulings to maintaining the stability of the regime and continuous access to material and ideational resources, such as funding or reputation.[65] These concerns, or a combination of them, influence how international courts behave and, ultimately, the outcome of their

[64] Oliver C. Robinson, "Sampling in Interview-Based Qualitative Research: A Theoretical and Practical Guide," *Qualitative Research in Psychology* 11, no. 1 (2014): 32.

[65] Leslie Johns, *Strengthening International Courts: The Hidden Costs of Legalization* (Ann Arbor: University of Michigan Press, 2015).

decisions.[66] For example, based on its mandate, the European Court can be described as a "community-serving" human rights court.[67] Its primary motivation should therefore be upholding and advancing rights protected under the Convention. However, at the same time, it is an institution with conservative origins.[68] It has certain organizational needs,[69] such as obtaining funding, securing respect for its decisions, and maintaining legitimacy in the eyes of its member states and the international community.[70]

How do these competing motivations or concerns influence the Court's behaviour? I argue that this complexity has compelled the Court to oscillate between audaciously expanding the definitions under the Convention and showing forbearance and considering states' sensitives. While the former behaviour is a manifestation of the Court's progressive mandate and intentions, the latter is prompted by the need for political expediency. Law develops in between these tactical moves. It is practically impossible to understand what motivates such moves without considering the Court's institutional characteristics and its relation to member states and the broader legal community. There is therefore a strong link between the transformation of the norm and the transformation of the institution that effectuates this process. This book sets out to explain this link. It traces the norm against torture and inhuman or degrading treatment and how it has been shaped by the institutional transformation of the European Court over five decades.

Theoretical Expectations

International courts are situated in a political context, where they interact with various stakeholders. In this configuration, they are particularly attuned to their relationship with member states. States have such a prominent role because they not only enforce court decisions and uphold

[66] For an account of different political and institutional pressures that shape judicial behavior see, Martin Shapiro, *Courts: A Comparative and Political Analysis* (Chicago: University of Chicago Press, 1986); Diana Kapiszewski, "Tactical Balancing: High Court Decision Making on Politically Crucial Cases," *Law and Society Review* 45, no. 2 (2011): 471–506.

[67] Fuad Zarbiyev, "Judicial Activism in International Law – A Conceptual Framework for Analysis," *Journal of International Dispute Settlement* 3, no. 2 (2012): 247–78.

[68] Duranti, *The Conservative Human Rights Revolution.*

[69] Kapiszewski, "Tactical Balancing," 471–506.

[70] For more on the court legitimacy, see Harlan Grant Cohen et al., eds., *Legitimacy and International Courts* (Cambridge: Cambridge University Press, 2018); Armin von Bogdandy and Ingo Venzke, "In Whose Name? An Investigation of International Courts' Public Authority and Its Democratic Justification," *European Journal of International Law* 23, no. 1 (2012): 7–41.

courts' legitimacy, but they also provide courts with funding, resources, and personnel.[71] International tribunals are dependent on states; this dependency "endows courts with authority while also making them reliant on states for material, procedural and normative support."[72] As a result, international courts "wield *interdependent* lawmaking power" and are influenced by the preferences of states and other actors.[73] Therefore, they behave strategically to balance their objectives with the expectations of other actors, especially states.[74]

The importance of states is a source of fragility for international courts. This is because, unlike domestic courts, international courts do not channel government power or unconditional support. Instead, international courts come with a sovereignty cost that states might contest, especially if it grows over time.[75] This cost could be even higher for courts that receive complaints brought by individuals against member states, as is the case for the European Court. In order to balance the costs while cultivating and maintaining state support, courts may occasionally offer trade-offs or turn to judicial avoidance.[76] This might mean overriding their organizational imperative to suit state preferences or not using their institutional prerogatives to the maximum to signal that they can function at a lower-sovereignty cost.[77] In a way, international courts may need to negotiate their continued existence, relevance, and reputation.

71 Andreas Follesdal, "Survey Article: The Legitimacy of International Courts," *Journal of Political Philosophy* 28, no. 4 (2020): 2.

72 Courtney Hillebrecht, *Saving the International Justice Regime: Beyond Backlash against International Courts* (Cambridge and New York: Cambridge University Press, 2021), 36.

73 Tom Ginsburg, "Bounded Discretion in International Judicial Lawmaking," *Virginia Journal of International Law* 45, no. 3 (2005): 633.

74 Ibid., 657–58.

75 Kenneth W. Abbott and Duncan Snidal, "Hard and Soft Law in International Governance," *International Organization* 54, no. 3 (2000): 437.

76 Miles Jackson, "Judicial Avoidance at the European Court of Human Rights: Institutional Authority, the Procedural Turn, and Docket Control," *International Journal of Constitutional Law* 20, no. 1 (2022): 112–140.

77 Emilie M. Hafner-Burton, Edward D. Mansfield, and Jon C. W. Pevehouse, "Human Rights Institutions, Sovereignty Costs and Democratization," *British Journal of Political Science* 45, no. 1 (2015): 1–27. Mikael Rask Madsen explains how the European Court has re-negotiated its sovereignty cost to ensure that it would not pose a significant threat to the contracting states' sovereignty. For more see, Mikael Rask Madsen, "Protracted Institutionalization of the Strasbourg Court: From Legal Diplomacy to Integrationist Jurisprudence," in *The European Court of Human Rights between Law and Politics*, ed. Jonas Christoffersen and Mikael Rask Madsen (New York: Oxford University Press, 2011), 56–57.

Jeffrey Dunoff and Mark Pollack successfully demonstrate some of the trade-offs that international courts face.[78] They explain that courts cannot be highly accountable, transparent, and independent at the same time. High judicial accountability (i.e., subjecting judges to periodic assessment and reappointment) and high judicial transparency (i.e., compelling judges to write separate opinions) mean there is less emphasis on judicial independence.[79] Shai Dothan is another scholar that evaluates such judicial strategies. Inspired by game theory, Dothan proposes a framework to investigate court tactics intended to ensure member state compliance with their judgments. Dothan essentially argues that courts must first make strategic moves to improve their reputation. Only after a positive reputation has been established can an international court afford to risk issuing onerous judgments and still expect to secure compliance.[80]

In a similar vein, an international court might strategise to balance its core functions with its need to gain member state support and preserve its reputation.[81] As Nuno Garoupa and Tom Ginsburg argue, maintaining a good judicial reputation in the eyes of multiple audiences (i.e., states, the legal community, academia, etc.) is a condition for courts to be effective.[82] This requires careful balancing. Court incentives to push forward long-term progressive change in International Law might be interrupted by the short-term necessity of holding back to accommodate member state interests. While pushing forward may increase a court's reputational capital in the eyes of the international legal community, its reputational credit may simultaneously be depleted in the eyes of member states. In order to ensure member states' continued support, a court may choose to issue "unadventurous" decisions that accommodate state interests – bolstering the Court's reputation and replenishing its future credit.[83] Even if

[78] Jeffrey L. Dunoff and Mark A. Pollack, "The Judicial Trilemma," *American Journal of International Law* 111, no. 2 (2017): 227.

[79] Ibid. 238.

[80] Shai Dothan, "Judicial Tactics in the European Court of Human Rights," *Chicago Journal of International Law* 12, no. 1 (2011); Shai Dothan, *Reputation and Judicial Tactics: A Theory of National and International Courts*, Comparative Constitutional Law and Policy (Cambridge: Cambridge University Press, 2014).

[81] Nuno Garoupa and Tom Ginsburg, *Judicial Reputation: A Comparative Theory* (Chicago: University of Chicago Press, 2015), 2.

[82] Ibid., 2–4.

[83] For example, Miles Jackson calls for judicial avoidance to shield the Court from a potential political pushback. For more, see Jackson, "Judicial Avoidance at the European Court of Human Rights," 28.

this relationship may appear to be transactional, it also contributes to the overall mission of maintaining the Court's image as a legitimate authority "that can rightly influence or constrain [states'] political discretion."[84]

In order to account for the prominence and consequences of trade-offs influencing the Court's changing attitudes, I rely on the concepts of audacity and forbearance. I define audacity as using "one's institutional prerogatives in an unrestrained way" and forbearance as abstaining from doing so.[85] This definition is built upon the concept of forbearance introduced by Alisha Holland,[86] as well as Steven Levitsky and Daniel Ziblatt, who use Holland's definition.[87] In her groundbreaking book, Holland defines forbearance as "intentional and revocable government leniency toward violations of the law" and distinguishes forbearance from weak enforcement that oftentimes results from lack of capacity.[88] Instead, she characterises forbearance, the under-utilisation of one's institutional power, as a "political choice" and argues that governments resort to forbearance to appeal to poor voters.[89] Developed, thus, to understand domestic processes, the concept of forbearance helps one capture how governments further their electoral interests while also meeting some of their poor constituencies' distributive demands.[90]

I argue that the main logic behind this concept is applicable to international courts that are also sometimes willing to underutilise their powers to appeal to states as their main constituencies and meet their redistributive claims. Moreover, building upon this concept, I argue that forbearance has an antithesis: audacity. While under-utilising one's authority is a political choice, so is over-utilizing it. That is to say, audacity is also a strategy and not just a natural tendency. I chose to use *forbearance* together with *audacity* to capture tactical balancing that takes place in the course of supranational legal review.

84 Andreas Follesdal, Johan Karlsson Schaffer, and Geir Ulfstein, "International Human Rights and the Challenge of Legitimacy," in *The Legitimacy of International Human Rights Regimes: Legal, Political and Philosophical Perspectives*, ed. Andreas Føllesdal, Johan Karlsson Schaffer, and Geir Ulfstein (Cambridge: Cambridge University Press, 2013), 4.

85 Steven Levitsky and Daniel Ziblatt, *How Democracies Die* (New York: Crown Publishing, 2018), 63. Their definition of forbearance is borrowed from Alisha Holland, *Forbearance as Redistribution: The Politics of Informal Welfare in Latin America* (Cambridge: Cambridge University Press, 2017).

86 Holland, *Forbearance as Redistribution.*

87 Levitsky and Ziblatt, *How Democracies Die.*

88 Holland, *Forbearance as Redistribution*, 13.

89 Alisha C. Holland, "Forbearance," *American Political Science Review* 110, no. 2 (2016): 233.

90 Holland, *Forbearance as Redistribution*, 15–17.

International courts may choose to use their institutional prerogatives in an audacious way by pronouncing progressive decisions, regardless of how such decisions impact state interests. Alternatively, they may resort to forbearance and not fully use their institutional prerogatives in order to win over state support. I identify these two behaviour types as strategies for institutional survival and resilience – employed at measured doses and appropriate intervals suitable to maintaining an institution's image and ensuring its continued access to resources.

I measure the degree of audacity and forbearance in reference to two observations. The first is the willingness to recognise new obligations or new rights (*novel claims*); the second is the propensity for finding a violation overall (*propensity*). I argue that a higher rate of accepting novel claims and a higher rate of propensity to find states in violation are signs of audacity. International courts' recognition of novel claims requires a high degree of audacity since they not only recognise these claims as legally valid claims but also lower the thresholds to find a violation in the future.[91] In other words, the first violation rulings that accept novel claims are costlier than subsequent rulings that simply build on them as precedents. Although there is no clear rule recognizing the authority of judicial precedents in International Law, invoking existing precedents helps increase the legitimacy of legal reasoning and conclusions.[92] In a similar fashion, finding states in violation at a higher rate calls for judicial courage and demonstrates a given court's audacity.[93] While audacious courts will have a higher score for both of these measures, forbearing courts will have a lower score. By implication, while audacity expands the protections offered to the victims, forbearance leads to retractive rulings reversing this expansion or upholding the status quo.

To be sure, forbearance and audacity are not the only strategies expected from institutions. Theoretically, courts may also refuse to perform their mandate (dereliction) or go beyond it (excess or *ultra-vires*). However, these two types of behaviour take place outside of the courts' delegated zone of discretion. Dereliction occurs when an institution intentionally does

[91] Ezgi Yildiz et al., "New Norms in Old Regimes: Judicial Strategies for Importing Environmental Norms," *Unpublished Manuscript*, 2022.

[92] Harlan Cohen, "Theorizing Precedent in International Law," in *Interpretation in International Law*, ed. Andrea Bianchi, Daniel Behn, and Matthew Windsor (Oxford: Oxford University Press, 2015), 268–89.

[93] Scholars take no violation rulings as a sign of restraint. See for example Øyvind Stiansen and Erik Voeten, "Backlash and Judicial Restraint: Evidence from the European Court of Human Rights," *International Studies Quarterly* 64, no. 4 (2020): 770–84.

not deliver its mandate, whereas excess refers to an institution's overuse of its powers. In other words, dereliction describes an actor's choice not to do what they must, and excess concerns an actor's choice to do what they must not. In this book, I will only be focusing on audacity and forbearance as types of behaviour that fall within the competence of courts and other institutions without creating serious legitimacy concerns.

Audacity and forbearance bear a resemblance to what legal scholarship identifies as judicial activism and judicial restraint. Judicial activism is often associated with courts going beyond applicable law "in a way that furthers social justice" or the prescription of "non-traditional remedies aimed at ameliorating social problems."[94] Judicial restraint, on the other hand, suggests that the judiciary assumes a more limited and deferential role. The proponents of judicial restraint argue that judges should respect the executive and legislative branches and minimise their interference.[95] While judicial activism portrays judges as norm entrepreneurs, judicial restraint views them as neutral arbiters.

There is conceptual compatibility between judicial activism/restraint and audacity/forbearance, yet I have chosen to use the latter pair for three reasons. First, the concepts of judicial activism and restraint explain judicial behaviour based on judges' worldviews, attitudes, and convictions about their role and the scope of their powers.[96] They are more about fixed attributes and less about strategies.[97] As we will see in this book, international courts, like the European Court, may not have a uniform or static vision about how to treat a certain claim. Their attitudes may change based on the characteristics and the salience of the subject matter, as well as the requirements of political expediency at the time.

Second, and relatedly, judicial activism and restraint concepts do not fully capture the institutional and relational dynamics unique to international courts. While they are suitable for studying judicial philosophies on a granular level (micro level), often with reference to judges'

[94] Stephen Breyer, "Judicial Activism: Power without Responsibility?," in *Judicial Activism: Power without Responsibility?*, ed. Benjamin Kiely (Melbourne: The University of Melbourne, 2006), 72.

[95] J. Clifford Wallace, "Jurisprudence of Judicial Restraint: A Return to the Moorings," *George Washington Law Review* 50, no. 1 (1981): 8.

[96] Stefanie A. Lindquist and Frank B. Cross, *Measuring Judicial Activism* (Oxford University Press, 2009); Frank B. Cross and Stefanie A. Lindquist, "The Scientific Study of Judicial Activism," *Minnesota Law Review* 91, no. 6 (2007): 1752–84.

[97] I have argued this point elsewhere. For more, see Ezgi Yildiz, "A Court with Many Faces: Judicial Characters and Modes of Norm Development in the European Court of Human Rights," *European Journal of International Law* 31, no. 1 (2020).

self-identification,[98] their explanatory power diminishes at the organizational level (meso-level). International courts' compositions are different from domestic courts. The influence of international judges elected for limited terms is more diffuse, as we will see in Chapter 2.[99] Permanent legal staff, partaking not only in legal review but also in prioritizing institutional objectives and storing institutional memory, play an important role. The members of the secretariat and other permanent staff are also concerned with "the long-term health" and the "integrity and reputation" of the institution.[100] Hence, their input and the influence of the courts' common institutional culture should also be considered when analyzing judicial strategies.

Third, the concepts of forbearance and audacity are more generalizable. While judicial activism and restraint were developed to examine only the judiciary, forbearance and audacity may explain the strategies of actors or organizations beyond the judiciary. Engaging in politics of institutional resilience is something international courts and other international organizations with delegated authority have in common. The concepts of forbearance and audacity help answer the questions about how organizations balance their institutional imperatives while also attempting to avoid political pushback or backlash. They thus enable studying international courts in comparison to, or in conjunction with, other organizations.

Determinants of Forbearance and Audacity

As this book makes clear, international courts need an important quality to be audacious: a large discretionary space. Discretionary space (or zone of discretion) represents the freedom of choice that an institution enjoys *above what it must do* (dereliction) and *below what it must not do* (excess).[101] Figure I.1 displaces the scope of the discretionary space as well as the location of my key concepts within this space:

[98] Geoffrey R. Stone, "Selective Judicial Activism," *Texas Law Review* 89, no. 6 (2011): 1423.

[99] It is difficult, if not impossible, to trace the impact of individual judges on norms' interpretative evolution, which is embedded in the broader sociopolitical context. For more, see Ezgi Yildiz, "Interpretative Evolution of the Norm Prohibiting Torture and Inhuman or Degrading Treatment under the European Convention," in *Language and Legal Interpretation in International Law*, ed. Anne Lise Kjaer and Joanna Lam (New York: Oxford University Press, 2022), 295–314.

[100] David D. Caron, "Towards a Political Theory of International Courts and Tribunals," *Berkeley Journal of International Law* 24, no. 2 (2006): 24.

[101] Alec Stone Sweet and Thomas L. Brunell, "Trustee Courts and the Judicialization of International Regimes: The Politics of Majoritarian Activism in the European Convention on Human Rights, the European Union, and the World Trade Organization," *Journal of Law and Courts* 1, no. 1 (2013): 65.

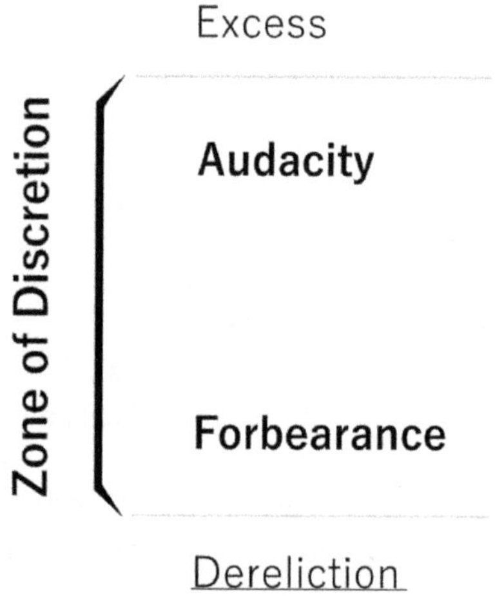

Figure I.1 Representation of zone of discretion

Theoretically, the bounds of this space are defined by formal rules, and within this space, courts have the liberty to decide as they wish – without venturing into excess and dereliction. But, in practice, are international courts truly free to choose their own interpretive preferences within their zone of discretion?

According to the existing scholarly works, institutions with an expansive discretionary space, such as constitutional courts, tend to generate "sweeping outcomes that are frequently unanticipated."[102] That is to say, when an international court's zone of discretion is wide, it can be audacious across the board. Yet, when this zone is narrow, or there is a credible threat that this zone may shrink, it ought to be careful not to undermine state interests.[103] My theoretical framework follows a similar logic. When international courts' zone of discretion is narrow, they lean toward forbearance to signal that their operations have low sovereignty costs. They tend to issue forbearing rulings overall while being selectively audacious. In such instances, the issue characteristics matter more. While courts will not be motivated to venture into progressive understandings that conflict

[102] Mark Thatcher and Alec Stone Sweet, "Theory and Practice of Delegation to Non-Majoritarian Institutions," *West European Politics* 25, no. 1 (2002): 16.

[103] Such credible threats may only materialise when member states unite under the objective of court-curbing. Karen J. Alter, "Agents or Trustees? International Courts in Their Political Context," *European Journal of International Relations* 14, no. 1 (2008): 37.

Table I.1 *Expectations regarding court responses to changes in discretionary space and negative feedback*

		Widespread negative feedback	
		Yes	No
Discretionary space	Narrow	General forbearance (1)	Selective audacity (2)
	Wide	Selective forbearance (3)	General audacity (4)

with state interests, they may still pronounce certain right-expansive rulings concerning matters of low salience to states. By doing so, they build confidence, and perhaps in the future, they will be given a larger discretionary space. On the contrary, courts with wide discretionary space may act audaciously across the board unless there is a risk that their operations will spur negative feedback or backlash, which in extreme situations, may also shrink their discretionary space.

Hence, in addition to the breadth of discretionary space, negative political feedback matters. As the literature explains, courts may be influenced by political signals, public opinions, or "policy moods."[104] Instead of direct control, states may indirectly control courts through "feedback politics."[105] Negative feedback is often geared toward "communicating dissatisfaction,"[106] and, in extreme cases, signalling state intent to undermine a given court's authority,[107] or which scholars of domestic judicial politics identify as "court curbing."[108] Negative feedback is a sustained criticism that goes beyond isolated outcries. When negative feedback is widespread, voiced by multiple member states or states that normally constitute a court's support base, the need for forbearance increases.

Table I.1 outlines how international courts are expected to behave based on their discretionary space and the negative feedback they receive.

104 Laurence R. Helfer and Erik Voeten, "Walking Back Human Rights in Europe?," *European Journal of International Law* 31, no. 3 (2020): 802; Richard Steinberg, "Judicial Lawmaking at the WTO: Discursive, Constitutional, and Political Constraints," American Journal of International Law 98, no. 2 (2004): 247–75; Garoupa and Ginsburg, *Judicial Reputation*.

105 Daniel Abebe and Tom Ginsburg, "The Dejudicialization of International Politics?," *International Studies Quarterly* 63, no. 3 (2019): 525.

106 Ibid., 525.

107 Hillebrecht, *Saving the International Justice Regime*, 27–30; Steinberg, "Judicial Lawmaking at the WTO," 263–64.

108 Mark A. Pollack, "International Court Curbing in Geneva: Lessons from the Paralysis of the WTO Appellate Body," *Governance*, accessed June 5, 2022, https://doi.org/10.1111/gove.12686.

The strategies that courts can adopt vary in the degree to which they are associated with progressive attitudes – in ascending order from (1) general forbearance to (2) selective audacity, (3) selective forbearance, and finally, (4) general audacity. When international courts enjoy only a narrow discretionary space, and when they receive widespread negative feedback, they will tend toward *general forbearance*. On the contrary, when courts with limited discretionary space do not receive widespread negative feedback, they can afford to be *selectively audacious*, especially regarding noncontentious issues with lower stakes. When courts enjoy a wide discretionary space but face widespread negative feedback, they still tend to be overall audacious, but *selectively forbearing*. Their selective forbearance will be tailored to issue areas where they receive the most criticism to mitigate actual or potential political pushback and backlash. Finally, courts that enjoy wide discretionary space and that are free from widespread negative feedback can be *generally audacious*.

While these expectations are listed independently here, they might occasionally influence each other. For example, the reason why a given court has only narrow discretionary space may be the widespread negative feedback that has resulted from previous audacious behaviour. More concretely, applying these expectations to the European Court, we can surmise that when the Court has a narrow discretionary space, it will be overall forbearing; because it is forbearing, it will not face widespread negative feedback or backlash. When the Court has wide discretionary space, it will tend toward audacity. If this audacity spurs negative feedback (or backlash in extreme cases), the Court will only be selectively forbearing.

The institutional history of the European Court includes three phases and presents us with an interesting in-case variation. These phases are *the old Court* (1959–1998), *the new Court* (1998–2010), and *the reformed Court* (2010–present). Each of these distinct phases is marked by different zones of discretion and different degrees of negative feedback. The old Court is the first incarnation and covers the period until 1998 – when the European human rights system underwent an institutional transformation. The pre-1998 old Court was a part-time body working alongside the European Commission of Human Rights (the Commission) – a separate institution in charge of filtering applications from individual complainants. Member states could choose whether to accept the Court's jurisdiction or allow individuals' right to bring complaints. Hence delegation was not automatic, and the Court was not entirely in control of its docket. As a result, it could enjoy only a *narrow discretionary space*.

This model changed with Protocol 11 in 1998. A new full-time Court was created, and the Commission was abolished. Moreover, individuals gained direct access to the Court, which became a permanent body with compulsory jurisdiction. Due to these changes, the new Court began its life as a court with a *wide discretionary space*. While this institutional structure mostly stayed the same, the new Court entered into a reform phase in 2010. Member states organised a series of High-Level Conferences to discuss the future of the Court, which heralded a new era where voicing criticism and directing negative feedback became more commonplace.[109] Different from its previous versions, the post-2010 reformed Court has been confronted with *widespread negative feedback*.

This institutional transformation influenced the way the Court operated in its different incarnations. During the time of the old Court, norm development under Article 3 was overshadowed by two overarching concerns regarding member states: avoiding interference in states' national security policies and not generating resource-intensive positive obligations (some of which also required finding states liable for the conduct of private actors). Nevertheless, the old Court would pass more audacious rulings when reviewing cases concerning issues with low political stakes. Notably, the Court saved its right-expansive rulings when addressing issues around which there was already a general agreement in Europe, such as the inhumane nature of corporal punishment or the death row phenomenon.[110]

The new Court, however, became more audacious across the board after 1998. Within a span of a few years, it launched a series of resource-intensive positive obligations. It certified the absolute nature of the prohibition against torture, which cannot be justified even in self-defence. The reformed Court has not fully taken up this progressive trend. While remaining audacious overall, the reformed Court has been selectively forbearing, especially when reviewing claims related to the *non-refoulement*

[109] There is an interesting debate on the impact of this period on the Court's authority and practices. For more, see Mikael Rask Madsen, "Two-Level Politics and the Backlash against International Courts: Evidence from the Politicisation of the European Court of Human Rights," *The British Journal of Politics and International Relations* 22, no. 4 (2020): 728–38; Helfer and Voeten, "Walking Back Human Rights in Europe?"; Alec Stone Sweet, Wayne Sandholtz, and Mads Andenas, "Dissenting Opinions and Rights Protection in the European Court: A Reply to Laurence Helfer and Erik Voeten," *European Journal of International Law* 32, no. 3 (2021): 897–906; Alec Stone Sweet, Wayne Sandholtz, and Mads Andenas, "The Failure to Destroy the Authority of the European Court of Human Rights: 2010–2018," *The Law and Practice of International Courts and Tribunals* 21, no. 2 (2022): 244–77.

[110] The term refers to the emotional stress felt by prisoners waiting to be executed.

principle (i.e., cases about forcing refugees and asylum seekers to return to a country where they may face torture and inhuman or degrading treatment).

This differential treatment indicates that the main driver behind the Court's selective forbearance might not be the election of more state-friendly judges. Such a cohort would issue forbearing rulings across the board. Rather, the differential treatment of the *non-refoulement* principle directly corresponds to several European governments' requests for greater forbearance in judicial review, especially in cases concerning refugees and asylum seekers.[111] This finding calls for greater scrutiny of the reformed Court's bifurcated approach toward the norm against torture and inhuman or degrading treatment.

As Mikael Rask Madsen explains, the current elected judges sitting in the new Court and the reformed Court are different from those that served in the old Court.[112] Madsen observes that they are significantly younger, more experienced in human rights law, and less connected to politics and diplomacy in and around the Court.[113] On the surface, this might increase the audacity of a given court. However, this is not necessarily always the case with the European Court, as we will see in Chapter 7. Especially the reformed Court, the most recent incarnation of the Court, shows selective forbearance concerning politically sensitive issues (e.g., the *non-refoulement* principle) while being highly audacious when it comes to less controversial topics (e.g., curbing police brutality). This bifurcated approach indicates that the Court's audacious or forbearing tendencies may not be entirely (or only) determined by the preferences of the judges elected for limited terms, as I will discuss further in Chapter 2.

Conditions for Audacity

In addition to the importance of the width of the discretionary space and feedback politics, my findings show that the European Court's

[111] Helfer and Voeten, "Walking Back Human Rights in Europe?," 798; Laurence R. Helfer and Erik Voeten, "Walking Back Dissents on the European Court of Human Rights: A Rejoinder to Alec Stone Sweet, Wayne Sandholtz and Mads Andenas," *European Journal of International Law* 32, no. 3 (2021): 911.

[112] Mikael Rask Madsen, "The Legitimization Strategies of International Judges: The Case of the European Court of Human Rights," in *Selecting Europe's Judges: A Critical Review of the Appointment Procedures to the European Courts*, ed. Michal Bobek (Oxford: Oxford University Press, 2015), 259–76.

[113] Ibid., 262.

audacity is likely to increase when its decisions are: (1) in line with widespread societal needs, (2) supported by legal principles and jurisprudence developed by other courts or institutions, and (3) actively promoted by civil society groups.

First, unsurprisingly, it is easier to generate change when that change reflects societal needs.[114] International courts do take societal trends into account when reviewing and adjusting existing norms, whether considering changing moral values (e.g., increased acceptance of LGBTQ communities),[115] technological advancements (e.g., the use of in vitro fertilization),[116] or new awareness around emerging crises (e.g., environmental degradation or climate change).[117] Proving a demonstrable link between a particular complaint and an emerging societal need not only creates a sense of urgency but also grants courts the social legitimacy necessary to engage in progressive change.

Second, legal developments initiated by other international treaties, courts, or expert bodies can be influential by setting precedents and establishing clear directions for change. International courts may rely on the principles exported from other treaties, decisions, or expert body reports to establish a stronger legal basis for the norm's expansion.[118] For example, when further developing the norm against torture, the European Court has often relied on the case law of the UN Committee against Torture and the reports of the Committee for the Prevention of Torture created under the European Convention for the Prevention of Torture.[119] Similarly, Nahide's case benefited from the principles set by the CEDAW and Belém do Pará Convention.

[114] See for example George Letsas, "The ECHR as a Living Instrument: Its Meaning and Legitimacy," in *Constituting Europe: The European Court of Human Rights in a National, European and Global Context*, ed. Andreas Føllesdal, Birgit Peters, and Geir Ulfstein (New York: Cambridge University Press, 2013), 106–41.

[115] See for example Laurence R. Helfer and Erik Voeten, "International Courts as Agents of Legal Change: Evidence from LGBT Rights in Europe," *International Organization* 68, no. 1 (2014).

[116] Lyria Bennett Moses, "Understanding Legal Responses to Technological Change of In Vitro Fertilization," *Minnesota Journal of Law, Science and Technology* 6, no. 2 (2005): 505–618.

[117] For an illustration see, Jaap Spier, "There Is No Future without Addressing Climate Change," *Journal of Energy and Natural Resources Law* 37, no. 2 (2019): 181–204.

[118] See for example Nina Reiners, *Transnational Lawmaking Coalitions for Human Rights* (Cambridge and New York: Cambridge University Press, 2021).

[119] Forowicz, *The Reception of International Law in the European Court of Human Rights*, 201–13.

Finally, civil society organizations may play an active role in generating change with what is commonly known as strategic litigation.[120] This term refers to coordinated campaigns for effecting social change by bringing exemplary cases before judicial bodies.[121] Strategic litigation includes various legal tools such as representing the applicants before courts, providing them with legal advice, or submitting observations (*amicus curiae*) on an ongoing case.[122] Civil society groups can be influential because they can bring similar cases before the same institution or before different institutions to maximise impact. This increases the chances of successfully obtaining a violation decision supporting their cause. As this book reveals, civil society organizations also benefit from three working methods: specialization, transfer of expertise, and cross-fertilization of legal standards – that is, utilization of standards developed in other legal regimes.

Contributions

The framework and the accompanying analysis provide theoretical, conceptual, and empirical contributions to the rich scholarship on international norms and judicial politics. They offer empirical evidence for, and theoretical explanation of, why and when courts generate progressive change and when they refrain from doing so. The framework developed here can be adjusted to explain delegated institutions' motivations to resort to forbearance to signal that they can operate at a lower-sovereignty cost to the states. While organizations may set their own agendas and chart their courses by occasionally even pushing the limits of their mandates, they might also consciously do the reverse to maintain their institutional reputation and secure access to resources. Unlike previous

[120] Loveday Hodson, "Activating the Law: Exploring the Legal Responses of NGOs to Gross Rights Violations," in *Making Human Rights Intelligible: Towards a Sociology of Human Rights*, ed. Mikael Rask Madsen and Gert Verschraegen (Oxford and Portland: Hart Publishing, 2013), 278; Laura Van den Eynde, "An Empirical Look at the Amicus Curiae Practice of Human Rights NGOs before the European Court of Human Rights," *Netherlands Quarterly of Human Rights* 31, no. 3 (2013): 271–313.

[121] James Goldston, "Public Interest Litigation in Central and Eastern Europe: Roots, Prospects, and Challenges," *Human Rights Quarterly* 28 (2006): 496.

[122] See for example Catherine Corey Barber, "Tackling the Evaluation Challenge in Human Rights: Assessing the Impact of Strategic Litigation Organisations," *The International Journal of Human Rights* 16, no. 3 (2012): 411–35; Rachel A. Cichowski, "Civil Society and the European Court of Human Rights," in *The European Court of Human Rights between Law and Politics*, ed. Jonas Christoffersen and Mikael Rask Madsen (Oxford: Oxford University Press, 2011); Heidi Nichols Haddad, *The Hidden Hands of Justice: NGOs, Human Rights, and International Courts* (New York: Cambridge University Press, 2018).

studies on judicial behavior, the framework works on the meso-level. It assesses judicial behaviour not only as an expression of the preference of the judges elected for a limited term, but instead as an institutional strategy adopted by all members of the judicial elite at the Court.[123]

In addition, the book presents an analysis of the development of the prohibition of torture and inhuman or degrading treatment and the judicial motivations shaping this process. By demonstrating what this norm entails and how much its contents have changed over time, the book helps identify the pace and magnitude of legal change. This empirically rich assessment complements existing doctrinal analysis on the European Court[124] and its jurisprudence on the prohibition of torture and inhuman or degrading treatment,[125] and in particular positive obligations.[126] However, the relevance of this close-up analysis goes beyond the specialised debate on the European Court or its jurisprudence by offering insights for audiences interested in understanding the development of international norms and law and the role of international courts in this regard in three key ways.

First, the findings presented here have broader implications for the literature on international norms. They showcase the importance of courts and court-like bodies in norm development and transformation.[127]

[123] See for example Erik Voeten, "The Impartiality of International Judges: Evidence from the European Court of Human Rights," *American Political Science Review* 102, no. 4 (2008): 417–33.

[124] See for example Kanstantsin Dzehtsiarou, *Can the European Court of Human Rights Shape European Public Order?* (Cambridge: Cambridge University Press, 2021); Jens T. Theilen, *European Consensus between Strategy and Principle* (Baden-Baden: Nomos Publishers, 2021); Alastair Mowbray, "Subsidiarity and the European Convention on Human Rights," *Human Rights Law Review* 15, no. 2 (2015): 313–41; Steven Greer and Luzius Wildhaber, "Revisiting the Debate about 'Constitutionalising' the European Court of Human Rights," *Human Rights Law Review* 12, no. 4 (2012): 655–87.

[125] See for example Mavronicola, *Torture, Inhumanity and Degradation under Article 3 of the ECHR*; Corina Heri, *Responsive Human Rights: Vulnerability, Ill-Treatment and the ECtHR* (Gordonsville: Hart Publishing, 2021); Lutz Oette, "The Prohibition of Torture and Persons Living in Poverty: From the Margins to the Centre," *International and Comparative Law Quarterly* 70, no. 2 (2021): 307–41; Webster, *Dignity, Degrading Treatment and Torture in Human Rights Law*.

[126] See for example Felix E Torres, "Reparations: To What End? Developing the State's Positive Duties to Address Socio-Economic Harms in Post-Conflict Settings through the European Court of Human Rights," *European Journal of International Law* 32, no. 3 (2021): 807–34; Stoyanova, "Fault, Knowledge and Risk within the Framework of Positive Obligations under the European Convention on Human Rights"; Lavrysen, *Human Rights in a Positive State*.

[127] For other studies on norm change see, Wayne Sandholtz, "International Norm Change," *Oxford Research Encyclopedia of Politics*, June 28, 2017, https://doi.org/10.1093/acrefore/9780190228637.013.588; Wayne Sandholtz and Kendall W. Stiles, *International*

In norms literature, courts are often not portrayed as norm entrepreneurs. This could be because they are viewed as neutral bodies only able to react when activated or as lacking the proactiveness that norm entrepreneurs like states, non-state actors, or individuals may possess.[128] However, as we see in this book, international courts are actors of a complex nature, driven by multiple (and not always compatible) motivations, and they can show proactiveness when the conditions are right.

Moreover, courts are uniquely positioned to effectuate rule modification, and they play a significant role in consolidating meaning and resolving norm collisions.[129] International courts not only solve legal disputes but also serve as venues where abstract norms are discussed, negotiated, and grounded as legal standards. Therefore, it is essential to understand what prompts courts to adopt progressive agendas and what encourages them to display reticence instead.

Second, the framework introduced here contributes to the legal scholarship and the literature on international courts.[130] It offers conceptual tools to analyze what motivates courts to either effectuate progressive legal change or refrain from doing so. It also allows a glimpse of how courts operate under normal circumstances versus how they balance their priorities when under pressure. This inquiry carries particular importance today amidst a wave of backlash against liberal-leaning international institutions. As the guardians of international norms, international courts have had their fair share of resistance and pushback.[131] This book elucidates the precursors and implications of the recent backlash against the

Norms and Cycles of Change (Oxford and New York: Oxford University Press, 2008); Martha Finnemore and Kathryn Sikkink, "International Norm Dynamics and Political Change," *International Organization* 52, no. 4 (1998): 887–917.

128 Harald Müller and Carmen Wunderlich, eds., *Norm Dynamics in Multilateral Arms Control: Interests, Conflicts, and Justice* (Athens and London: University of Georgia Press, 2013).

129 Druscilla Scribner and Tracy Slagter, "Recursive Norm Development: The Role of Supranational Courts," *Global Policy* 8, no. 3 (2017): 322–32; Tobias Berger, *Global Norms and Local Courts: Translating the Rule of Law in Bangladesh* (Oxford and New York: Oxford University Press, 2017). See also, Sassan Gholiagha, Anna Holzscheiter, and Andrea Liese, "Activating Norm Collisions: Interface Conflicts in International Drug Control," *Global Constitutionalism* (2020) 9, no. 2, 1–28.

130 See for example Ingo Venzke, *How Interpretation Makes International Law: On Semantic Change and Normative Twists* (Oxford and New York: Oxford University Press, 2012); Helfer and Voeten, "International Courts as Agents of Legal Change," 77–110; Laurence R. Helfer and Karen J. Alter, "Legitimacy and Lawmaking: A Tale of Three International Courts," *Theoretical Inquiries in Law* 14, no. 2 (2013): 479–503.

131 See for example Voeten, "Populism and Backlashes against International Courts," 1–16; Madsen, Cebulak, and Wiebusch, "Backlash against International Courts," 197–220.

European Court and provides insights into how backlash permeates institutions, shapes their preferences, and hinders progressive agendas.

Third, the empirical analysis of the transformation of the norm against torture and inhuman or degrading treatment reveals what human rights entail and what legal change implies. On the surface, a norm such as the prohibition of torture and inhuman or degrading treatment remains the same over time, banning torture and other forms of ill-treatment. However, its interpretive transformation and changing standards of accountability have real-life implications for the victims (right-holders) and the states (duty-bearers).[132] The analysis presented here suggests that the debate on torture should be broader. It should include new victim groups recognised under this prohibition, such as domestic violence victims or irregular immigrants, and new state obligations, such as the provision of legal protection and remedy. However, my analysis also cautions that this normative development may not always be linear and on the increase. Progression can stall and even give way to regression.

The Structure of the Book

The Introduction lays out the building blocks of the theoretical framework, which lists the conditions under which the European Court may be expected to issue audacious rulings. This framework relies on previous literature and insights gathered from expert interviews. According to this framework, for courts like the European Court to be audacious, they need wide discretionary space. Chapter 1 introduces this concept and discusses how the boundaries of this space are determined. It also examines how states might attempt to influence the Court through negative feedback and how the Court might realign its priorities based on this feedback to preserve its institutional image and reputation and secure access to resources. Finally, the chapter introduces a range of supplementary factors that increase the likelihood of audacious rulings (i.e., changing societal needs, legal developments external to the regime, and civil society campaigns). The framework helps explain why the norm changed in the way it did and

[132] Christopher J. Fariss, "Respect for Human Rights Has Improved over Time: Modeling the Changing Standard of Accountability," *American Political Science Review* 108, no. 2 (2014): 297–318; Christopher J. Fariss, "The Changing Standard of Accountability and the Positive Relationship between Human Rights Treaty Ratification and Compliance," *British Journal of Political Science* 48, no. 1 (2018): 239–71; Christopher J. Fariss and Geoff Dancy, "Measuring the Impact of Human Rights: Conceptual and Methodological Debates," *Annual Review of Law and Social Science* 13, no. 1 (2017): 273–94.

lays out the conditions under which the Court may be audacious enough to generate progressive change in the future.

In the first part of Chapter 2, I look at the Court's inner workings and how it functions by relying on expert interviews and previous research. Expanding this assessment beyond the elected judges, I argue that the Court defines its organizational priorities as a collective body. This essentially implies that all members of the judicial elite working at the Court contribute to defining their collective purpose and determining if there is a need for tactical balancing. In the second part of the chapter, I analyze the Court's institutional structure and dynamics influencing the breadth of the Court's discretionary space over time. In particular, I give an account of the Court's institutional transformation from a part-time Court to a full-time Court in 1998 and the subsequent reform processes.

Chapter 3 explains my methodological choices and introduces my original dataset and main results. This dataset is built based on content analysis of all Article 3 judgments issued between 1967 and 2016. It specifically includes information on the responding government, the type of obligation engaged, the outcome of the ruling, and the Court's reasoning for not finding a violation. By disaggregating the norm against torture and inhuman or degrading treatment into its components, I map out different types of obligations under the prohibition of torture. I also capture the moment when positive obligations were acknowledged and record their share of the general Article 3 jurisprudence. In addition to jurisprudential mapping, I use the data gathered from this analysis to measure the degree of audacity and forbearance demonstrated by the Court in its three different incarnations.

Chapter 4 provides an overview of how the modern understanding of the norm against torture and inhuman or degrading treatment first came to be before assessing its subsequent gradual transformation under the old Court's watch. Taking the Convention drafters' stated intentions as a baseline, it traces the norm's development through several landmark judgments. Relying on legal analysis, I show that the boundaries of the norm against torture were initially limited to appease member states. The old Court could expand the norm only when it was safe to do so – that is, when stakes were low and there was an emerging consensus around an issue. This constraint influenced the way the norm against torture and inhuman or degrading treatment developed in the early days of the European human rights regime.

Chapter 5 explores how, immediately after its inception in 1998, the new Court took to progressive interpretation and generated a foundational change in the way this prohibition is understood and applied. In particular, it takes a closer look at how the new Court introduced positive obligations and expanded the definition of this prohibition by enforcing ever-lower thresholds of severity for qualifying violations. I argue that, with these changes, the new Court reversed the compromises that the old Court made, especially regarding member states' national security concerns. Differing from the old Court, the new Court also showed a new willingness to recognise resource-intensive positive obligations and violations committed by private actors. I also discuss the areas where this progress was slower by looking at the Court's treatment of claims arising from systemic racism.

In Chapter 6, I apply my framework of analysis to explain how and why the norm against torture and inhuman and degrading treatment dramatically expanded after 1998. I look particularly at the conditions that made the new Court audacious enough to acknowledge these resource-intensive obligations. First, the Court secured a wide discretionary space after becoming a full-time court with compulsory jurisdiction. Second, it had reasons to believe that positive obligations were much needed in European societies, particularly in the aftermath of the accession of the formerly communist countries (known as the Eastward expansion). Third, introducing positive obligations was less likely to raise eyebrows as they were already established in the jurisprudence of other international courts and actively promoted by civil society groups.

In Chapter 7, I examine the current trends and the future of the norm against torture against the backdrop of recent reform initiatives and the general atmosphere of backlash since 2010. Relying on the results from my large-N analysis, insights from elite interviews, and legal analysis of some landmark rulings, I examine the reformed Court's selective forbearance and differential attitude toward different obligations under Article 3. I compare the reformed Court's recent decisions concerning the rights of irregular migrants, refugees, and asylum seekers with rulings concerning police brutality. I show that the reformed Court began to backtrack on the progressive policies developed in the late 1990s and early 2000s concerning the rights of migrants in general while increasing the standards of protection for countering police brutality, for example. This regressive trend directly corresponds to the degree of negative feedback that the Court has received from the Western European countries and indicates that the reformed Court is willing to heed member states' concerns while maintaining and improving human rights protection in other areas.

In the **Conclusion,** I revisit the key turning points in the Court's jurisprudence and unpack the reasons behind them. I also discuss the implications of the Court's varied attitudes on the norm's development and the degrees of protection it offers to victims. Finally, I discuss the applicability of the framework and associated key concepts to other studies on international courts and institutions.

1

The Conditions for Audacity

Why did the Court shape the norm against torture and inhuman or degrading treatment in the way it did? What explains the peculiarity of the late 1990s – the period when the Court effectuated a sudden and foundational change in the way this prohibition is understood? This chapter presents a framework that will help us answer these questions. The theoretical framework provides an institutional explanation for understanding norm change by situating the transformation of the norm within the broader transformation of the Court. It is built upon insights gathered from secondary sources and elite interviews. It aims to serve as a heuristic tool to explain the conditions under which international courts, such as the European Court of Human Rights, can be expected to be audacious or forbearing.

While the framework was created with the example of the European Court in mind, it is meant to be applicable to other courts and tribunals. The framework is composed of one core component and three contributing factors. Having a large discretionary space, with no or limited negative feedback, is a necessary condition for courts to issue more audacious rulings across the board. However, there are several other sociopolitical factors that can facilitate the Court's audacity, such as emerging societal needs, the legal developments introduced by other courts or institutions, and civil society campaigns.

This framework and the accompanying analysis that will be presented in Chapters 6 and 7 contribute to the rich literature on the politics of international courts, and International Relations and International Law scholarship in general.[1] Most of the existing legal literature would

[1] See, for example, Laurence R. Helfer and Erik Voeten, "International Courts as Agents of Legal Change: Evidence from LGBT Rights in Europe," *International Organization* 68, no. 1 (2014): 77–110; Karen J. Alter, *The New Terrain of International Law: Courts, Politics, Rights* (Princeton and Oxford: Princeton University Press, 2014); Laurence R. Helfer and Karen J. Alter, "Legitimacy and Lawmaking: A Tale of Three International Courts," *Theoretical Inquiries in Law* 14 (2013): 479–503; Ingo Venzke, *How Interpretation Makes International Law: On Semantic Change and Normative Twists* (Oxford and New York:

agree that lawmaking is an ordinary part of adjudication[2] and that legal change is one of its intentional or inadvertent outcomes.[3] Yet, this literature overlooks the question of when we can expect international courts to engage in progressive lawmaking or to resort to forbearance. The framework deals with this important question, promising to shed light on what motivates courts to serve as change agents and what hinders their progressive agendas.

The Core Component: Discretionary Space

A large discretionary space – either given to or carved out by courts – is a necessary condition for international courts to be audacious enough to generate progressive change. The discretionary space, or the zone of discretion, is the strategic space within which courts carry out their functions in line with their preferences.[4] The bounds of this zone are delimited by the constraints set by formal rules. Within this space, courts have room for maneuver[5] and may "operate creatively."[6] This concept comes out of the rationalist institutionalist literature.[7] It is tailored

Oxford University Press, 2012); Karen J. Alter and Laurence R. Helfer, "Nature or Nurture? Judicial Lawmaking in the European Court of Justice and the Andean Tribunal of Justice," *International Organization* 64, no. 4 (2010): 563–92; Ingo Venzke, "Between Power and Persuasion: On International Institutions' Authority in Making Law," *Transnational Legal Theory* 4, no. 3 (2013): 354–73.

2 See, for example, Fuad Zarbiyev, "Judicial Activism," in *Max Planck Encyclopedia of International Procedural Law (EiPro)* (Oxford: Oxford University Press, 2018).

3 Studies have critically analyzed judicial lawmaking and its consequence, for example, Armin von Bogdandy and Ingo Venzke, "In Whose Name? An Investigation of International Courts' Public Authority and Its Democratic Justification," *European Journal of International Law* 23, no. 1 (2012): 7–41; Tom Ginsburg, "Bounded Discretion in International Judicial Lawmaking," *Virginia Journal of International Law* 45, no. 3 (2005): 631–73; Helfer and Voeten, "International Courts as Agents of Legal Change," 77–110.

4 Alec Stone Sweet, "The European Court of Justice and the Judicialization of EU Governance," *Living Reviews in European Governance* 5, no. 2 (2010): 15.

5 Mark Thatcher and Alec Stone Sweet, "Theory and Practice of Delegation to Non-Majoritarian Institutions," *West European Politics* 25, no. 1 (2002): 5.

6 Mark A. Pollack, "Delegation, Agency, and Agenda Setting in the European Community," *International Organization* 51, no. 1 (1997): 129.

7 Mark A. Pollack, "Learning from the Americanists (Again): Theory and Method in the Study of Delegation," *West European Politics* 25, no. 1 (2002): 200–19; Pollack, "Delegation, Agency, and Agenda Setting in the European Community," 99–134; Mark A. Pollack, *The Engines of European Integration: Delegation, Agency, and Agenda Setting in the EU* (Oxford: Oxford University Press, 2003); Jonas Tallberg, "Delegation to Supranational Institutions: Why, How, and with What Consequences?," *West European Politics* 25, no. 1 (2002): 23–46; Jonas Tallberg, "The Anatomy of Autonomy: An Institutional Account of Variation in Supranational Influence," *JCMS: Journal of Common Market Studies* 38, no. 5 (2000): 843–64.

to study non-majoritarian institutions like courts.[8] What is distinctive about non-majoritarian institutions is that they exercise "specialised public authority" without being "elected by the people, nor [are they] directly managed by elected officials."[9] Courts are a special case of non-majoritarian institutions. They are delegated with authority to carry out functions such as supervising the implementation of a treaty, interpreting and applying its provisions, settling disputes, and (possibly) developing further rules.[10]

While the zone of discretion may appear to be an elusive concept, it can be pinned down in reference to other measures, in particular, court autonomy and authority. Autonomy concerns a court's independence from member states and parent organizations.[11] Authority, on the other hand, refers to a court's credibility and ability to influence its audience by serving as a reference point,[12] which goes beyond the question of whether court judgments are complied with.[13] High degrees of authority and autonomy should ideally yield a wide zone of discretion.

For international courts and tribunals, complete independence may not be possible because they derive their authority from a constitutive treaty signed and enforced by states. Moreover, it is these states that elect or appoint the judges sitting on these courts. Therefore, international courts

[8] See Alec Stone Sweet and Thomas Brunell, "Trustee Courts and the Judicialization of International Regimes: The Politics of Majoritarian Activism in the ECHR, the EU, and the WTO." *Journal of Law and Courts* 1, no. 1 (2013)." See also Sweet, "The European Court of Justice and the Judicialization of EU Governance," 1–50.

[9] Thatcher and Sweet, "Theory and Practice of Delegation to Non-Majoritarian Institutions," 2.

[10] Kenneth W. Abbott et al., "The Concept of Legalization," *International Organization* 54, no. 3 (2000): 401–19.

[11] Complete independence from member states is not entirely possible. This is because international courts and tribunals have a subordinate nature since they derive their authority from a constitutive treaty signed and enforced by states or because their judges are elected or appointed by states. However, courts, as in the case of the European Court, may be able to carve out a space of autonomy for themselves over time. See John Merrills, "International Adjudication and Autonomy," in *International Organizations and the Idea of Autonomy: Institutional Independence in the International Legal Order* (New York: Routledge, 2011).

[12] Authority exists in different forms, and it may have different marks; for more information, see Fuad Zarbiyev, "Saying Credibly What the Law Is: On Marks of Authority in International Law," *Journal of International Dispute Settlement* 9, no. 2 (2018): 291–314; Nico Krisch, "Liquid Authority in Global Governance," *International Theory* 9, no. 2 (2017): 237–60.

[13] This definition is inspired by the ones offered in Ingo Venzke, "Understanding the Authority of International Courts and Tribunals: On Delegation and Discursive Construction," *Theoretical Inquiries in Law* 14, no. 2 (2013): 398; Karen J. Alter, Laurence R. Helfer, and Mikael Rask Madsen, "How Context Shapes the Authority of International Courts," *Law and Contemporary Problems* 79, no. 1 (2016): 1–36.

are by nature subordinate and depend on states.[14] That said, courts may be granted, or they may carve out, a space of autonomy for themselves over time, as was the case with the European Court.[15] According to Mikael Rask Madsen, the Court lacked autonomy when it was first instituted, but it then acquired "a higher degree of legal autonomy." This was due to "a set of interdependent processes of institutionalization, legalization, and even scientification of European human rights."[16] Darren Hawkings and Wade Jacoby provide a similar narrative.[17] They find that while the Court had limited autonomy in the 1960s and 1970s, its autonomy increased from the early 1980s onward.[18]

Authority, on the other hand, concerns the courts' standing in the eyes of member states and the broader international legal community. In theory, authority is derived from a court's reputation and credibility as an independent body in settling disputes in light of the law. In practice, a court's authority is certified when its decisions are respected and not challenged by member states.[19] Madsen, in another study, finds that the European Court's authority, like its autonomy, has increased over time.[20] The Court maintained narrow legal authority from its inception until the mid-to-late 1970s, but then it began to enjoy extensive authority in the 1990s and became "the *de facto* Supreme Court of human rights in Europe" with "a steady and growing docket."[21]

Indeed, the European Court began enjoying a larger discretionary space after the late 1990s, as Alec Stone Sweet and Thomas Brunell show in their study.[22] This is due to various reasons. First, the Court has been endowed

[14] Courtney Hillebrecht, *Saving the International Justice Regime: Beyond Backlash against International Courts* (Cambridge and New York: Cambridge University Press, 2021), 32.

[15] Mikael Rask Madsen, "From Cold War Instrument to Supreme European Court: The European Court of Human Rights at the Crossroads of International and National Law and Politics," *Law and Social Inquiry* 32, no. 1 (2007): 143.

[16] Ibid., 138.

[17] Darren Hawkins and Wade Jacoby, "Agent Permeability, Principal Delegation and the European Court of Human Rights," *The Review of International Organizations* 3, no. 1 (2008): 1–28.

[18] Ibid., 16–24.

[19] This definition is inspired by the one offered in Alter, Helfer, and Madsen, "How Context Shapes the Authority of International Courts," 1–36. More specifically, they measure authority based on the extent to which international courts' decisions are respected and the domestic authorities take measures to implement them.

[20] Mikael Rask Madsen, "The Challenging Authority of the European Court of Human Rights: From Cold War Legal Diplomacy to the Brighton Declaration and Backlash," *Law and Contemporary Problems* 79, no. 1 (2016).

[21] Ibid., 143.

[22] Sweet and Brunell, "Trustee Courts and the Judicialization of International Regimes," 61.

with compulsory jurisdiction to authoritatively interpret the Convention since 1998. Second, the Court has been able to expand its own zone of discretion by interpreting the Convention and the scope of its powers.[23] An important illustration of such judicial constructs is the principle of evolutive interpretation (i.e., the living instrument doctrine).[24] This principle has provided justifications for progressive interpretation in light of present-day circumstances and for expanding the Court's interpretive authority. Finally, states have not attempted to override any of the Court's important decisions regarding the interpretation of the European Convention by means of treaty revision.[25]

What Stone Sweet and Brunell do not remark upon in their study is that the European Court has also been known to engage in more forbearing treaty interpretation and to generate interpretive concepts that have the effect of narrowing the scope of its powers. Prominent examples falling under this category are the principle of subsidiarity and the margin of appreciation doctrine – both require the Court to act deferent to domestic authorities and to their authority to guarantee rights protection at the national level.[26] The existence and use of such principles do not mean that the Court's zone of discretion is effectively contracted. Instead, they signal that the Court does not have the sole intention to use its authority to the maximum. It may also have the instinct to use less discretion and assume a more circumscribed role.

Such a trade-off might be necessary for obtaining essential resources to survive and be secure (e.g., funding, state support, or legitimacy).[27] As Michael Barnett and Liv Coleman argue, institutions have diverse preferences that range from surviving to furthering their mandate and

[23] Sweet, "The European Court of Justice and the Judicialization of EU Governance," 15.

[24] Kanstantsin Dzehtsiarou, "European Consensus and the Evolutive Interpretation of the European Convention on Human Rights," *German Law Journal* 12, no. 10 (2011): 1731–45; George Letsas, "The ECHR as a Living Instrument: Its Meaning and Legitimacy," in *Constituting Europe: The European Court of Human Rights in a National, European and Global Context*, ed. Andreas Føllesdal, Birgit Peters, and Geir Ulfstein (New York: Cambridge University Press, 2013): 106–41.

[25] Sweet and Brunell, "Trustee Courts and the Judicialization of International Regimes," 66–67.

[26] Marisa Iglesias Vila, "Subsidiarity, Margin of Appreciation and International Adjudication within a Cooperative Conception of Human Rights," *International Journal of Constitutional Law* 15, no. 2 (2017): 393–413; Eva Brems, "Positive Subsidiarity and Its Implications for the Margin of Appreciation Doctrine," *Netherlands Quarterly of Human Rights* 37, no. 3(2019).

[27] Michael Barnett and Liv Coleman, "Designing Police: Interpol and the Study of Change in International Organizations," *International Studies Quarterly* 49, no. 4 (2005): 593–619.

protecting their autonomy. Institutions make trade-offs to pursue these goals.[28] In this book, I argue that this has been precisely the case for the European Court. The Court has used these diverse judicial tools to make trade-offs and adjust its behaviour to prevent or mitigate widespread negative feedback and political pushback.[29]

Determinants of the Width of Discretionary Space: State Control

As the case of the European Court shows, the zone of discretion is not a static space. Once the initial zone of discretion is established by formal powers and controls, it can be subsequently readjusted. Court activities may spur reactions from states, especially when they create domestic distributional consequences by issuing controversial rulings that are financially or politically costly to implement.[30]

In order to better understand what determines the bounds of discretionary space, it is worth briefly revisiting the theories on institutional design and delegation.[31] Most existing work agrees that international courts come with a "sovereignty cost" that can grow over time.[32] What they disagree on is the extent to which states can recover some of this cost by exerting control over courts.

Rationalist design scholars view states as the principals that delegate authority to courts as their agents, based on a contractual agreement.[33] While the expectations might be clear at the outset, courts – just like other institutions with delegated authority – may grow to have their own

[28] Ibid., 615.

[29] Martin Shapiro and Alec Stone Sweet, *On Law, Politics, and Judicialization*, 1st edition (Oxford and New York: Oxford University Press, 2002), 130.

[30] Hillebrecht, *Saving the International Justice Regime*, 36–37.

[31] See, for example, Darren G. Hawkins et al., eds., *Delegation and Agency in International Organizations*. Political Economy of Institutions and Decisions (Cambridge: Cambridge University Press, 2006); Thatcher and Sweet, "Theory and Practice of Delegation to Non-Majoritarian Institutions"; Tallberg, "Delegation to Supranational Institutions"; Karen J. Alter, "'Delegating to International Courts: Self-Binding vs. Other-Binding Delegation," *Law and Contemporary Problems* 71, no. 1 (2008); Manfred Elsig and Mark A. Pollack, "Agents, Trustees, and International Courts: The Politics of Judicial Appointment at the World Trade Organization," *European Journal of International Relations* 20, no. 2 (2014): 391–415.

[32] Kenneth W. Abbott and Duncan Snidal, "Hard and Soft Law in International Governance," *International Organization* 54, no. 3 (2000): 437.

[33] Pollack, "Delegation, Agency, and Agenda Setting in the European Community"; Pollack, "Learning from the Americanists (Again)," 200–219; Kenneth W. Abbott and Duncan Snidal, "Why States Act through Formal International Organizations," *Journal of Conflict Resolution* 42, no. 1 (1998): 3–32.

preferences,[34] or may evade control mechanisms (i.e., agent slack).[35] They might be inclined to exploit their discretion and act autonomously.[36] In order to prevent this, states often prefer to exert direct control over delegated institutions – including, for example, withholding delegation,[37] imposing bureaucratic and budgetary restrictions,[38] and overruling judgments.[39] While agreeing that international courts are special cases of delegated authority and are more prone to being autonomous, most scholars in this camp theorise about the ways in which states may exert direct or indirect influence on courts.[40]

There are others who disagree with characterizing courts as agents, opting instead to characterise international courts as trustees.[41] They find that, while it might be appealing to control courts to prevent them from solely pursuing their own preferences, in reality, states enforce only limited control on courts.[42] This is because the functions that the courts typically carry out require "substantive levels of discretion."[43] In other words, courts need independence in order to preserve their own legitimacy and the legitimacy of their judgments.[44] In addition, courts are not solely dependent on their delegated authority; they may also derive some

[34] Hawkins and Jacoby, "Agent Permeability, Principal Delegation and the European Court of Human Rights."

[35] Karen J. Alter, "Agents or Trustees? International Courts in Their Political Context," *European Journal of International Relations* 14, no. 1 (2008): 34; Richard H. Steinberg, "The Decline of Global Trade Negotiations – and the Rise of Judicial and Regional Alternatives," *Journal of Scholarly Perspectives* 5, no. 1 (2009).

[36] Tallberg, "Delegation to Supranational Institutions," 28.

[37] Curtis Bradley and Judith Kelley, "The Concept of International Delegation," *Law and Contemporary Problems* 71 (2008): 20.

[38] Hillebrecht, *Saving the International Justice Regime*, 25.

[39] Clifford J. Carrubba and Matthew Gabel, "International Courts: A Theoretical Assessment," *Annual Review of Political Science* 20, no. 1 (2017): 55–73; Richard H. Steinberg, "Judicial Lawmaking at the WTO: Discursive, Constitutional, and Political Constraints," *American Journal of International Law* 98, no. 2 (2004): 247–75.

[40] Hawkins and Jacoby, "Agent Permeability, Principal Delegation and the European Court of Human Rights," 10.

[41] Alter, "Agents or Trustees?," 33; Thatcher and Sweet, "Theory and Practice of Delegation to Non-majoritarian Institutions," 7.

[42] Alter, "Delegating to International Courts"; Alter, "Agents or Trustees?

[43] Tallberg, "Delegation to Supranational Institutions," 26.

[44] Independence can be understood as impartiality and political insularity – the notion that judges will decide on the basis of facts and law and will not be employed as tools for furthering political goals. Christopher M. Larkins, "Judicial Independence and Democratization: A Theoretical and Conceptual Analysis," *American Journal of Comparative Law* 44, no. 4 (1996): 609.

authority from their normative functions.[45] Finally, courts might even expand their authority by building alliances with sub-state actors and compliance constituencies (e.g., advocacy networks, domestic judges, and officials from administrative agencies).[46] Such transnational coalitions may provide courts with an alternative source of support and reduce their dependency on states.

Even starting from the assumption that states are less likely to put in place intrusive control mechanisms over international courts,[47] we can reasonably expect that states may still attempt to reduce the sovereignty cost by resorting to indirect or more informal measures.[48] Laurence Helfer and Anne-Marie Slaughter describe these as "a range of structural, political, and discursive mechanisms to ensure that independent judges are nevertheless operating within a set of legal and political constraints."[49] These reactions often may not amount to full dejudicialization or re-contracting – a complicated formal process to amend courts' constitutive treaties and the scope of their delegated authority.[50] Instead, indirect means may include the appointment of judges who favour deferring to state policies,[51] communicating dissatisfaction,[52] threatening withdrawals,[53] or a variety of other court curbing strategies.[54] As Mark Pollack highlights in his study of the paralysis of the Appellate Body of the World Trade Organization (WTO), such attacks or threats thereof are common.[55]

45 Hillebrecht, *Saving the International Justice Regime*, 18.

46 Alter and Helfer, "Nature or Nurture?," 563. Karen J. Alter, James T. Gathii, and Laurence R. Helfer, "Backlash against International Courts in West, East and Southern Africa: Causes and Consequences," *European Journal of International Law* 27, no. 2 (2016): 293–328.

47 Tallberg, "The Anatomy of Autonomy," 861.

48 For more details on the list of strategies designed to undermine courts' authority, see Heidi Nichols Haddad, "Judicial Institution Builders: NGOs and International Human Rights Courts," *Journal of Human Rights* 11, no. 1 (2012): 134.

49 Laurence R. Helfer and Anne-Marie Slaughter, "Why States Create International Tribunals: A Response to Professors Posner and Yoo," *California Law Review* 93, no. 3 (2005): 902.

50 Alter, "Agents or Trustees?"; Daniel Abebe and Tom Ginsburg, "The Dejudicialization of International Politics?," *International Studies Quarterly* 63, no. 3 (2019): 525.

51 Erik Voeten, "The Politics of International Judicial Appointments: Evidence from the European Court of Human Rights," *International Organization* 61, no. 4 (2007): 669–701.

52 Abebe and Ginsburg, "The Dejudicialization of International Politics?," 525.

53 Ginsburg, "Bounded Discretion in International Judicial Lawmaking," 557–58; Steinberg, "Judicial Lawmaking at the WTO," 263–64.

54 Mark A. Pollack, "International Court Curbing in Geneva: Lessons from the Paralysis of the WTO Appellate Body," *Governance* (2022), https://doi.org/10.1111/gove.12686.

55 Ibid., 21.

Such reactions, when concerted or systematic, might compel the courts to adjust their practices and interpretive preferences.[56] In this sense, courts, just like other institutions, may act strategically to ensure their survival and increase their reputation, relevance, and resources.[57] As this book argues, forbearance is the collective term to depict judicial strategies geared toward such aims. It essentially means that a given court chooses to underutilise its prerogatives and refrains from issuing sweeping judgments with significant adjustment or implementation costs. This dynamic implies that even courts that enjoy a wide discretionary space occasionally may be constrained by the preferences of other actors, especially states.[58] Only when such constraints are lifted can international courts afford to be audacious and pursue more progressive agendas unrestrained by state interests.

Negative Feedback and Signaling

When could widespread negative feedback influence court behaviour? Serving as a tool of indirect control, negative feedback is not only about punishing courts for past behaviour; it is also for future signalling.[59] The influence of negative feedback may work in two ways. First, when accumulated, negative feedback can erode the state or public support for an institution. The mechanism behind this dynamic can be best explained by drawing inspiration from recent Historical Institutionalist accounts that focus on endogenous drivers of change – rather than exogenous ones such as geopolitical shifts, recessions, crises, or other shocks.[60] The

[56] This adjustment might involve a combination of rational and cognitive processes. For more details, see Ezgi Yildiz and Umut Yüksel, "Understanding the Limitations of Behavioralism: Lessons from the Field of Maritime Delimitation," *German Law Journal* 23, no. 3 (2022): 413–30.

[57] Barnett and Coleman, "Designing Police."

[58] Ginsburg, "Bounded Discretion in International Judicial Lawmaking," 632.

[59] Joost Pauwelyn and Manfred Elsig, "The Politics of Treaty Interpretation: Variations and Explanations across International Tribunals," in *Interdisciplinary Perspectives on International Law and International Relations: The State of the Art*, ed. Jeffrey L. Dunoff and Mark A. Pollack (Cambridge: Cambridge University Press, 2012), 445–74.

[60] See, for example, Wolfgang Streeck and Kathleen Thelen, eds., *Beyond Continuity: Institutional Change in Advanced Political Economies* (Oxford and New York: Oxford University Press, 2005). For a general overview of this literature, see Orfeo Fioretos, "Historical Institutionalism in International Relations," *International Organization* 65, no. 2 (2011): 367–99; Giovanni Capoccia, "When Do Institutions 'Bite'? Historical Institutionalism and the Politics of Institutional Change," *Comparative Political Studies*

source of change can be the institutions themselves. As explained by James Mahoney and Kathleen Thelen, institutions generate distributional effects; those that are not advantaged by this effect are likely to challenge the institutions.[61] Such negative feedback might have a diffusion effect and culminate in social and political pressures undermining the institutions.[62] This observation is applicable to international courts whose outputs might generate negative feedback and erode their "political support bases over time."[63] The erosion of support might trigger formal or informal processes that threaten international courts' authority and autonomy.

Second, negative feedback and signalling can inform courts' organizational priorities. Chief among those priorities is maintaining a good reputation in the eyes of member states, which oftentimes is a condition for securing resources and enhancing courts' political and social influence.[64] Courts' concern for reputation and authority can be a constraint on their choices and activities, and can compel them to prioritise their "organizational imperatives" over pursuing unequivocally progressive agendas – a phenomenon coined as the "authority trap."[65] In order to maintain their reputation and authority, international courts may respond to negative feedback by engaging in strategies for institutional survival and resilience, which include judicial avoidance,[66] or showing deference.[67] In so doing, they

49, no. 8 (2016): 1095–1127; Giovanni Capoccia and R. Daniel Kelemen, "The Study of Critical Junctures: Theory, Narrative, and Counterfactuals in Historical Institutionalism," *World Politics* 59, no. 3 (2007): 341–69.

61 James Mahoney and Kathleen Thelen, "A Theory of Gradual Institutional Change," in *Explaining Institutional Change: Ambiguity, Agency, and Power*, ed. James Mahoney and Kathleen Thelen (New York: Cambridge University Press, 2010), 8.

62 Wolfgang Streeck and Kathleen Thelen, "Introduction: Institutional Change in Advanced Political Economies," in *Beyond Continuity: Institutional Change in Advanced Political Economies*, ed. Wolfgang Streeck and Kathleen Thelen (Oxford: Oxford University Press, 2005), 1–39.

63 Alan M. Jacobs, "Social Policy Dynamics," in *The Oxford Handbook of Historical Institutionalism*, ed. Orfeo Fioretos, Tulia G. Falleti, and Adam Sheingate (Oxford: Oxford University Press, 2016), 351.

64 Nuno Garoupa and Tom Ginsburg, *Judicial Reputation: A Comparative Theory* (University of Chicago Press, 2015), 5.

65 This concept created for international nongovernmental organizations has relevance for international courts whose concern for authority or reputation may serve as a driver for forbearing and constrained strategies. Sarah S. Stroup and Wendy H. Wong, *The Authority Trap: Strategic Choices of International NGOs* (Ithaca: Cornell University Press, 2017).

66 Steinberg, "Judicial Lawmaking at the WTO," 269.

67 Øyvind Stiansen and Erik Voeten, "Backlash and Judicial Restraint: Evidence from the European Court of Human Rights," *International Studies Quarterly* 64, no. 4 (2020): 770.

underutilise their discretionary space and signal back to the states that they can operate on lower sovereignty costs.[68]

Strategies for Institutional Survival and Resilience: Between Tactical Balancing and Trade-Offs

International courts are sensitive to the threat of negative feedback and such feedback itself. They engage in tactical balancing exercises to fend off negative criticism and to preserve the institution and its public image. This self-preservation exercise is a collective strategy undertaken not only by the judges who are elected for a limited term but also by the Secretariat staff employed on a more permanent basis, as we will discover in Chapter 2. Hence, all members of the judicial elite working at the Court can partake in fashioning strategies and trade-offs for institutional survival or resilience.

The literature on courts provides insights into how this trade-off might look. For example, Diana Kapiszewski argues that judicial review is not a strictly mechanical exercise and that it is accompanied by tactical balancing.[69] That is to say, judges read the content of each politically important case and the case's context. They simultaneously balance multiple considerations, including their own ideology and life view, how they perceive the interest of the institution they serve, the political and economic implications of their decision, the opinion of the public, and the state of International Law.[70] Kapiszewski's theory convincingly portrays how judicial decisions are shaped by "multiple political and institutional pressures."[71] It also explains how judges can be selectively assertive when the context calls for it.

This depiction is directly applicable to the case of the European Court. When the Court's zone of discretion is narrow, issue characteristics matter more; the Court can be assertive only in select instances. The likelihood

[68] Emilie M. Hafner-Burton, Edward D. Mansfield, and Jon C. W. Pevehouse, "Human Rights Institutions, Sovereignty Costs and Democratization," *British Journal of Political Science* 45, no. 1 (2015): 1–27.

[69] Diana Kapiszewski, "Tactical Balancing: High Court Decision Making on Politically Crucial Cases," *Law and Society Review* 45, no. 2 (2011): 471–506.

[70] According to Kapiszewski's framework, judges have six considerations: (1) their own ideology, (2) judicial institutional interests, (3) elected branch preferences, (4) the possible economic or political consequences of their decision, (5) popular opinion regarding the case, and (6) the law and legal considerations. Kapiszewski, "Tactical Balancing," 472–73.

[71] Ibid., 472.

of the Court being assertive and audacious increases as its zone of discretion enlarges. This is what Mikael Rask Madsen captures in his study of the history of the European human rights regime. Madsen introduces the concept of "legal diplomacy" to depict the old European Court and the Commission's attempts to provide legal and extra-legal solutions to the disputes they settled up until the 1970s. He also remarks that legal diplomacy gave way to more progressive trends in the subsequent period, especially in the late 1990s, when the new Court secured a larger zone of discretion.[72]

The interviews I gathered at the Court provide insights into how this tactical balancing might look today. Almost all of the judges I interviewed confirmed, either explicitly or implicitly, that judges do consider the broader implications that their decisions might generate. During an interview, an experienced judge clarified the distinction between political decisions and legal decisions that may have a political impact. According to them, the Court refrains from making political decisions. This does not, however, mean the Court is unaware of the political effects of its decisions. It takes them into consideration when delivering judgments.[73] Another judge underlined that the Court cannot function in isolation and that "the European Court is particularly well placed to observe the general trends in the society."[74] Similarly, a judge from a Western European country explained that, normatively, the Court should not be influenced by external factors when delivering decisions; however, empirically that is the case. They avowed the following:

> We are human beings. I am a human being like yourself, with blood and flesh. I read the newspapers. I understand what is happening in the environment. I am sure, at least subconsciously, we, as judges, are influenced by external factors, and whether we are more prone to take more human rights viewpoint or more government viewpoint is a matter of personality. It depends on where you are coming from. A lot of the judges come from the human rights community, so they instinctively perhaps are willing to listen to human rights views, and some come from the civil service sector, and they pay more attention to the state side. Empirically, judges are

[72] Mikael Rask Madsen, "Protracted Institutionalization of the Strasbourg Court: From Legal Diplomacy to Integrationist Jurisprudence," in *The European Court of Human Rights between Law and Politics*, ed. Jonas Christoffersen and Mikael Rask Madsen (New York: Oxford University Press, 2011), 56–57"; Madsen, "The Challenging Authority of the European Court of Human Rights."

[73] Interview 18.

[74] Interview 11.

> influenced by factors. International judges cannot be so naive as to do their jobs without taking account of external factors. It is all about legitimacy, trust, and the community believing that they are doing what they are supposed to be doing. So normatively, no; they should not take account of external factors, but yes, empirically, they do in different ways for different reasons.[75]

Another judge from an Eastern European country explained the dynamics of tactical balancing and argued that judges "cannot decide the cases without having a general political background." They then added that "This is completely normal. We are aware of the developments around us, and we have to look at [judicial review] from a certain perspective."[76]

Some judges supported their view on the necessity of tactical balancing with examples. One judge from Eastern Europe referred to *Hirst (No. 2)* v. *the United Kingdom*,[77] and *Greens and M.T.* v. *the United Kingdom*,[78] where the Court found that issuing a blanket ban on prisoners' voting rights violated the Convention.[79] They disclosed that the Court felt the need to find the United Kingdom in violation due to changing trends in Europe, as well as the strong signals sent from the Parliamentary Assembly against voting rights restrictions.[80] Similarly, another judge from Western Europe brought up *Lautsi* v. *Italy*,[81] a controversial decision about the display of crucifixes in state schools.[82] In the Chamber judgment of 2009, the Court unanimously found Italy in violation of Article 2 of Protocol 1 (right to education) in conjunction with Article 9 (freedom of thought, conscience, and religion). The case was then appealed to the Grand Chamber, which reversed this decision in 2011; this change, the judge later explained, was due to state pressure. They specifically underlined that, alongside ten member states of the Council of Europe, thirty-three members of the European Parliament collectively sent submissions in favour of the Italian

[75] Interview 15.

[76] Interview 13.

[77] *Hirst (No. 2)* v. *the United Kingdom*, app. no. 74025/01, ECHR [GC] (October 6, 2005).

[78] *Greens and M.T.* v. *United Kingdom*, app. nos. 60041/08 and 60054/08, ECHR (November 23, 2010).

[79] Interview 4.

[80] Parliamentary Assembly, Resolution on the Abolition of Restrictions on the Right to Vote 1459 (2005) (June 24, 2005); Parliamentary Assembly, Recommendation 1714 (2005) (June 24, 2005), which urged the Committee of Ministers to appeal that member states reconsider existing restrictions on electoral rights of prisoners and military personnel.

[81] *Lautsi and Others* v. *Italy*, app. no. 30814/06, ECHR (November 3, 2009).

[82] Interview 10.

government's position.[83] This was the largest group of third-party interveners ever in the Court's history, collectively appealing to the Court to be more forbearing.[84] As these examples show, legal review is often accompanied by tactical balancing, whereby judges gauge the importance of the case and the repercussions it might generate – albeit under the condition of imperfect information.[85]

Tactical balancing accompanies crucial cases with political and legal complexity in particular, as the examples above show. But tactical balancing in itself is a neutral exercise that might result in forbearing or audacious decisions. One argument proposed in this book is that the Court may tactically decide to act more forbearing when its zone of discretion is limited or when it receives overwhelming negative feedback. Alternatively, tactical balancing yields more audacious decisions when the Court's discretionary space is wide. Yet, as we will see in the following section, other factors can also facilitate the Court's assertiveness.

Contributing Factors for Increased Audacity

In addition to the zone of discretion, which is the cornerstone, there are other sociopolitical and legal factors considered in the framework. The Court's likelihood of being audacious increases when its decisions are in line with (1) widespread societal needs, (2) the precedents or legal principles set by other courts and institutions or in other treaties, and (3) civil society campaigns. The expectation is that when the Court enjoys a large discretionary space, unrestrained by negative feedback, it will weigh these contributing factors more than its need to pay heed to state interests.

The existing literature has already identified the importance of these factors on the Court's behaviour and decisions. First, the Court may be more willing to effectuate change concerning matters around which European societies agree. As sociolegal scholars and legal historians such as Mikael Rask Madsen and Ed Bates explain, sociopolitical context constrains or enables the Court's tendencies to be more progressive.[86] There are also

83 The intervening countries were Armenia, Bulgaria, Cyprus, the Russian Federation, Greece, Lithuania, Malta, Monaco, Romania, and the Republic of San Marino.

84 Interview 10.

85 Abebe and Ginsburg, "The Dejudicialization of International Politics?," 524.

86 See, for example, Mikael Rask Madsen, "International Human Rights and the Transformation of European Society: From 'Free Europe' to the Europe of Human Rights," in *Law and the Formation of Modern Europe: Perspectives from the Historical Sociology of Law*, ed. Mikael Rask Madsen and Chris Thornhill (Cambridge: Cambridge University

studies that explain how changing social trends may compel the Court to be more progressive and justify decisions with wider implications.[87] For example, Sarah Lucy Cooper finds that, while the Court rejected the notion of same-sex relationships as family units in the 1980s, it began to be receptive to the idea only in the 1990s when it had already become socially acceptable in Europe.[88]

This generally implies that successful attempts at change concern emerging societal needs or issues unlikely to provoke political resistance. The Court has traditionally checked this by looking at whether there are repeated complaints about an issue and whether a European consensus exists around a practice.[89] The existence of repeated complaints, especially brought against multiple countries, is a sign of the pervasiveness of the problem. For example, introducing procedural obligations under the prohibition of torture was a response to a problem demonstrated by the systemic rule of law deficiencies in several member states.[90] The Court can also discern general trends by carrying out European consensus analysis (i.e., assessing whether there is unified agreement around a certain practice in Europe).[91] To illustrate, the Court justified its decision that states would not have a positive obligation to facilitate euthanasia by looking at the general trends in Europe. Noting that "assisted suicide and consensual killing are unlawful in all Convention countries except the Netherlands,"

Press, 2014); Madsen, "From Cold War Instrument to Supreme European Court"; Ed Bates, *The Evolution of the European Convention on Human Rights: From Its Inception to the Creation of a Permanent Court of Human Rights* (Oxford and New York: Oxford University Press, 2010).

87 The European consensus doctrine works on this idea. European consensus refers to the common position of the majority of member states within the Council of Europe and indicates that, if in doubt, the Court will interpret in favor of this common position. Dzehtsiarou, "European Consensus and the Evolutive Interpretation of the European Convention on Human Rights."

88 Sarah Lucy Cooper, "Marriage, Family, Discrimination and Contradiction: An Evaluation of the Legacy and Future of the European Court of Human Rights' Jurisprudence on LGBT Rights," *German Law Journal* 12, no. 10 (2011): 1746–63.

89 Dzehtsiarou, "European Consensus and the Evolutive Interpretation of the European Convention on Human Rights."

90 Eva Brems and Laurens Lavrysen, "Procedural Justice in Human Rights Adjudication: The European Court of Human Rights," *Human Rights Quarterly* 35, no. 1 (2013): 176–200.

91 See more, Kanstantsin Dzehtsiarou, *European Consensus and the Legitimacy of the European Court of Human Rights* (Cambridge: Cambridge University Press, 2015); Panos Kapotas and Vassilis P. Tzevelekos, *Building Consensus on European Consensus: Judicial Interpretation of Human Rights in Europe and Beyond* (Cambridge: Cambridge University Press, 2019).

the Court ruled that states do not have an obligation to sanction euthanasia under Article 3 in *Pretty* v. *the United Kingdom* in 2002.[92]

Second, the Court may channel judicial innovations created or promoted by other courts and institutions or in other treaties, as Magdalena Forowicz shows in her work.[93] Innovations and changes initiated elsewhere may inform the Court about general trends in International Law. More practically, other institutions or treaties may set precedents and open the gateways for change. It is plausible to assume that emulating legal change launched by another institution would be less costly.[94] Therefore, these precedents provide the Court not only with guidance, but also with legally valid justifications to effectuate change within the European human rights system. Particularly in the context of the prohibition of torture, the global anti-torture regime – composed of specialised treaties, expert bodies, and committees that carry out on-site visits – and other Council of Europe instruments against torture and inhuman or degrading treatment have provided the Court with evidence or legal grounds to proactively develop the norm. For example, when recognizing Nahide's victimhood under Article 3 in *Opuz* v. *Turkey*, the European Court relied on the Convention on the Elimination of Discrimination against Women (CEDAW) and the Belém do Pará Convention.[95]

Finally, as previous studies established, civil society organizations can shape and inform court decisions by strategically litigating key cases and actively promoting the principles set out in these cases.[96] In particular, the influence of third-party interventions has been subjected to systematic studies.[97] For example, Yaël Ronen and Yale Naggan argue that although

[92] *Pretty* v. *the United Kingdom*, application no. 2346/02, ECHR (April 29, 2002), §28.

[93] Magdalena Forowicz, *The Reception of International Law in the European Court of Human Rights* (Oxford and New York: Oxford University Press, 2010), 195.

[94] Yildiz et al., "New Norms in Old Regimes: Judicial Strategies for Importing Environmental Norms." *Unpublished Manuscript*, 2022.

[95] *Opuz* v. *Turkey*, application no. 33401/02, ECHR (June 9, 2009).

[96] Rachel A. Cichowski, "Civil Society and the European Court of Human Rights," in *The European Court of Human Rights between Law and Politics*, ed. Jonas Christoffersen and Mikael Rask Madsen (Oxford: Oxford University Press, 2011); Loveday Hodson, *NGOs and the Struggle for Human Rights in Europe* (Oxford and Portland: Hart Publishing, 2011); Heidi Nichols Haddad, *The Hidden Hands of Justice: NGOs, Human Rights, and International Courts* (New York: Cambridge University Press, 2018).

[97] For an extensive analysis of the third-party interventions before the European Court, see Laura Van den Eynde, "An Empirical Look at the Amicus Curiae Practice of Human Rights NGOs before the European Court of Human Rights," *Netherlands Quarterly of Human Rights* 31, no. 3 (2013): 271–313."

there are relatively few cases in which *amicus curiae* briefs are submitted to the European Court, these submissions are often mentioned in the text of the judgment.[98] They find a correlation between third-party interventions and the Court finding a violation on the grounds that they intervene.[99] Other scholars portrayed the role of civil society organizations in creating positive change for a range of groups from minorities[100] to victims of gross violations in Chechnya and Turkey's Kurdish regions.[101]

Civil society can be influential because they provide the Court with vital information about the systematic nature of certain problems. They do so by acting as repeat players, bringing similar cases before the Court to draw attention to pervasive or protracted human rights violations. For example, their active promotion has helped the Court understand the scale of discrimination toward the Roma in Central and Eastern Europe.[102] The European Roma Rights Centre (ERRC), Interights, and the Open Society Justice Initiative intervened as third parties on the side of the applicants in *Nachova and Others* v. *Bulgaria* – a case about racially motivated police violence.[103] The ERRC also represented the applicants in *Moldovan and Others* v. *Romania [No.2]*.[104] This case concerned state authorities' failure to provide a legal remedy following the destruction of their home due to racially motivated mob violence. Finally, the ERRC and the Roma Center for Social Intervention and Studies ("the Romani CRISS") represent the

98 Yael Ronen and Yale Naggan, "Third Parties," in *The Oxford Handbook of International Adjudication*, ed. Cesare P. R. Romano, Karen J. Alter, and Yuval Shany (Oxford and New York: Oxford University Press, 2013), 824.

99 Ibid., 824.

100 James A. Goldston, "The Struggle for Roma Rights: Arguments That Have Worked," *Human Rights Quarterly* 32, no. 2 (2010): 311–25.

101 Freek van der Vet, "Seeking Life, Finding Justice: Russian NGO Litigation and Chechen Disappearances before the European Court of Human Rights," *Human Rights Review* 13, no. 3 (2012): 303–25; Dilek Kurban, "Protecting Marginalised Individuals and Minorities in the ECtHR: Litigation and Jurisprudence in Turkey," in *The European Court of Human Rights and the Rights of Marginalised Individuals and Minorities in National Context*, ed. Dia Anagnostou and Evangelia Psychogiopoulou (Boston and Leiden: Martinus Nijhoff, 2010), 159–82; Dilek Kurban, *Limits of Supranational Justice: The European Court of Human Rights and Turkey's Kurdish Conflict* (Cambridge and New York: Cambridge University Press, 2020).

102 James A. Goldston, "Public Interest Litigation in Central and Eastern Europe: Roots, Prospects, and Challenges," *Human Rights Quarterly*, no. 2 (2006): 492–527; Goldston, "The Struggle for Roma Rights."

103 *Nachova and Others* v. *Bulgaria*, application no. 43577/98 and 43579/98, ECHR [GC] (July 6, 2005).

104 *Moldovan and Others* v. *Romania [No.2]*, application no. 41138/98 and 64320/01, ECHR (July 12, 2005).

applicant in *Stoica* v. *Romania* – another case concerning racially motivated ill-treatment.[105] In all of these cases, various civil society organizations called attention to racial motivations behind police violence and authorities' failure to provide a legal remedy. They relentlessly challenged the Court by using litigation to portray the systemic discrimination against the Roma in Central and Eastern Europe. The Court finally acknowledged racial motivations behind ill-treatment and police violence in *Stoica* in 2008.[106]

In addition to the existing literature, my interviewees at the Court referred to these three contributing factors when explaining the change in Article 3 jurisprudence. In 2014, I asked fifteen current and two former judges a series of questions about what influences them when carrying out judicial review and sources of legal change.[107] Concerning the basic drivers of interpretive change, all seventeen of them underlined the relevance of changing times and societal needs. One judge with an academic background elucidated that legal change is due to the changing societal dynamics in Europe. They then added that "We have to interpret the Convention guarantees in the line of these new developments and new threats."[108] Another judge, who previously served as a supreme court justice, identified the source of change as "the life itself…the Convention as a living instrument. We cannot always be ahead of our time, but we cannot afford to be left behind."[109] Finally, a judge from a Western European country described that

> To some extent, this whole notion of a changing norm within the changing societal dynamics is inevitable. (…) Nobody expected a homosexual relationship would constitute a family in the 1950s, but now we accept it. (…) If this issue was to be brought up in the 50s or 60s, the Court would unanimously decide that same-sex relationships are not protected under Article 8 [right to private and family life]. It would be a lot more difficult to come back to this issue in the 80s and 90s for this claim. So, the strategy should not be naive but timely.[110]

Ten of them also mentioned that other treaties, courts, and institutions might also provide the Court with encouragement and inspiration to effectuate change within the European system. One judge explained

[105] *Stoica* v. *Romania*, application no. 42722/02, ECHR (March 4, 2008).
[106] Ibid, §111–114.
[107] Current judges are those who were serving – and some of whom are still serving – at the Court in 2014 and 2015 when I carried out the interviews.
[108] Interview 9.
[109] Interview 13.
[110] Interview 15.

that other courts and treaties provide them with a "fresh perspective" and update them about what is at stake at the international level.[111] Another judge disclosed that other courts' case law gives a direction to the Court.[112] Finally, a Western European judge clarified that they may sometimes turn to "other tribunals or expert bodies to determine what the situation is at the international level."[113] They added that although the judgment will be decided on the basis of the Convention, "of course, we will think twice before we go against an established international practice."[114]

Unprompted, judges did not immediately talk about the role of civil society. When asked specifically, eleven of them confirmed that civil society groups may play an important role. They divulged that what makes civil society groups particularly influential is the fact that they bring new information about the legal developments taking place elsewhere, present the opinion of the public, and provide legal counsel to victims who otherwise may not be able to represent themselves.[115]

There was no clear agreement about the extent of civil society's influence in shaping the case law, however. Some judges argued that what matters is the legal arguments and not necessarily who brings them.[116] Others viewed civil society groups' role to be essential.[117] One judge expressed that "without them, we would have a partial picture."[118] Another judge explained their relevance as follows: "On issues such as segregation of Roma children, we do not get a lot of information from the governments, but the NGOs provide us with data and information. They bring us good cases too."[119] Similarly, a former judge observed that civil society groups are often "very useful with mapping out general problems."[120] Finally, one Western European judge described third-party submissions as "often interesting and occasionally challenging for the Court." They then added, "I would not say that entire judgments have been shaped on the basis of the intervention of an NGO. But certainly, they have contributed to shaping the case law."[121]

[111] Interview 3.
[112] Interview 5.
[113] Interview 6.
[114] Ibid.
[115] Interview 4; Interview 5; Interview 12; Interview 14; Interview 17.
[116] Interview 1; Interview 10; Interview 13.
[117] Interview 2; Interview 6; Interview 9.
[118] Interview 2.
[119] Interview 3.
[120] Interview 17.
[121] Interview 16.

Conclusion

In this chapter, I have laid out the building blocks of my theoretical framework, which catalogues the conditions under which international courts, like the European Court, may be expected to issue audacious rulings. This framework relies on previous literature and insights gathered from interviews in and around the Court. The necessary condition for an audacious court is a wide discretionary space within which that court may act without fearing repercussions from states. Yet, such a wide discretionary space is not always given; when it is given, states might still attempt to influence courts through direct or indirect means. Such means include threatening to close down a court's discretionary space and threatening widespread negative feedback, as well as actually taking either action. International courts, in turn, are often compelled to (re)align their priorities in order to react to or pre-empt the use of such means. This (re)alignment is a form of tactical balancing whereby courts adjust their behaviour to ensure their continued access to resources and preserve their reputation and image. Finally, I have introduced additional factors that increase the likelihood of audacious rulings (i.e., congruence with changing societal needs, legal developments external to the regime, and civil society campaigns). In Chapter 2, I will take a look inside the Court and further explore how it operates, what its trade-offs are, and how its discretionary space changes over time.

2

Inside the Court

Its Trade-Offs and Zone of Discretion

In the first part of this chapter, I take a closer look at the Court to shed light on what kind of actor the Court is. What motivates it to oscillate between audacity and forbearance? To answer this question, I rely on the existing accounts of the Court's inner workings and the insights gained from the interviews I carried out in 2014 and 2015. I consider the Court's internal character as a collective actor composed of different groups of agents (i.e., elected judges, permanent staff, and support services). The Court's smooth operation depends on a division of labour and close collaboration among these different groups. Beyond its functional benefits, this collaboration cultivates a coherent legal culture and gives the Court a collective purpose. In the second part of the chapter, I turn to the Court's institutional transformation and how this transformation has influenced the width of its discretionary space. In particular, I describe how the part-time old Court transformed into the full-time new Court with compulsory jurisdiction and how the new Court transitioned into the reformed Court due to a series of reform processes that started in 2010. I will then elaborate on the implications of these shifts on the way the Court operated in different stages of its lifetime.

Who Is the Court?

The European Court of Human Rights (the Court) is "the crown jewel" of the human rights regime embedded in the Council of Europe, located in Strasbourg, France.[1] The Court was created to oversee the application of

[1] Laurence R. Helfer, "Redesigning the European Court of Human Rights: Embeddedness as a Deep Structural Principle of the European Human Rights Regime," *European Journal of International Law* 19, no. 1 (2008): 125–59. The Council of Europe is different from the European Union. In fact, the former predates the latter. It was specifically created to coordinate European countries' social policies, promote cooperation and prevent another European war. See David P. Forsythe, *Human Rights in International Relations* (New York: Cambridge University Press, 2006), 111.

the European Convention of Human Rights (the Convention).[2] The Registry is its largest organ, with roughly 640 staff members, a considerable number of whom are employed on a permanent basis. The Registry's staff includes lawyers, administrative staff, translators, and the Jurisconsult in charge of ensuring the consistency of jurisprudence.[3]

The Court is organised into five sections, each with its own judicial chamber, President and Vice President (elected from among the judges), Section Registrar, and Deputy Section Registrar. The sections are the Court's administrative units; each unit includes nine or ten judges who are assisted by members of the Registry.[4] Judges assigned to these administrative units may serve in one of the following four formations: (1) *Single-judge formation*, which is mainly responsible for filtering inadmissible cases, (2) *Committee of three judges* that decides on the admissibility and merits of cases where case law is already well-established, (3) *Chamber of seven judges* that reviews admissibility and merits of non-repetitive cases, and (4) *Grand Chamber of seventeen judges* that serves as an appeal mechanism over relinquished or referred cases.[5]

The entire case processing system relies on a synergetic interaction between the Registry's legal team and elected judges. As Nina-Louisa Arold, who conducted a research stay at the Court, rightly points out, "[the permanent staff] remain in Strasbourg so long that their domestic legal

[2] Other bodies of the Council of Europe, such as the Committee of Ministers and the Parliamentary Assembly, support the Court in this regard. The Committee of Ministers, a body composed of foreign ministers and permanent representatives of all forty-six member states, monitors the execution of the Court's judgments. The Parliamentary Assembly consists of parliamentarians of member states and elects the Court's judges. There is also the Secretariat, which consists of the Secretary General, the Deputy Secretary General, and other staff members.

[3] European Court of Human Rights, "ECHR Registry," available at www.echr.coe.int/Documents/Registry_ENG.pdf

[4] For more on the Court's organization and deliberation practices, see Helen Keller and Corina Heri, "Deliberation and Drafting: European Court of Human Rights (ECtHR)," in *Max Planck Encyclopedia of International Procedural Law (EiPro)* (Oxford Public International Law, May 2018).

[5] Appeal to the Grand Chamber is exceptional and takes place through referral or relinquishment; namely, either party can request a referral, or the Chamber relinquishes the case to the Grand Chamber "if the case raises serious questions affecting the interpretation of the Convention." In addition, according to Article 45 of the Convention (on infringement proceedings), the Grand Chamber can also be referred to if a member state refuses to abide by a Court's judgment. Article 45: "if the Committee of Minister (by a two-thirds majority) finds a state is refusing to abide by a Court judgment, it can be referred back to the Grand Chamber for an infringement finding which will then be referred back to the Committee to take action."

cultures become secondary to their experience of the Strasbourg system," and judges serving for a limited term "bring the necessary fresh knowledge of the national law into the system."[6] The existence of the permanent staff, some of whom have worked for the Registry for several decades, contributes to the maintenance of the legal culture and the "stability and continuity of legal reasoning."[7] Similarly, Cosette Creamer and Zuzanna Godzimirska describe the Registry's role as being "largely related to ensuring continuity and coherence in the Court's caselaw and maintaining the institutional memory of the Court."[8] One former judge also highlighted this point in an interview, where he described the Registry's role as "keeping the Court intact and preventing it from going into different schools."[9]

Judges are a much smaller group.[10] There are currently forty-six judges, one from each member state of the Council of Europe, holding nonrenewable nine-year terms.[11] The Parliamentary Assembly elects one judge per member state.[12] The number of judges decreased from forty-seven to forty-six when Russia ceased to be a party to the European Convention on September 16, 2022.[13] Elected judges often have diverse professional

[6] Nina-Louisa Arold, *The Legal Culture of the European Court of Human Rights* (Leiden; Boston: Brill Nijhoff, 2007), 46.

[7] Ibid., 46.

[8] Cosette D. Creamer and Zuzanna Godzimirska, "Trust in the Court: The Role of the Registry of the European Court of Human Rights," *European Journal of International Law* 30, no. 2 (2019): 670.

[9] Interview 17.

[10] The criteria for office, the election process, and the terms of office are regulated in Articles 21–23 of the Convention as amended by Protocol 14, which came into force in 2010. Every Member State proposes three candidates before the Parliamentary Assembly of the Council of Europe, which selects one judge among the candidates. Judges cannot be reelected. Their terms of office expire when they reach seventy.

[11] Council of Europe, "ECHR Registry," www.echr.coe.int/Pages/home.aspx?p=court/howitworks&c= [September 20, 2019]. Additionally, the Member States have begun seconding legal staff in order to contribute to the work of the Court, which was encouraged in the Interlaken, Izmir, and Brighton declarations. The seconded legal officials are only employed at the filtering divisions, where they decide the admissibility of the cases.

[12] Each member state transmits a list of three candidates, and the Assembly elects one judge per member state, in line with the majority rule. Parliamentary Assembly, "Procedure for Electing Judges to the European Court of Human Rights," AS/Cdh/Inf (2015) 02 Rev 1$ (2015).

[13] At the time of writing this book, the number of member states decreased from forty-seven to forty-six with Russia's exit from the Council of Europe. Russia was officially expelled from the Council of Europe on March 22, 2022, due to Russia's refusal to "cease its aggression against Ukraine." Committee of Ministers, on legal and financial consequences of the cessation of membership of the Russian Federation in the Council of Europe, *Resolution CM/Res (2022)3* (March 23, 2022). While the process of Russia's expulsion was underway, Russia announced its withdrawal from the Council of Europe on March 15, 2022.

backgrounds, though typically hold academic, judicial, or public office positions in their home countries before being elected.[14] Although elected judges are a minority of the Court's staff, their work carries major significance since they hold the official responsibility of issuing rulings.[15]

As became clear in the course of the interviews I carried out at the Court, judges have different views concerning the Court's role. Seven out of the fifteen sitting judges I interviewed told me they considered their role to be the simple application of the Convention.[16] These seven were mostly from Western European countries. Four other judges, mostly from Eastern European countries, told me that the Court's role is to protect human rights and enforce the rule of law. The remaining four judges saw their role as setting standards across Europe. Some of the judges elaborated on their vision of the Court. According to one judge: "the Court is there to uphold the values of our civilization."[17] Another judge with an academic background said that the Court's role is "to build a Europe of Rights."[18] Some believe that the Court's role should be more limited. A judge from Western Europe defined the Court's role as ensuring that "the High Contracting parties observe the Convention's provisions."[19] He further added the following: "I have a very traditional sense of what it is to be a judge. I am not a policymaker. I am not a politician. I am here to decide on a case-by-case basis whether the member states have respected human rights as provided by the Convention."[20] Finally, another judge, who previously served on a constitutional court, argued that the primary role of the Court is to decide whether states have complied with their obligations arising from the Convention.[21] He then added:

> The secondary or collateral role of the Court is that of a standard setter. (...) a third, even perhaps more collateral – but at the same time vitally important – the role is that of ensuring that the Convention remains a credible document. This credibility could be undermined if the Court were

[14] For an assessment of the judges' changing backgrounds, Mikael Rask Madsen, "The Legitimization Strategies of International Judges: The Case of the European Court of Human Rights," in *Selecting Europe's Judges: A Critical Review of the Appointment Procedures to the European Courts*, ed. Michal Bobek (Oxford: Oxford University Press, 2015), 259–76.

[15] Arold, *The Legal Culture of the European Court of Human Rights*, 46.

[16] Interview 1; Interview 2; Interview 3; Interview 6; Interview 10; Interview 14; Interview 15.

[17] Interview 8.

[18] Interview 9.

[19] Interview 15.

[20] Ibid.

[21] Interview 10.

> to interpret and apply the Convention in such a way that some member States would consider it as re-writing the Convention. This could happen with unnecessary forays into areas such as ethics and morality.[22]

Eight out of fifteen judges argued that it is within the Court's prerogative to refine the norms in line with societal needs and changing moral values.[23] In contrast, three judges, all from Western European countries, argued that the Court's role does not extend into creating new rights.[24] One judge especially cautioned that the Court must be careful when generating legal change in order to avoid causing backlash from member states.[25]

Scholars have considered how it is that judges coming from different countries, with different prior experiences and understandings, work together as a part of a collective body. In one study, Erik Voeten investigated whether judges exhibited national bias. He concluded that the heterogeneity of judges' national legal cultures does not compromise their impartiality.[26] Nina-Louisa Arold, on the other hand, found that the Court provides a space within which national legal cultures or professional backgrounds are fused into a common legal culture.[27] Judges bring fresh perspectives and experiences that complement the Court's long-term legal tradition, which is well guarded by the Registry's permanent team.

According to my interviews, the synergetic interaction between elected judges and the Registry's permanent staff is what fuels the Court's operations.[28] What became evident in our conversations was that judgments are not just "made" by the judges sitting on the bench. Instead, they are the outcome of a process in which many nameless individuals – such as law clerks, nonjudicial rapporteurs, or editors – are also involved.[29] Judgments are the products of the Court as an institution. "They are public documents," one judge explained.[30] They are decided either

[22] Ibid.

[23] Interview 1; Interview 5; Interview 10; Interview 11, Interview 12; Interview 13; Interview 15.

[24] Interview 2; Interview 8; Interview 14.

[25] Interview 2.

[26] Erik Voeten, "The Impartiality of International Judges: Evidence from the European Court of Human Rights," *American Political Science Review* 102, no. 4 (2008): 417–33; Erik Voeten, "The Politics of International Judicial Appointments: Evidence from the European Court of Human Rights," *International Organization* 61, no. 4 (2007): 669–701. See also Jeffrey L. Dunoff and Mark A. Pollack, "The Judicial Trilemma," *American Journal of International Law* 111, no. 2 (2017): 225–76.

[27] Arold, *The Legal Culture of the European Court of Human Rights*, 80.

[28] Interview 10, Interview 16, Interview 17, Interview 18, Interview 19, Interview 20, and Interview 25.

[29] Interview 19, Interview 17, Interview 20, and Interview 24.

[30] Interview 4.

unanimously or by majority vote and are signed by the entire Chamber, the Committee, or the Grand Chamber. In this regard, they are different from separate opinions authored and owned by an individual judge or a group of judges.

Judgments become institutional documents also because of the way they are produced. The case processing system is complicated and requires the entire staff's collaboration – from judges to the Registry's legal and support services teams. When an application is submitted, it is transferred to one of the Sections and assigned to a reporting judge (judge rapporteur).[31] The judge rapporteur and the Registry's clerks who assist them have an important role in this case throughout the proceedings.[32] Their tasks include submitting a draft report on admissibility, requesting further information from the parties when needed, and proposing a draft judgment to the Chamber to be discussed during deliberations.[33]

Following an initial examination, the judge rapporteur decides whether the case will be reviewed by a single-judge formation, a Committee, or a Chamber.[34] The cases that appear to be inadmissible at first glance (manifestly ill-founded cases) are passed to a single-judge formation or to a Committee.[35] These units are in charge of "disposing of the weakest cases."[36] Assisted by a nonjudicial rapporteur, single judges may declare a case inadmissible or strike it out of the list. Similarly, a Committee of three judges may issue admissibility decisions or strike a case out of the list

[31] Judge rapporteur's identity serving a given case is strictly confidential. For more, see Keller and Heri, "Deliberation and Drafting," § 38.

[32] Arold, *The Legal Culture of the European Court of Human Rights*, 61.

[33] European Court of Human Rights, "Rules of the Court" (2014), www.echr.coe.int/Documents/Rules_Court_ENG.pdf, §Rules 48–50.

[34] Philip Leach, *Taking a Case to the European Court of Human Rights*, 3rd edition (Oxford and New York: Oxford University Press, 2011), 41.

[35] According to the Court's admissibility guide, "[m]anifestly ill-founded complaints can be divided into four categories: 'fourth-instance' complaints [complaints that ask the Court to question the findings of the conclusions of the domestic Courts, putting the Court in a position of a supreme court], complaints where there has clearly or apparently been no violations, unsubstantiated complains and, finally confused or far-fetched complaints." For more, see European Court of Human Rights, "Practical Guide on Admissibility Criteria," January 1, 2014, available at www.echr.coe.int/Documents/Admissibility_guide_ENG.pdf [September 20, 2019], at 83§320.

[36] Leach, *Taking a Case to the European Court of Human Rights*, 41. One disadvantage of being reviewed by a single judge formation or a Committee is that the applicants will not receive an explanation as to why their application was declared inadmissible, and therefore, rejected.

if the decision is unanimous.[37] In the event that the Committee cannot reach a unanimous decision, the case is reviewed by a Chamber.[38]

When there is no apparent reason to declare a case inadmissible, it is communicated to the responding government. The government is then required to submit written observations or reply to specific questions. The applicant is also invited to submit observations in response.[39] Based on the parties' written submissions (or oral hearings, if applicable),[40] the Court assesses both the admissibility and the merits of the case and issues a judgment.[41] If a case raises important questions concerning the Convention's interpretation or the jurisprudence's consistency, then that case is relinquished to the Grand Chamber.[42] Parties may also request a Chamber judgment to be sent to the Grand Chamber for a final review.

This procedure through which a case traverses between different case processing units may seem to be automatic. However, in practice, case processing is realised by means of the tedious work of drafting and redrafting documents and expressing grievances as legal problems.[43] It is the Registry's legal team that administers the case processing steps.[44] They draft the case correspondence, admissibility decisions, and judgments for consideration by single judges or judge rapporteurs.[45] In addition, the facts of the cases are always processed and written by the Registry.[46] The

[37] Ibid.

[38] Additionally, the Committee may issue judgments on the merits of the case, if the case concerns an issue that is well-established in the case law or repetitive violations (manifestly well-founded case). Leach, *Taking a Case to the European Court of Human Rights*, 42.

[39] Ibid., 43–44.

[40] As Philip Leach explains, "the European Convention system is primarily a written rather than an oral procedure. (…) The vast majority of European Court cases will not include an oral hearing. If any Court hearing is held at all, it usually takes less than half a day from start to finish"; Ibid., 44.

[41] The Court may only examine the admissibility of the complaints in some cases. However, the usual practice is to consider both admissibility and merits at the same time, which is considered more efficient. Ibid., 48.

[42] Ibid., 48. The parties can raise objections to the relinquishment decision. However, it is not clear whether their objections amount to a veto, which prevents relinquishment. Protocol 15, which entered into force on August 1, 2021, has a provision that abolishes the parties' right to object.

[43] For an account of the daily tasks of legal practitioners, see Bruno Latour, *The Making of Law: An Ethnography of the Conseil d'Etat* (Cambridge: Polity Press, 2010).

[44] For a good assessment of the authority of international bureaucracies, see Julia Fleischer and Nina Reiners, "Connecting International Relations and Public Administration: Toward a Joint Research Agenda for the Study of International Bureaucracy," *International Studies Review* 23, no. 4 (2021): 1230–47.

[45] Leach, *Taking a Case to the European Court of Human Rights*, 27.

[46] Interview 17.

lawyers may also inform the judge rapporteurs about the relevant national law, or even applicable European jurisprudence if the judge is new or less experienced.[47]

Helen Keller, a former judge at the Court, and Corina Heri explain that the deliberations for Chamber and Grand Chamber judgments differ. Before the deliberations at the Chamber, the judges receive "a thick file from the Registry that already contains a draft judgment or decision."[48] They also receive a document about the Court's caselaw from the Jurisconsult in order to ensure consistency.[49] The judge rapporteur presents the draft opinion to the Chamber at the deliberations.[50] Participating judges express their opinions and take a preliminary vote. The clerks revise the draft judgment based on this feedback. Keller and Cori explain that "there is usually no second deliberation in the Chamber proceedings, as there is often no need for one: generally, the Chamber judges approve the draft judgments or decisions before them."[51]

The discussions at the deliberation are not reflected in the final ruling, which is decided either unanimously or by majority vote.[52] The judgment, which is the text of the majority, does not give a hint about how the Chamber reached a decision. Since deliberations take place in secrecy, one cannot know whether the decision is fully based on the draft proposed by the judge rapporteur and clerks, or a version modified to some degree.[53] It is impossible to discern the judges' individualised input in the final judgment's text. However, judges who do not fully agree with the majority tend to announce their position in separate opinions annexed to the judgment.[54]

Grand Chamber proceedings are like those of the Chamber. However, judges do not receive draft judgments before deliberations at the Grand Chamber. Instead, the judges receive a note from the judge rapporteur (rapporteur's note) and reports from the Registry.[55] While the Chamber usually uses the draft judgment as a template to inform the final decision,

[47] Arold, *The Legal Culture of the European Court of Human Rights*, 62.
[48] Keller and Heri, "Deliberation and Drafting," § 27.
[49] Ibid., §39.
[50] National judge also participates in deliberations and provides further information concerning the national legal system if needed.
[51] Keller and Heri, "Deliberation and Drafting," §43.
[52] Arold, *The Legal Culture of the European Court of Human Rights*, 63.
[53] Ibid., 75.
[54] European Court of Human Rights, Rules of the Court, §Rule 74(2).
[55] Keller and Heri, "Deliberation and Drafting," §27.

the Grand Chamber does not have such a template. Rather it finds a way to resolve the dispute during the course of deliberations, in line with the information provided by the judge rapporteur and the Registry.[56] Grand Chamber proceedings generally start with a public hearing.[57] At the end of the first deliberation session, the Grand Chamber's president selects a drafting committee of up to five judges – including a Judge Rapporteur. The Registry clerks draft a judgment based on the discussions held at the deliberation. The Judge Rapporteur reviews the draft and sends it to the drafting committee. The drafting committee may further revise it, preparing it for a discussion at the second (and final) deliberation meeting.[58]

The entire case processing system, conducted mostly behind the scenes under the cloaks of anonymity, works toward the institutional reproduction of judgments.[59] This largely disguises any given individual's input. Case processing becomes a collective activity. It is the Registry's clerks who process the case files and propel the system.[60] The degree of judges' involvement is a matter of their personality and the importance of the case.[61] For example, Grand Chamber proceedings may require more involvement than those of single-judge formations. However, overall, when it comes to the case-writing process, "it is more the exception than the rule that the judges will intervene," as one former judge explained. This is because "[judges] cannot handle the workload."[62]

Both the judges and the clerks acknowledged the importance of the Registry's role in determining the Court's working methods and the significance of the collaboration between the judges and the clerks.[63] One judge, in particular, laid out the Registry's role as follows: "The judges often depend on the Registrars and their teams. Sometimes the cooperation goes so far that the clerk proposes a draft that will later be used by the judges as the basis for the judgment."[64] Similarly, a senior clerk described

56 Ibid., §31.
57 There are exceptions to this rule. The judge rapporteur may request not to hold a hearing.
58 Keller and Heri, "Deliberation and Drafting," §49–59.
59 For an interesting overview of how international courts function, see Jeffrey L. Dunoff and Mark A. Pollack, "International Judicial Practices: Opening the Black Box of International Courts," *Michigan Journal of International Law* 40, no. 1 (2018): 47–114.
60 Arold, *The Legal Culture of the European Court of Human Rights*, 44–46.
61 Creamer and Godzimirska, "Trust in the Court," 679.
62 Interview 17.
63 Interview 18, Interview 19, and Interview 4.
64 Quoted from an interview in Arold, *The Legal Culture of the European Court of Human Rights*, 46.

his colleagues as "established civil servants" who have been in the system for a long time. He underlined that they are highly skilled in efficiently drafting judgments.[65] What was evident from these discussions was that this working method is the only viable way to process the Court's overwhelming caseload.[66] It requires different groups of agents to cooperate, and it creates a sense of collective ownership over judgments.[67]

This working method and these procedures are the most likely explanation for how the Court can enjoy a coherent common legal culture and formulate a collective purpose. As one Western European judge highlighted, "the system is stronger and larger than the individual. The system is sophisticated and absorptive. The Court remains ideologically homogenous, even with the new and changing personnel."[68] This is why it is plausible to assume that Court's motivations to be audacious and forbearing are not determined by only a few judges, but instead decided collectively. The Court's permanent and temporary agents maintain a coherent narrative about the Court's core concerns and priorities. Together, they may maintain or progress rights in line with their core objective as a human rights court or offer trade-offs in order to secure necessary resources for institutional survival. Regardless, they take this decision as a collective body – albeit the weight of their contributions may vary based on their roles and functions, with judges having the official responsibility of rendering judgments.

European Court at Different Phases of Its Existence

The European human rights system in its early days was different from the one we know today. This difference is primarily related to changes in its institutional design. Design changes are not simply structural reorganization, however. They have an important bearing on the Court's autonomy

[65] Interview 18.

[66] Interview 18 and Interview 10. This does not mean that this relationship is always harmonious. A bone of contention, for example, is the extent of the Registry's functions. Judges held mixed views concerning the role of the Registry. To illustrate, one current judge expressed their concern about the extent of the Registry's power and noted that "the Convention says that the Court shall have a Registry, but it should have been written in the other way around; the Registry shall have a Court." They found judges' limited involvement in writing judgments problematic (Interview 10). Another judge, on the other hand, expressed their satisfaction with the way the Convention system is working and the facilitator role of the Registry (Interview 4).

[67] Arold, *The Legal Culture of the European Court of Human Rights*, 154.

[68] Quoted from an interview in Arold, 83.

and authority and by implication its zone of discretion, as we see in the following section.[69]

The Old Court, 1959–1998: An Institution Built upon a Compromise

The European human rights regime was a product of the political climate in the aftermath of the Second World War.[70] From the devastation that the War brought along still in living memory, European leaders agreed to create a regional human rights regime. Its constitutive treaty, the European Convention, was written in reaction to the atrocities committed during the War.[71] Representing a clear break from the past, this regime was created to embody European values, to prevent democracies from relapsing into dictatorships,[72] and to contain the threat of a communist expansion in Europe.[73]

The Convention took legal effect in 1953, three years after its approval in Rome. The document included a range of civil and political rights, such as the right to life; freedom from slavery; the right to a fair trial; freedom of expression; and freedom of thought, conscience, and religion. The original signatories were the governments of Belgium, Denmark, France, Germany, Iceland, Ireland, Italy, Luxembourg, the Netherlands, Norway, the Saar Protectorate, Turkey, and the United Kingdom. The enactment of the Convention was the first step in launching the European human rights regime. This regime would then go on to shape the political and legal landscape in Europe, becoming an authoritative forum for human rights protection.[74]

69 Darren Hawkins et al., eds, *Delegation and Agency in International Organizations* (New York: Cambridge University Press, 2006).

70 Transnational groups took up an important role too. While few human rights organizations strove to contribute to this effort within the UN framework, they assumed an important role in the European case. Samuel Moyn, *The Last Utopia* (Cambridge and Massachusetts: Harvard University Press, 2010).

71 Luzius Wildhaber, "Rethinking the European Court of Human Rights," in *The European Court of Human Rights between Law and Politics*, ed. Jonas Christoffersen and Mikael Rask Madsen (New York: Oxford University Press, 2011), 206.

72 Andrew Moravcsik, "The Origins of Human Rights Regimes: Democratic Delegation in Postwar Europe," *International Organization* 54, no. 2 (2000): 217–52.

73 Ed Bates, "The Birth of the European Convention on Human Rights – and the European Court of Human Rights," in *The European Court of Human Rights between Law and Politics*, ed. Jonas Christoffersen and Mikael Rask Madsen (New York: Oxford University Press, 2011), 40.

74 Helfer, "Redesigning the European Court of Human Rights," 126.

The circumstances surrounding the creation of the European human rights regime were not free from controversy. The most glaring of those was the fact that some of the founding members were colonial powers at the time of the Convention's drafting. The French and the British took the lead in drafting the Convention, even as they were implicated in serious human rights violations within their colonies.[75] Their colonial heritage was reflected in the way the Convention was written, giving the impression that the rights safeguarded were for only "a select group of individuals."[76] Take, for example, Article 56 (territorial application clause). This infamous colonial clause acknowledged the existence of "overseas territories" and specified that it was up to member states to choose whether to extend the Convention to "all or any of the territories for whose international relations it is responsible." This effectively meant that this protection system, created for Europeans, would not automatically be applied to those people living in European colonies.

Although the drafters agreed on this particular matter, they disagreed about others. At the June 1950 Conference in Strasbourg, where the Convention's text was finalised, the drafters argued over whether to create a supranational tribunal and how much power to give it. This matter immediately became a point of contestation because this supranational court would receive complaints brought by member states against other states (interstate complaints) and individuals against states (individual applications). The very idea of a regional court spurred spirited discussions during the drafting sessions.[77] Member states were wary about the sovereignty cost of establishing a supranational review mechanism.[78] To the sceptics, this effectively meant that member states' domestic affairs would be under the scrutiny of a European Court. Allowing individuals to bring cases before the Court appeared equally threatening. Communist sympathisers and other figures aiming to discredit the West could activate

[75] Mikael Rask Madsen, "From Cold War Instrument to Supreme European Court: The European Court of Human Rights at the Crossroads of International and National Law and Politics," *Law and Social Inquiry* 32, no. 1 (2007): 144.

[76] Jonas Christoffersen and Mikael Rask Madsen, "Introduction: The European Court of Human Rights between Law and Politics," in *The European Court of Human Rights between Law and Politics*, ed. Jonas Christoffersen and Mikael Rask Madsen (New York: Oxford University Press, 2011), 1.

[77] Bates, "The Birth of the European Convention on Human Rights – and the European Court of Human Rights," 40.

[78] For more on this, see Karen Alter, "Delegating to International Courts: Self-Binding vs. Other-Binding Delegation," *Law and Contemporary Problems* 71, no. 1 (2008): 37–76.

the Court for disingenuous reasons.[79] On the other hand, supporters of the supranational court believed that the European human rights regime could not be fully realised without it. A clear majority of the countries – such as Denmark, Greece, Netherlands, Norway, Sweden, Turkey, and the United Kingdom – were in the sceptical camp, and only Belgium, France, Ireland, and Italy were in favour.[80]

Belgium, France, Greece, Ireland, Italy, Luxembourg, Sweden, and Turkey proposed a compromise. According to this new scheme, member states could choose whether to accept the Court's jurisdiction or to allow the individuals' right to bring cases before the Court (right to petition). Even though the Netherlands and the United Kingdom – two colonial powers at the time – strongly rejected this proposal initially, these two compromise clauses resolved the differences between member states at the time of the Convention's adoption in 1950.[81] The Convention, therefore, did not automatically require a loss of sovereignty to supranational review, but left the choice to the member states.[82] Accepting the Court's jurisdiction and an individual's right to petition remained optional until the introduction of Protocol 11 in 1998.

In the same spirit, the original design features of the European human rights regime favoured a more limited and state-centric course of action.[83] The regime was created as a two-tier system composed of one quasi-judicial filtering mechanism and one judicial body.[84] In the first tier, the European Commission of Human Rights (established in 1954) would receive individual complaints and decide their admissibility.[85] It would then launch the cases that it deemed admissible before the Court on behalf

[79] Ed Bates, *The Evolution of the European Convention on Human Rights: From Its Inception to the Creation of a Permanent Court of Human Rights* (Oxford and New York: Oxford University Press, 2010), 96.

[80] Bates, "The Birth of the European Convention on Human Rights – and the European Court of Human Rights," 28.

[81] Ibid., 37.

[82] Mikael Rask Madsen, "International Human Rights and the Transformation of European Society: From 'Free Europe' to the Europe of Human Rights," in *Law and the Formation of Modern Europe: Perspectives from the Historical Sociology of Law*, ed. Mikael Rask Madsen and Chris Thornhill (Cambridge University Press, 2014), 256.

[83] Bates, "The Birth of the European Convention on Human Rights – and the European Court of Human Rights," 38.

[84] Solomon T Ebobrah, "International Human Rights Courts," in *The Oxford Handbook of International Adjudication*, ed. Cesare Romano, Yuval Shany, and Karen J. Alter (Oxford and New York: Oxford University Press, 2014), 230.

[85] Ilias Bantekas and Lutz Oette, *International Human Rights Law and Practice* (New York: Cambridge University Press, 2013), 230.

of the individual applicants if the responding state recognised the Court's jurisdiction.[86] This model gave a more prominent role to the Commission which functioned as a quasi-judicial filter and carried out initial screening of individual applications.[87] In the second tier, the European Court of Human Rights (the Court, founded in 1959), would review the cases referred by either the Commission or another member state.

These design features yielded limited authority and autonomy and thereby a narrow zone of discretion.[88] What limited the Court's zone of discretion was the compromise upon which the system was created: *optional* jurisdiction and right of individual petition. These two conditions would severely limit the individuals' access to the Court and the inflow of cases. In the early days, few countries accepted individual petition rights or the Court's jurisdiction. At the time the Convention entered into force in 1953, only Denmark, Ireland, and Sweden agreed to grant the right of individual petition. Denmark and Ireland were the sole members that accepted the Court's jurisdiction.[89] Even when states submitted to the Court's jurisdiction, they did not do so unconditionally but often on two-to-five-year renewable terms. As a result, few cases reached the Commission and the Court, and both operated only on a part-time basis and met when needed.[90]

Member states' initial resistance to being fully on board sent a clear signal to the Court and the Commission that they had to be cautious to offset this resistance. In order to prove that the system was not there to threaten the member states, the Court and the Commission carried out their legal functions with diplomatic sensitivity.[91] This was a specific form of

[86] The Commission was abolished with Protocol 11, which came into force in 1998 and allowed individuals to take cases to the Court directly.

[87] Bantekas and Oette, *International Human Rights Law and Practice*, 224.

[88] These two concepts are also intricately linked to a third concept, legitimacy. For more on the constitutive elements of legitimacy, see Başak Çali, Anne Koch, and Nicola Bruch, "The Legitimacy of Human Rights Courts: A Grounded Interpretivist Analysis of the European Court of Human Rights," *Human Rights Quarterly* 35, no. 4 (2013): 955–84.

[89] Bates, "The Birth of the European Convention on Human Rights – and the European Court of Human Rights," 40.

[90] As for the other design features, both the Commission and the Court would work on the principle of one member and one judge per member state. While the commissioners would be elected by the Committee of Ministers for a period of six years, the judges would be elected by the Consultative Assembly (today's Parliamentary Assembly) for nine years. Commissioners and judges could run for re-election.

[91] Mikael Rask Madsen, "Protracted Institutionalization of the Strasbourg Court: From Legal Diplomacy to Integrationist Jurisprudence," in *The European Court of Human Rights between Law and Politics*, ed. Jonas Christoffersen and Mikael Rask Madsen (New York: Oxford University Press, 2011), 46.

tactical balancing that led the Court and the Commission to adopt more conservative positions in the 1950s and 1960s.[92] They each paid greater attention to member states' national interests and provided both legal and extra-legal solutions to the disputes at hand, as Mikael Rask Madsen finds in his study.[93]

This cautious approach limited the number and nature of decisions in the early period. As Sir Humphrey Waldock – then President of the Commission – explained, they were not there to name and shame member states. Rather, their main function was "to conduct confidential negotiations with the parties and to try and set right unobtrusively any breach of human rights that may have occurred."[94] Underscoring their diplomatic role, he emphasised that the Commission "was not primarily established for the purpose of putting states in the dock and registering convictions against them."[95] He signalled that the European human rights regime would not be the forum to discredit the West at the height of the Cold War rivalry. Following this logic, the Commission adopted a stringent approach when deciding on the admissibility of cases in the early days.[96] The Court contributed to this diplomatic effort by showing deference to domestic authorities with regard to protecting rights and delivering justice.[97] The most effective tools for deference were the margin of appreciation doctrine and Article 15 (derogation clause).[98] The former

[92] Darren Hawkins and Wade Jacoby, "Agent Permeability, Principal Delegation and the European Court of Human Rights," *The Review of International Organizations* 3, no. 1 (2008): 24.

[93] Madsen, "International Human Rights and the Transformation of European Society: From 'Free Europe' to the Europe of Human Rights," 259.

[94] Bates, *The Evolution of the European Convention on Human Rights*, 2010, 223.

[95] Ibid., 223.

[96] In 1966, for example, out of 303 applications, only five were declared admissible; in 1974, out of 445 applications, only six were declared admissible. For more, see Bates, *The Evolution of the European Convention on Human Rights*, 241–45.

[97] The margin of appreciation doctrine results from the fact that the diverse cultural background of the member states made it difficult to establish a uniform European standard for human rights across the board. This principle largely "refers to the room for maneuver the Strasbourg institutions are prepared to accord national authorities in fulfilling their obligations under the European Convention on Human Rights." Steven C. Greer, *The Margin of Appreciation: Interpretation and Discretion under the European Convention on Human Rights* (Strasbourg: Council of Europe, 2000).

[98] Article 15 reads as follows: (1) In time of war or other public emergency threatening the life of the nation any High Contracting Party may take measures derogating from its obligations under this Convention to the extent strictly required by the exigencies of the situation, provided that such measures are not inconsistent with its other obligations under international law; (2) No derogation from Article 2, except in respect of deaths resulting

granted the member states flexibility in fulfilling their Convention obligations, and the latter allowed states to reduce some of their obligations in times of emergency – except for the provisions concerning torture, slavery, servitude, right to life, and punishment without law.[99]

These strategies must have surely worked, because in the early 1970s, there was a sudden increase in the number of ratifications and acceptance of optional clauses – that is, submission to the Court's jurisdiction and the right to individual petition.[100] By 1974, thirteen out of eighteen member states accepted the optional clauses.[101] As confidence in the European human rights regime grew stronger over the decades, more member states accepted the individual petition right. By 1990, all member states (twenty-two at the time) allowed their citizens to bring cases before the European Court.[102] This trend decreased the need for legal diplomacy and increased the flow of cases into the Court's docket. The Court had effectively boosted its autonomy and authority.[103]

The end of the Cold War contributed to this upward trend. When the formerly communist countries joined the ranks of the Council of Europe, the Court's reputation and caseload exponentially grew due to what has become known as the "Eastward expansion." The expansion started in 1990 when Hungary ratified the Convention and became a Council of Europe member. Within a few years, the number of member states grew from twenty-one to forty-one. The European human rights regime significantly broadened its geographical reach when Russia, the largest country in Europe, ratified the Convention in 1998.

The war in the Former Yugoslavia had propelled the expansion of the European human rights regime. Europe was stunned and horrified by another war on the continent in which gross human rights violations were being committed. As a response, the Council of Europe member states

from lawful acts of war, or from Articles 3, 4 (paragraph 1), and 7 shall be made under this provision; (3) Any High Contracting Party availing itself of this right of derogation shall keep the Secretary General of the Council of Europe fully informed of the measures which it has taken and the reasons therefor. It shall also inform the Secretary General of the Council of Europe when such measures have ceased to operate and the provisions of the Convention are again being fully executed.

99 Madsen, "From Cold War Instrument to Supreme European Court," 151.

100 Bates, *The Evolution of the European Convention on Human Rights*, 2010, 278.

101 Madsen, "Protracted Institutionalization of the Strasbourg Court," 53.

102 European Court of Human Rights, "Annual Report 2011" (Strasbourg: Registry of the European Court, 2012).

103 Bates, *The Evolution of the European Convention on Human Rights*, 283.

issued the Vienna Declaration of October 9, 1993.[104] Members extended their invitation to the newly independent countries and declared that new members' accession to the Convention System would be "a central factor in the process of European construction." This invitation marked a colossal shift in the European human rights system's objectives, from that of fine-tuning well-functioning democracies to helping countries transition to democracy.

Shortly after ratification, the new members accepted the Court's jurisdiction and individual petition right.[105] In the aftermath, the Court was entrusted not only with a new role but also with an exponentially growing caseload.[106] There already had been steady growth in the number of applications since the 1980s; this further escalated with the Eastward expansion. The number of applications increased from 404 in 1981 to 4,750 in 1997.[107] The Court began having trouble clearing its docket and faced a different challenge: a large backlog of cases.[108]

Protocol 11 was introduced to tackle the caseload problem in 1998. This protocol also reversed the compromise made during the drafting of the Convention and created the European human rights system as we know it now. It abolished the Commission and created the new Court with compulsory jurisdiction. The new Court would work on a full-time basis and receive applications directly from the individual complainants.[109] As one judge explained, the system's structural transformation represented a colossal change in the Court's approach. The Commission's abolition increased "the rhythm and the pace" of legal evolution.[110] The Court began receiving cases that it would not normally have received. This presented the Court with an opportunity to launch the legal change analyzed in Chapters 3 and 4.

The New Court: From Euphoria to Reform

The new institutional setup of the new Court yielded more autonomy and authority, but it did not guarantee smooth sailing. The 1990s brought not

104 Council of Europe, "Vienna Declaration," October 9, 1993.
105 Bates, *The Evolution of the European Convention on Human Rights*, 447.
106 Christoffersen and Madsen, "Introduction," 3.
107 Karen Schlüter, "The Council of Europe, the Standard Setter," in *Human Rights in Europe: A Fragmented Regime?*, ed. Malte Brosig (Frankfurt am Main: Peter Lang AG, 2006), 40.
108 Helfer, "Redesigning the European Court of Human Rights," 126. In 2017, this number rose to 63,350, according to the Court's "Analysis of Statistics 2017."
109 European Court of Human Rights, "Annual Report 2011," 12.
110 Interview 14.

only major new opportunities for the Court but also major challenges. First came euphoria about the expansion of the European human rights regime with the inclusion of the former socialist countries in the East. Then came waves of reform initiatives attempting to limit the Court's roles and functions.[111]

Once the Eastward expansion was completed in the early 2000s, the Court was charged with reviewing human rights practices of an entire region of nearly 800 million people. In addition to the increase in the volume of applications, the nature of issues brought before the Court changed in this period. Until the 1990s, the Court received cases only from states with long democratic traditions.[112] After the expansion, the cases coming from new members included entrenched problems, such as systemic violations openly targeting ethnic groups or the lack of sufficient domestic remedies.[113] These cases indicated a need to instruct such countries in European human rights standards. Therefore, the Court often took a pedagogical role in cultivating human rights traditions in the newly independent countries.[114]

Although the increased caseload posed an administrative challenge to the Court, it also reinforced its institutional authority. Motivated by a political ambition to consolidate their democracies, the formerly communist states were eager to respect the Court's authority. As Michael O'Boyle, former Deputy Registrar of the Court, explains: "while adding significantly to the Court's docket, [the Eastward expansion] has arguably not weakened or undermined the system but strengthened it. It has created a new and unexpected geopolitical dimension for the institution which *ipso facto* engenders renewed political support."[115]

The Court had been crippled with insurmountable caseloads and delays in the implementation of judgments since the early 2000s. To address these problems, member states initiated a series of reform proposals,

[111] Mikael Rask Madsen, "The Challenging Authority of the European Court of Human Rights: From Cold War Legal Diplomacy to the Brighton Declaration and Backlash," *Law and Contemporary Problems* 79, no. 1 (2016).

[112] Bates, *The Evolution of the European Convention on Human Rights*, 2010, 473.

[113] Aisling Reidy et al., "Gross Violations of Human Rights: Invoking the European Convention on Human Rights in the Case of Turkey," *Netherlands Quarterly of Human Rights* 15, no. 1 (1997): 172.

[114] Robert Harmsen, "The European Convention on Human Rights after Enlargement," *The International Journal of Human Rights* 5, no. 4 (2010): 33. Also, Interview 16.

[115] Michael O'Boyle, "The Imperiled Success of the European Court of Human Rights," in *Trente Ans de Droit Européen Des Droits de l'Homme. Études à La Mémoire de Wolfgang Strasser*, ed. Hanno Hartig (Brussels: Nemesis/Bruylant, 2007), 261.

which spurred structural and behavioural changes – starting the era of the reformed Court. First, member states introduced additional protocols to the Convention and generated significant structural changes. The most important such development came in 2010 with Protocol 14. This protocol modified the Court's internal organization. The original one-judge-per-member-state rule remained the same.[116] Yet, judges' terms of office changed from six years renewable to nine years nonrenewable.[117] The protocol also revamped the admissibility criteria to simplify the application process,[118] and changed the Court's composition to include the following units that are used today: single-judge formations, Committees of three judges, Chambers of seven judges, and Grand Chambers of seventeen judges. These changes – especially the single-judge filtering mechanisms and the three-judge committees – were much needed to tackle the increasing caseload and to streamline the case processing procedures. After this restructuring, the Court announced in October 2013 that its backlog had been reduced from 160,200 in 2011 to 111,350.[119]

Member states have also started a dialogue to address the challenges that the new Court had been facing. They initiated a series of High-Level Conferences on the Future of the Court in Interlaken, Switzerland; İzmir, Turkey; Brighton, the United Kingdom; Brussels, Belgium; and Copenhagen, Denmark, between 2010 and 2018. All of these meetings gathered ministers or high-level officials from each Council of Europe

[116] The selection of the judges takes place in a two-stage process whereby the member states send a shortlist of three candidates to the Parliamentary Assembly, which selects one of these three candidates.

[117] Originally, the Convention stipulated judges' terms of office as nine years renewable. Protocol 11 reduced it to six years renewable.

[118] Admissibility criteria are covered under Article 35 of the Convention: (1) The Court may only deal with the matter after all domestic remedies have been exhausted, according to the generally recognised rules of international law, and within a period of six months from the date on which the final decision was taken. (2) The Court shall not deal with any application submitted under Article 34 that (a) is anonymous; or (b) is substantially the same as a matter that has already been examined by the Court or has already been submitted to another procedure of international investigation or settlement and contains no relevant new information. (3) The Court shall declare inadmissible any individual application submitted under Article 34, which it considers incompatible with the provisions of the Convention or the protocols thereto, manifestly ill-founded, or an abuse of the right of application. (4) The Court shall reject any application, which it considers inadmissible under this Article. It may do so at any stage of the proceedings.

[119] European Court of Human Rights, "Reform of the Court: Filtering of Cases Successful in Reducing Backlog," *Press Release, ECHR 312 (2013)*, October 24, 2013. By 2017 this number dropped even further to 56,250. European Court of Human Rights, "Analysis of Statistics 2017."

member states. Meetings were concluded with declarations that serve as road maps to improving the European human rights regime. What is striking about these declarations is that they gave the member states the opportunity to express their visions for the Court and the extent of its functions while also suggesting practical measures to address the backlog of cases. According to Judge Spano, former President of the European Court, these meetings heralded the dawn of "the age of subsidiarity," re-emphasizing that the supranational review carried out by the Court is subsidiary to the one provided at the national level.[120] Indeed, these meetings represented a turning point in the Court's reform history and influenced the way the Court carries out its judicial functions today.[121] For this reason, I call the post-2010 Court the "reformed" Court and highlight ways in which its practices differed from the new Court. This distinction allows me to assess the influence of the reform process on the Court's interpretive preferences and tendencies for forbearing or audacious interpretations.

The reform Court period is still underway, with the Court facing further structural changes and political challenges.[122] For example, the Committee of Ministers adopted two additional protocols amending and adding to the European Convention. Protocol 15, which entered into force on August 1, 2021, amends the Convention by setting out changes to the case processing mechanism and the Preamble. Notably, it reduces the time limit to bring an application before the European Court from six months to four months, and adds the principle of subsidiarity and margin of appreciation to the Preamble. Protocol 16, on the other hand, adds to the Convention and enables national courts to seek advisory opinions from the Court. Protocol 16 came into force on August 1, 2018, in respect of sixteen member states that ratified it: Albania, Andorra, Armenia, Bosnia and Herzegovina, Estonia, Finland, France, Georgia, Greece, Lithuania, Luxembourg, Netherlands, San Marino, Slovak Republic, Slovenia, and Ukraine.[123]

[120] Robert Spano, "Universality or Diversity of Human Rights? Strasbourg in the Age of Subsidiarity," *Human Rights Law Review* 14, no. 3 (2014): 487–502; Robert Spano, "The Future of the European Court of Human Rights – Subsidiarity, Process-Based Review and the Rule of Law," *Human Rights Law Review* 18, no. 3 (2018): 473–94.

[121] Mikael Rask Madsen, "Rebalancing European Human Rights: Has the Brighton Declaration Engendered a New Deal on Human Rights in Europe?," *Journal of International Dispute Settlement* 9, no. 2 (2018): 199–222.

[122] For a discussion of authoritarian challenges that the Court faces, see Başak Çali, "Autocratic Strategies and the European Court of Human Rights," *European Convention on Human Rights Law Review* 2, no. 1 (March 10, 2021): 11–19.

[123] This information was verified on April 27, 2022, through the Council of Europe webpage, available at www.coe.int/en/web/conventions/full-list?module=signatures-by-treaty&treatynum=214

In addition to these structural changes, the Council of Europe and the reformed Court have been confronted with several political challenges. These range from Turkey's withdrawal from the Istanbul Convention on Violence against Women in March 2021 to the Russian invasion of Ukraine in February 2022. The Council of Europe condemned Russia, and both the Parliamentary Assembly and the Committee of Ministers arrived at the conclusion that Russia "can no longer be a member state."[124] In the meantime, the European Court granted urgent interim measures on 1 March, 2022, underlining that "the current military action which commenced on 24 February 2022 in various parts of Ukraine (...) gives rise to a real and continuing risk of serious violations of the Convention rights of the civilian population."[125] Before the Committee of Ministers took a vote on expelling Russia, Russia announced its withdrawal from the Council of Europe and the European Convention on Human Rights.[126] While Russia's withdrawal, or Rexit, is likely to ease the Court's caseload (since 24.20% of all pending cases concern Russia, according to the Court's 2021 statistics), this will imply a serious gap in the protection of the rights both in Russia and in Ukraine with respect to violations perpetrated by Russia.[127] As Chapter 3 will show, cases brought against Russia constitute a clear majority of the Article 3 jurisprudence.

Conclusion

This chapter is composed of two connected parts. The first part has looked at the European Court of Human Rights' inner workings and the way it functions. Expanding this assessment beyond the elected judges, the chapter has argued that the Court defines its organizational priorities as a collective body. This collective body includes not only the judges elected for limited terms but also law clerks and other legal professionals at the Registry, most of whom are hired on a permanent basis. This essentially

[124] The Council of Europe, "The Russian Federation can no longer be a member State of the Council of Europe, PACE says" (March 16, 2022) available at www.coe.int/en/web/portal/-/the-russian-federation-can-no-longer-be-a-member-state-of-the-council-of-europe-pace-says

[125] European Court of Human Rights, "The European Court grants urgent interim measures in application concerning Russian military operations on Ukrainian territory," Press release, *ECHR 068(2022)* (March 1, 2022).

[126] "'Rexit': Russia withdraws from Council of Europe ahead of expulsion vote," *Euronews* (March 16, 2022), available at www.euronews.com/my-europe/2022/03/16/rexit-russia-withdraws-from-council-of-europe-ahead-of-expulsion-vote.

[127] European Court of Human Rights, *The ECHR in Facts and Figure 2021* (February 2022), available at www.echr.coe.int/Documents/Facts_Figures_2021_ENG.pdf

implies that all members of the judicial elite working at the Court contribute to defining the Court's collective purpose and determining if there is a need for tactical balancing – thus shaping the tendency for forbearance or audacity. The second part has offered a historical overview of the Court's institutional transformation. Created in 1959, the European Court once operated as a part-time institution. The Court then became a full-time institution in 1998; its structure was further refined during the reform processes that officially began with the first High-Level Conference on the Future of the Court in 2010.

3

Mapping Out Norm Change

How did the Court refashion the norm against torture and inhuman or degrading treatment? Which elements of the norm were already present at the time of the Convention's inception, and which new dimensions were introduced at a later stage? The answers to these questions not only help one trace how the norm changed but also when and how much it did. To take on this task, this chapter closely examines the norm. Instead of treating the norm as a single unit, it breaks it down into components and assesses the norm's transformation over time by tracing when each component was introduced and what percentage of Article 3 jurisprudence they make up.

Norm disaggregation is particularly valuable for three reasons: First, it helps us understand what norms are made of. Norms are often thought to be vague or capacious.[1] Yet, by tracing the changing configuration of their contents, one gets closer to capturing norms in their entirety. Second, charting the range of obligations as they are introduced within a legal regime reveals the extent of judicial lawmaking. This is crucial because judicial lawmaking is often accompanied by the amnesia of creation. Such amnesia persists because courts resort to a narrative that they are not, in fact, introducing any new understandings; these new understandings were there all along.[2] Largely induced by courts' legitimacy concerns,

[1] For a good assessment of the definition and content of norms, see Michelle Jurkovich, "What Isn't a Norm? Redefining the Conceptual Boundaries of 'Norms' in the Human Rights Literature," *International Studies Review* 22, no. 3 (2020): 693–711.

[2] For a series of comprehensive analyses on judicial lawmaking, see Ingo Venzke, *How Interpretation Makes International Law: On Semantic Change and Normative Twists* (Oxford and New York: Oxford University Press, 2012); Karen Alter and Laurence Helfer, "Nature or Nurture?" Judicial Lawmaking in the European Court of Justice and the Andean Tribunal of Justice," *International Organization* 64, no. 4 (2010): 563–92; Tiago Fidalgo de Freitas, "Theories of Judicial Behavior and the Law: Taking Stock and Looking Ahead," in *Judicial Activism: An Interdisciplinary Approach to the American and European Experiences*, ed. Luís Pereira Coutinho, Massimo La Torre, and Steven D. Smith (Cham and New York: Springer, 2015), 105–17.

this narrative is often employed to ensure that courts are not seen to be creating new obligations not previously agreed to by states.[3] Finally, as this book makes clear, international courts may not adopt the same interpretative lenses toward different obligations falling under the same norm. For example, they might not evenly apply expansive (or right-restraining) interpretations across the board, which makes it harder to assess how progressive a certain court is. Disaggregating norms and studying them at the level of obligations is useful to measure whether a court is right-expansive across the board or selectively.

This approach complements existing International Relations and International Law scholarship on norm change in substantial ways. Norm scholars have explored the impact that norms have on state behaviour. Yet, they have undertheorised what happens to norms once they are legalised and codified.[4] A new generation of norm scholars has amended this to a great extent, examining how the meaning, validity, and application of norms are disputed.[5] Nevertheless, they also have continued to take treaties as their point of reference, tending not to focus on international courts' impact on norm transformation.[6] This is despite the fact that international courts have a crucial role to play in updating norms' formal validity by interpreting treaties, as well as by establishing divergence

[3] Tom Ginsburg, "Bounded Discretion in International Judicial Lawmaking" *Virginia Journal of International Law* 45, no. 3 (2005): 631–73; Laurence R. Helfer and Karen J. Alter, "Legitimacy and Lawmaking: A Tale of Three International Courts," *Theoretical Inquiries in Law* 14, no. 2 (2013): 479–504; Nienke Grossman et al., eds. *Legitimacy and International Courts* (Cambridge, New York: Cambridge University Press, 2018); Andreas Follesdal, "Survey Article: The Legitimacy of International Courts," *Journal of Political Philosophy* 28, no. 4 (2020): 476–99.

[4] Wayne Sandholtz, "Dynamics of International Norm Change: Rules against Wartime Plunder," *European Journal of International Relations* 14, no. 1 (2008): 101.

[5] Some examples include Mona Lena Krook and Jacqui True, "Rethinking the Life Cycles of International Norms: The United Nations and the Global Promotion of Gender Equality," *European Journal of International Relations* 18, no. 1 (2012): 103–27; Susanne Zwingel, "How Do Norms Travel? Theorizing International Women's Rights in Transnational Perspective," *International Studies Quarterly* 56, no. 1 (2012): 115–29; Amitav Acharya, "How Ideas Spread: Whose Norms Matter? Norm Localization and Institutional Change in Asian Regionalism," *International Organization* 58, no. 2 (2004): 239–75; Antje Wiener, *Contestation and Constitution of Norms in Global International Relations* (Cambridge: Cambridge University Press, 2018); Nicole Deitelhoff and Lisbeth Zimmermann, "Things We Lost in the Fire: How Different Types of Contestation Affect the Robustness of International Norms," *International Studies Review* 22, no. 1 (2020): 51–76.

[6] See, for example, Wiener, *Contestation and Constitution of Norms in Global International Relations*.

and convergence around meanings.[7] Legal scholars, on the other hand, have long remarked upon the importance of international courts in norm development.[8] What has been missing in such doctrinal accounts, however, is a systematic explanation of when and why norms change.[9] Instead, this scholarship has presented the most up-to-date standards by taking snapshots of the law at a particular moment in time. So far, it has limited itself to providing a wealth of normative work on the "right" way to interpret[10] or on timeless jurisprudential analyses of available legal principles.[11]

Between Forbearance and Audacity bridges two distinct scholarships and offers a new approach to systematically studying norm change. This approach helps trace how adjudication influences the development of an existing norm through norms' interpretation or application to concrete situations.[12] At its core, it advocates studying every decision regardless of its importance – not just poring over a few landmark decisions as

[7] There are a few exceptions, such as Druscilla Scribner and Tracy Slagter, "Recursive Norm Development: The Role of Supranational Courts," *Global Policy* 8, no. 3 (2017): 322–32; Tobias Berger, *Global Norms and Local Courts: Translating the Rule of Law in Bangladesh* (Oxford and New York: Oxford University Press, 2017); Zoltán I. Búzás and Erin R. Graham, "Emergent Flexibility in Institutional Development: How International Rules Really Change," *International Studies Quarterly* 64, no. 4 (2020): 821-33.

[8] For example, Kanstantsin Dzehtsiarou and Conor O'Mahony, "Evolutive Interpretation of Rights Provisions: A Comparison of the European Court of Human Rights and the U.S. Supreme Court," *Columbia Human Rights Law Review* 44 (2013 2012): 309–66; Steven Greer, "The Interpretation of the European Convention on Human Rights: Universal Principle or Margin or Appreciation," *UCL Human Rights Review* 3 (2010): 1–14; Ian Johnstone, *The Power of Deliberation: International Law, Politics and Organizations* (Oxford and New York: Oxford University Press, 2011).

[9] For a discussion on norm development, see Norbert Paulo, *The Confluence of Philosophy and Law in Applied Ethics* (London: Palgrave Macmillan, 2016).

[10] See, for example, Greer, "The Interpretation of the European Convention on Human Rights"; Kanstantsin Dzehtsiarou, "European Consensus and the Evolutive Interpretation of the European Convention on Human Rights," *German Law Journal* 12, no. 10 (2011): 1731–45; Alastair Mowbray, *The Development of Positive Obligations under the European Convention on Human Rights by the European Court of Human Rights* (Oxford and Portland: Hart Publishing, 2004); George Letsas, *A Theory of Interpretation of the European Convention on Human Rights* (Oxford: Oxford University Press, 2007); George Letsas, "Strasbourg's Interpretive Ethic: Lessons for the International Lawyer," *European Journal of International Law* 21, no. 3 (2010): 509–41.

[11] See, for example, Natasa Mavronicola, *Torture, Inhumanity and Degradation under Article 3 of the ECHR: Absolute Rights and Absolute Wrongs* (Oxford and New York: Hart Publishing, 2021), 128.

[12] On the distinction between norm interpretation and application, see Anastasios Gourgourinis, "The Distinction between Interpretation and Application of Norms in International Adjudication," *Journal of International Dispute Settlement* 2, no. 1 (2011): 31–57.

traditional legal analysis would require. This is what makes it possible to measure the magnitude, pace, and directionality of change.

We intuitively know that human rights improve over time in line with evolving societal needs. Yet, we cannot immediately guess when, why, and how much a norm can transform over time. This is precisely what can be revealed when norms are studied in a disaggregated manner by taking obligations as a reference. Tracing obligations demonstrates exactly when a norm fundamentally transforms and helps identify the type and magnitude of this transformation. Unlike previous studies that view legal change through the lenses of punctuated equilibrium theory (i.e., long phases of norm *stasis* disrupted by sudden and substantial adjustments),[13] this book makes it clear that there is no single way that norm change happens. Norm change sometimes occurs gradually, while other times, it appears in sudden bursts. Moreover, not every change episode would be of the same magnitude. In order to examine norm change using these different metrics, we need to disaggregate norms and study their transformation at the level of obligations.

This approach thus stands apart from those that investigate norms' strength or resilience by looking at norm clusters (i.e., a group of norms) in a more aggregated fashion.[14] While looking at norms as aggregated groups of standards makes sense to test their strength and resilience, such an approach does not allow the degree of precision necessary to trace how and how much norms transform within a given legal regime.

In addition to introducing this new approach to tracing norm change, this chapter also serves as an important stepping stone to the subsequent analysis. The results of the systematic content analysis presented below provide key information about when and how much the norm against torture and inhuman or degrading treatment changed over time. In so doing, they successfully illustrate the norm's trajectory in parallel with the European Court's institutional transformation.

[13] See, for example, Paul F. Diehl and Charlotte Ku, *The Dynamics of International Law* (Cambridge: Cambridge University Press, 2010).

[14] See, for example, Carla Winston, "Norm Structure, Diffusion, and Evolution: A Conceptual Approach," *European Journal of International Relations* 24, no. 3 (2018): 638–61; Eglantine Staunton and Jason Ralph, "The Responsibility to Protect Norm Cluster and the Challenge of Atrocity Prevention: An Analysis of the European Union's Strategy in Myanmar," *European Journal of International Relations* 26, no. 3 (2020): 660–86; Michal Ben-Josef Hirsch and Jennifer M. Dixon, "Conceptualizing and Assessing Norm Strength in International Relations," *European Journal of International Relations* 27, no. 2 (2021): 521-47.

Disaggregating Norms

Legal norms are composite constructs composed of obligations and correlative rights.[15] A common definition of a norm in International Relations is "a standard of appropriate behavior for actors with a given identity."[16] However, as Wayne Sandholtz rightly argues, this definition conflates norms with customs, traditions, values, or fashions.[17] Instead, he advocates Nicholas Onuf's definition of norms as standards of conduct that have a prescriptive quality in compelling agents to "behave in accordance with [them]."[18] This is a more compelling definition of legal norms and is the definition used in this book. Legal norms are part of the broader category of social norms, yet they still differ from other subcategories such as traditions, values, or fashions.[19] What distinguishes legal norms from social norms is the idiosyncratic way they are created – whether part of a body of hard law or soft law – and the manner in which they are argued, interpreted, and enforced.[20]

The fact that legal norms may entail multiple enforceable rights and obligations is the reason they should not be studied as highly abstract, singular units.[21] Focusing on a norm as a single unit would mean that only their most traditional elements are placed under the magnifying glass. For example, in the case of the prohibition of torture and inhuman

15 Here, I only refer to primary norms.

16 Martha Finnemore and Kathryn Sikkink, "International Norm Dynamics and Political Change," *International Organization* 52, no. 4 (1998): 891.

17 Sandholtz, "International Norm Change."

18 Nicholas Onuf, *International Legal Theory: Essays and Engagements, 1966–2006*, 1st edition (New York: Routledge-Cavendish, 2008), 450.

19 For nonlegal norms, see, for example, Erna Burai, "Parody as Norm Contestation: Russian Normative Justifications in Georgia and Ukraine and Their Implications for Global Norms," *Global Society* 30, no. 1 (2016): 67–77; Jessica L. Beyer and Stephanie C. Hofmann, "Varieties of Neutrality: Norm Revision and Decline," *Cooperation and Conflict* 46, no. 3 (2011): 285–311; Stephanie C. Hofmann and Andrew I. Yeo, "Business as Usual: The Role of Norms in Alliance Management," *European Journal of International Relations* 21, no. 2 (2015): 377–401; Alexander Cooley, "Authoritarianism Goes Global: Countering Democratic Norms," *Journal of Democracy* 26, no. 3 (2015): 49–63.

20 For more on this, see Jutta Brunnée and Stephen J. Toope, *Legitimacy and Legality in International Law: An Interactional Account* (Cambridge: Cambridge University Press, 2010); Joost Pauwelyn, "Is It International Law or Not, and Does It Even Matter?," in *Informal International Lawmaking*, ed. Joost Pauwelyn, Ramses A. Wessel, and Jan Wouters (Oxford: Oxford University Press, 2012), 125–61.

21 R. R. Baxter, "International Law in 'Her Infinite Variety,'" *The International and Comparative Law Quarterly* 29, no. 4 (1980): 549. See also Michael Bothe, "Legal and Non-Legal Norms – a Meaningful Distinction in International Relations?," *Netherlands Yearbook of International Law* 11 (1980): 65–95.

or degrading treatment, this is interrogative torture or ill-treatment. However, this norm's transformation cannot be fully understood without looking at its nontraditional elements – epitomised by the case of Nahide, a domestic violence victim. In order to understand norms and how they change, we need to take a closer look at what they embody. Legal change happens at the level of obligations (or rights), not at the level of norms. Therefore, the unit of analysis to study legal change should be each and every obligation falling under the same norm. It is the concrete obligations that root the abstract norms in a particular context. Norms become clearer as obligations become more specific. Norms grow stronger as the obligations reach taken-for-granted status.

Disaggregating norms offers certain benefits that other broad-brush approaches do not.[22] For example, disaggregation can tell us about the magnitude of change and whether this pertains to the norm's main logic or application (norm's core and periphery, respectively).[23] It can also reveal its unevenness. Indeed, while certain obligations are transformed at a higher rate and in sudden bursts, certain others might remain the same or change gradually over time. Focusing on norms globally without paying attention to their actual content prevents us from fully comprehending norms' nature, scope, or robustness. Such approaches do a special disservice to any attempt to understand their transformation. One cannot fully grasp how norms change if they are viewed as solid, singular, and confined behavioural standards. When looked at under the magnifying glass, each obligation that a norm embodies has the ability and potential to grow and take a direction of its own. Indeed, norms develop and are refined through expansion or adjustment of their scope or content.[24] What actually facilitates this refinement is the transformation or clarification of obligations (or rights) that they embody – and transformation for each obligation may not look the same, as we see in this book.

[22] Alison Brysk and Michael Stohl, *Contesting Human Rights: Norms, Institutions and Practice* (Cheltenham: Edward Elgar Publishing, 2019); Averell Schmidt and Kathryn Sikkink, "Breaking the Ban? The Heterogeneous Impact of US Contestation of the Torture Norm," *Journal of Global Security Studies* 4, no. 1 (2019): 105–22; Jeffrey S. Lantis, "Theories of International Norm Contestation: Structure and Outcomes," *Oxford Research Encyclopedia of Politics*, June 28, 2017; Anette Stimmer, "Beyond Internalization: Alternate Endings of the Norm Life Cycle," *International Studies Quarterly* 63, no. 2 (2019): 270–80.

[23] For an assessment of what norm's core are, see Deitelhoff and Zimmermann, "Things We Lost in the Fire"; see also Nicole Deitelhoff and Lisbeth Zimmermann, "Norms under Challenge: Unpacking the Dynamics of Norm Robustness," *Journal of Global Security Studies* 4, no. 1 (2019): 2–17.

[24] For a discussion on norm development, see Paulo, *The Confluence of Philosophy and Law in Applied Ethics*.

Types and Modes of Change

Norms change in a variety of ways.[25] Change can be in how they are applied (i.e., regarding the issue areas they cover), or it could be in their main logic.[26] The first form of change is peripheral change. Change can be peripheral when it concerns a norm's scope. That is to say, the existing obligations under the norm may begin covering new issues and victim groups, or the norm may come to include entirely new obligations. Alternatively, the scope may also retract when it is settled which obligations fall outside of the norm's coverage. In the context of the norm against torture, the norm's scope broadened when it was invoked to protect other vulnerable groups such as women, children, or disabled individuals.[27] For example, in *Romanov* v. *Russia,* the Court found that the treatment of a mentally ill detainee would fall under Article 3.[28] This meant a new victim group (mentally ill inmates or patients) could now seek protection under this norm. Likewise, the scope might be narrowed down when a judgment clearly indicates what a given obligation does not cover. To illustrate, the Court decided that states' obligation to prevent suffering does not go as far as facilitating euthanasia for terminally ill patients in *Pretty* v. *the United Kingdom.*[29] The rulings thereby set the limits of the norm. As these examples show, peripheral change concerns what a norm covers. It can be traced by taking the norm's scope as a reference and analyzing whether it has expanded or contracted.[30]

Sometimes, change can permeate the core of the norm, transforming its very logic.[31] For example, when the Court introduced positive obligations under the prohibition of torture in the late 1990s, it essentially rewired the norm's internal logic. This is because, traditionally, states

[25] These categories are heuristic devices to help understand and explain the ways in which norms may change. This book's objective is not to enumerate and exemplify each type or mode of change. Rather, it is to explain how and why court-effectuated legal change occurs in such manners.

[26] Or norm's core as it is identified in Deitelhoff and Zimmermann, "Things We Lost in the Fire," 59.

[27] Traditionally, this norm was considered to cover mostly detainees, prisoners, or terrorist suspects.

[28] *Romanov* v. *Russia,* application no. 63993/00, ECHR (October 20, 2005).

[29] *Pretty* v. *the United Kingdom,* application no. 2346/02, ECHR (April 29, 2002).

[30] For more on this, see Ezgi Yildiz, "A Court with Many Faces: Judicial Characters and Modes of Norm Development in the European Court of Human Rights," *European Journal of International Law* 31, no. 1 (2020).

[31] For a good explanation of what norms' core are, see Deitelhoff and Zimmermann, "Things We Lost in the Fire," 51–76.

were only responsible for acts actively committed by state agents (commission) under Article 3. After the introduction of positive obligations, the international community began to accept that the norm does not only entail obligations to refrain from doing something (i.e., torturing or subjecting someone to inhuman or degrading treatment). States became obligated to protect victims from acts perpetrated by their agents or private actors and started to bear responsibility for any failure to introduce necessary measures to protect vulnerable groups and prevent violations (omission).

The adoption of positive obligations generated both practical and ideational effects, transforming the norm's operating logic. On the practical level, positive obligations have enhanced protection under Article 3.[32] These new obligations require states to protect rights in a practical and effective way.[33] As one judge explained in an interview, they imply "a proactive approach by states to ensure that core values are actively promoted, pursued, and protected."[34]

On the ideational level, positive obligations have generated important changes in the way state obligations and individual rights are understood.[35] First, social rights have become less distinct from civil and political rights. Civil and political rights had typically been associated with negative obligations, and economic and social rights with positive obligations. Giving expression exclusively to civil and political rights, the European Convention was initially designed to impose only negative obligations. The Court's adoption of positive obligations reversed this separation. States are now required to take measures to actively protect rights rather than simply refrain from violating them.[36] Second, and relatedly, the prohibition of torture came to include other resource-intensive duties – such as investigating and punishing perpetrators, providing acceptable living conditions to detainees, refugees, and asylum seekers, and providing timely and sufficient medical treatment in detention facilities. Third, positive obligations

[32] Interview 5; Interview 9; Interview 27; Interview 28.

[33] Mowbray, *The Development of Positive Obligations under the European Convention on Human Rights by the European Court of Human Rights*, 2.

[34] Interview 10.

[35] By no means was the introduction of positive obligations only limited to the prohibition of torture. Positive obligations were also introduced under a variety of provisions, such as Article 2 (right to life) or Article 8 (right to respect for private and family life). Mowbray, *The Development of Positive Obligations under the European Convention on Human Rights by the European Court of Human Rights.*

[36] Interview 9.

made it possible to address human rights abuses that were committed by private agents.[37] States may bear responsibility when they fail to prevent abuse by non-state actors. This is a revolutionary interpretation of rights that were initially created to regulate states' behaviour toward their citizens. Now, states may be culpable for *not* stepping in to protect vulnerable groups against mistreatment perpetrated by private individuals.

Another important analytic dimension is the mode of change. Change can be incremental or sudden. Norms can be slowly sculpted by means of gradual change over a long period of time or quickly transformed in sudden bursts to address an emerging social need. For example, the minimum level of severity criteria (required for an act to be considered torture or inhuman or degrading treatment) has been gradually lowered over time, but the state obligation to prevent domestic violence was introduced much more swiftly – in the context of Nahide's case (*Opuz* v. *Turkey*).

Having distinguished these two modes of change, I should emphasise that gradual or sudden changes are not diametrically opposed categories. Rather, they may feed into each other. Years of gradual change might open the gateway for a sudden change. Alternatively, an episode of sudden change might be followed and further refined by gradual change. In order to categorise the ways a norm may change – be it gradual but peripheral or sudden and foundational – we need to disaggregate norms and study the transformation of each and every obligation falling under them. This is how I study the ways the prohibition against torture and inhuman or degrading treatment changed over time. I first break the norm into traceable components – obligations – in my analysis of the Court's jurisprudence. Then, I trace the type and mode of change by focusing on each and every obligation falling under Article 3.

Measuring Audacity and Forbearance

This analysis also helps understand the degree to which the European Court has been either forbearing or audacious over time. As explained in the Introduction, I measure audacity and forbearance with respect to two criteria. The first of these is a given court's willingness to recognise new state obligations or new rights (*novel claims*). The second is its propensity for finding states in violation (*propensity*). While audacious courts will have a higher score for both of these measures, forbearing courts will have a lower score.

[37] Sandra Krahenmann, "Positive Obligations in Human Rights Treaties" (Geneva, Graduate Institute of International and Development Studies, 2012), 3.

As the preceding discussion indicates, not every change episode is equal. Change proposals that transform the main logic of a norm, going beyond the adjustment of the scope of its application, are more audacious acts of change. Therefore, I consider the introduction of positive obligations under this norm in the late 1990s as an epitome of an audacious change, tracing the conditions that made this change possible in Chapter 6.

Data Collection and Analysis

My main methods for tracing legal change in the Court's anti-torture jurisprudence are legal analysis of a sample of rulings and content analysis of all Article 3 judgments. I collected every Article 3 judgment pronounced between 1967 and 2016 from HUDOC, the Court's official case repository.[38] This amounts to 2,294 rulings in total.[39] Figure 3.1 shows the distribution of Article 3 cases in ratio to the number of all cases for the period under study.

As Figure 3.1 shows, during the old Court and the new Court periods, Article 3 cases made up only 5% and 7% of all jurisprudence. This changed dramatically during the reformed Court period, where Article 3 cases constituted 21% of the jurisprudence.

Selection and Categorisation Rules

I have focused only on judgments from cases that passed an initial screening and were declared admissible for review.[40] My unit of analysis was

[38] This list also includes the Commission's decisions which were not referred to the Court. When there are both a Commission decision and a Court judgment about the same case, I have only looked at the latter.

[39] I have only assessed the final rulings issued by the highest body. This meant that I have privileged Grand Chamber rulings over Chamber rulings and the European Court rulings over the decisions of the European Commission except when these decisions were never referred to the Court. This total number includes 2,270 rulings issued by the European Court as well as 24 decisions that were issued and not reviewed by the Court. The 2,270 Court rulings include violation and no violation decisions separately. For the period under study, there are 1,929 judgments involving at least one violation decision and 652 judgments involving one no violation decision. In this count, some of the cases are counted twice because they involve at least one violation and at least one no violation decision.

[40] Every complaint brought before the Court is subjected to an admissibility test before being sent for judicial review. Article 35 of the Convention lays out criteria for admissibility decisions, according to which the applicant must exhaust all available domestic remedies and apply to the Court no more than six months after the final domestic court decision (prior to Protocol 15, which effectively reduces this time limit to four months). The Court

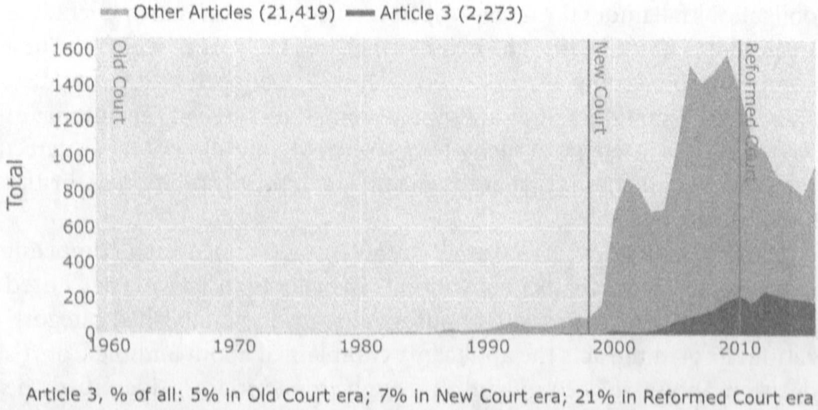

Figure 3.1 The evolution of the share of Article 3 cases in the entire jurisprudence

individual claims brought under Article 3. Because many cases involve claims concerning more than one obligation under Article 3, I separated out each complaint representing a distinct obligation.[41] For example, an applicant may have complained that she was subjected to inhuman treatment under custody (ill-treatment under custody) and that domestic authorities did not properly investigate her complaint (failure to fulfil procedural obligation). The Court may take a different position for each of these obligations.[42] It may find the responding state in violation concerning the first complaint but *not* in violation with respect to the second complaint. That is why looking at each complaint separately helps disentangle the Court's attitudes toward different obligations.

My first step was then to map out all the obligations that are associated with the norm against torture and inhuman or degrading treatment. To carry out this task systematically, I first ran a pilot study of decisions rendered between 1967 and 2006 with the goal of determining what types of

may declare any application inadmissible if the application is manifestly ill-founded (not based on facts or reliable evidence) or if the applicant has not suffered a significant disadvantage. Moreover, the Court may refuse to review a case if the applicant wishes the Court to revise and quash a decision taken by a domestic court – known as "fourth-instance" applications.

41 This total number includes violation and no violation decisions separately. For the period under study, there are 1,929 judgments involving at least a violation decision and 652 judgments involving a no violation decision. In this count, some of the cases are counted twice because there were both violations and no violations.

42 Yildiz, "A Court with Many Faces."

obligations fall under the norm against torture and inhuman or degrading treatment. I started with 1967 because that was the year in which the first complaint concerning Article 3 was reviewed.[43] I stopped in 2006 because, shortly thereafter, there was an unprecedented increase in the number of Article 3 cases. Analysis of such a long stretch of time allowed me to detect the types of obligations that are associated with the prohibition of torture and ill-treatment.

For the pilot study, I read each judgment and coded each complaint corresponding to a distinct obligation.[44] In order to cast a wide net, I used open coding. That is to say, without employing any established categorization, I noted the acts the applicants complained about and the Court's decision about each complaint. Through this exercise, I identified the types of acts that were considered Article 3 violations, as well as those that fell outside of the norm's scope.[45] Of the 284 cases pronounced between 1967 and 2006, some had more than one complaint relating to Article 3. To be exact, there were a total of 357 claims declared as Article 3 violations. Since my unit of analysis is isolated to obligations rather than the cases themselves, I reviewed all 357 separate claims.

When it comes to categorization, the circumstances and the location of ill-treatment determine what sort of obligation is involved. For example, if ill-treatment takes place after the arrest, then it is *ill-treatment during custody*; if it takes place during a riot control operation, then it is categorised as *police brutality*. Finally, if a complaint arises from unjustifiably stringent measures imposed on inmates, then it is categorised as *intrusive detention measures*. When categorizing obligations, I have made a distinction between positive and negative obligations. If an obligation calls upon state authorities to refrain from perpetrating an act (i.e., refrain from doing something), I list it as a *negative* obligation. If an obligation requires state authorities to take steps to ensure that individuals enjoy their rights (i.e., take active measures), then this obligation is categorised as a *positive* obligation. Tables 3.1 and 3.2 list the specific obligations identified, as well as related definitions.[46]

[43] The European Commission of Human Rights, *Heinz Zeidler-Kornmann* v. *The Federal Republic of Germany*, application no. 2686/65 (October 3, 1967).

[44] For more on content analysis and how to carry it out, see Klaus Krippendorff, *Content Analysis: An Introduction to Its Methodology* (SAGE Publications, 2018); Alan Bryman, *Social Research Methods*, 4th edition (Oxford and New York: Oxford University Press, 2012).

[45] This is mostly because my analysis is carried out on cases that passed the initial screening and were evaluated on their merits. That is, claims that evidently do not fall under this norm or those declared *inadmissible*, are not reviewed for this study.

[46] These categories and definitions served as a codebook during the coding exercise.

Table 3.1 *Claims concerning negative obligations*

Negative obligations
Ill-treatment during custody refers to a range of physical or mental abuse inflicted on victims after their arrest, namely during interrogation, detention, or imprisonment.
Refoulement constitutes a violation when a state places or transfers a person to somewhere they may face danger. The prohibition of *refoulement*, better known as the principle of *non-refoulement*, forbids states from extraditing, deporting, or expelling a person to a country where they might be tortured or ill-treated.
Torture is a (deliberate) infliction of severe pain to extract information or confession, to punish, or to intimidate.
Police brutality is excessive violence used during arrest attempts, police raids, security checks, road controls, or riot control operations.
Intrusive detention measures are unjustifiably stringent procedures imposed on inmates, such as strip searches, genital inspections, and solitary confinement without any compelling reason.
Destruction of property, homes, and livelihood constitutes a violation not due to the actual loss of property but due to the destruction's effect on victims' psychology and the extreme distress it generates.
Discrimination occurs when states implement unfavourable or unfair measures directed at certain groups or minorities based on their gender, sexual orientation, ethnicity, religion, or political beliefs.
Family separation refers to state authorities' unjustified decision to remove children from the custody of parents and place them with foster parents or childcare institutions, or to deport them without their parents, or to deport their parents.
Extrajudicial acts concern instances of unacknowledged detention, abduction, physical attack, and extrajudicial killing that are not officially documented and that allegedly take place with direct involvement or acquiescence of, state agents.

In the second part of my data analysis, I used the categories and coding rules in Tables 3.1 and 3.2 to analyze the remainder of the cases issued only by the European Court – leaving aside the decisions of the European Commission since it is an entirely separate body. For this study, I analyzed 2,270 Court judgments in total, which are made up of 3,553 separate complaints (including the 284 cases and 357 claims from the pilot study mentioned earlier). When coding judgments, I made use of the "case details" announced on the Court's website for each case. The case details include information on the Articles invoked, as well as on the conclusions reached.

Table 3.2 *Claims concerning positive obligations*

Positive obligations
Failure to provide legal protection/remedy arises when a state refuses to protect or its efforts fall short of protecting victims from abuse perpetrated by state agents or private individuals. This category also includes states' unwillingness or inability to offer a sufficient legal remedy or an effective recourse to legal remedy.
Failure to inform the relatives of disappeared persons occurs when states fail to conduct an effective investigation and inform the relatives (and sometimes the larger public) about the whereabouts of the disappeared persons in due course.
Failure to provide acceptable detention conditions occurs when a state is either unwilling or unable to provide detention facilities that comply with the minimum standards for the treatment of prisoners and detainees.
Failure to provide necessary medical care refers to deficiencies in supplying necessary medical assistance or appropriate conditions for sick and disabled inmates.
Failure to fulfil procedural obligations arises when states are unwilling or unable to carry out a timely and effective investigation into arguable claims of the victims or when they obstruct the proper administration of justice.
Failure to facilitate euthanasia refers to state authorities' refusal to help with euthanasia and assisted suicide by providing necessary substance and by not criminally charging the ones involved.
Failure to provide a healthy environment concerns state authorities' failure to take necessary and sufficient measures to ensure individuals can enjoy healthy living conditions without risks such as air pollution, water contamination, or chemical exposure.

Only in a few instances did the case details provide sufficient information for classification. A clear majority of the coding also required reading the judgment segments for Article 3, as well as the Court's conclusions. Two research assistants went over my codes, taking "case details" as a reference, to ensure that they were in line with the Court's records.

The resulting dataset includes information about the responding states and the number of claims that were ruled as violation or no violation of Article 3, amounting to 2,787 violation claims and 766 no violation claims, respectively. A higher percentage of claims concern violation decisions (around 78%), while only 12% of the claims concern a no violation decision. This could be because the analysis only focuses on the claims that passed the admissibility stage. The admissibility assessment might have selected cases that are more likely to be considered a violation of Article 3.

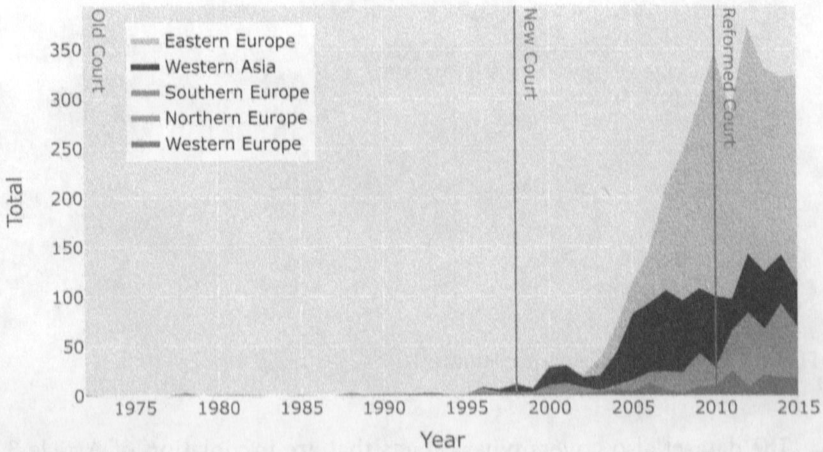

Figure 3.2 Distribution of Article 3 cases across different regions in Europe (UN Geoschemes)

This might explain the higher percentage of violation decisions captured in the dataset. While this appears to be a rather skewed finding, it does not pose a problem to my main objective, which is to chart out how the norm against torture and inhuman or degrading treatment transformed over time and how the Court's attitudes changed toward this norm.

Mapping Out the Anti-torture Jurisprudence

The first-cut analysis reveals the geopolitical distribution of the Court's anti-torture jurisprudence. As Figure 3.2 shows, the majority of Article 3 claims come from the Central and Eastern European countries (mostly formerly communist countries). Western Asia (e.g., Turkey, Armenia, and Azerbaijan) and Southern Europe (e.g., Italy, Greece, and Spain) come second and third, respectively. Northern Europe (e.g., Denmark, Norway, and Finland) and Western Europe (e.g., Germany, Belgium, and the Netherlands) are the least represented regions.

Further breaking down the results indicates that the Court's anti-torture jurisprudence is mostly driven by the claims brought against Russia, Turkey, Romania, Ukraine, and Bulgaria – two of which are also EU members (see Figure 3.3).[47]

[47] For the distribution of types of claims for each country, see the Annex.

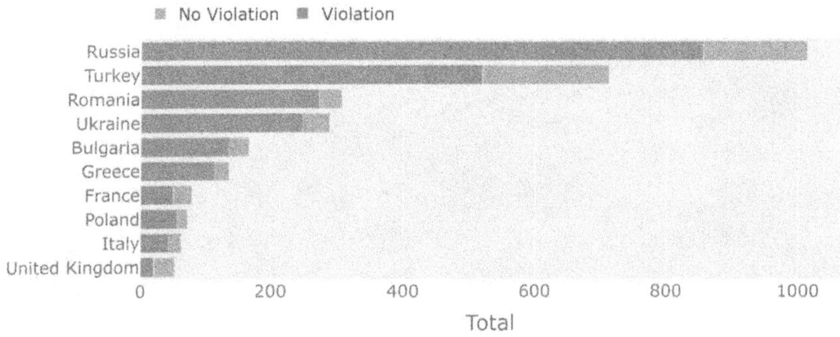

Figure 3.3 Number of claims per country[48]

The dataset also covers types of acts that are in violation of Article 3 and lists whether they concern negative or positive obligations. Figure 3.4 shows the distribution of claims invoking negative and positive obligations over time. It also gives information about whether the Court – or its different incarnations, to be exact – issued a violation or no violation ruling with respect to these claims.

Figure 3.4 portrays the total number of claims invoking negative obligations (on the left) and positive obligations (on the right). At first glance, we see that the claims concerning negative obligations and positive obligations are distributed differently over time. Negative obligations were recognised much earlier, during the old Court era. Positive obligations appeared on the Court's radar only in the late 1990s, during the reign of the new Court. The number of rulings invoking positive obligations rapidly increased after that, under the watch of the reformed Court, eclipsing the ones related to negative obligations. This figure offers us useful insights with respect to the pace of change (i.e., gradual and sudden change). While negative obligations have been refashioned in a more gradual manner spreading across time, positive obligations emerged suddenly in a relatively short time span in the period after the late 1990s.

As also seen, a clear majority of complaints, approximately 62%, invoke positive obligations. This is a counterintuitive finding. Considering that positive obligations as a category only emerged in the late 1990s, one would expect to see more claims to be invoking negative obligations. Indeed, negative obligations have long been established under Article 3.

[48] You can find the Court's propensity to find a violation against these countries in the Annex.

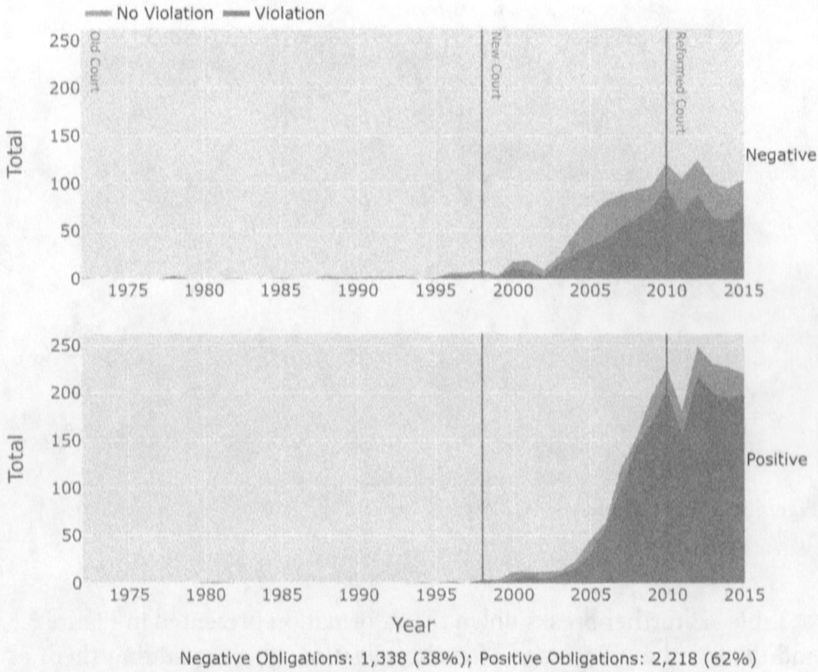

Figure 3.4 Distribution of claims by obligation type and outcome (violation or no violation)

Yet, the magnitude of positive obligations far surpasses that of negative obligations. In order to understand what is behind this pattern and which positive obligations have been frequently employed, Figure 3.5 and Table 3.3 further break down each category.

Figure 3.5 shows the breakdown of the total number of obligations falling under Article 3. What is interesting to observe here is that procedural obligations are the single most invoked obligation under this norm, with claims concerning detention conditions coming in as the not-so-distant second. Overall, we also see that there are significantly more violation decisions (shown in red or darker gray) than no violation decisions (shown in blue or lighter gray). That is to say, the Court is more likely to find a violation in cases that passed the admissibility stage. The admissibility review discards cases that are administratively flawed or are not likely to stand a chance in the legal review, otherwise known as manifestly ill-founded applications (i.e., cases that fail to provide evidence to support the legal arguments or those that include far-fetched complaints).

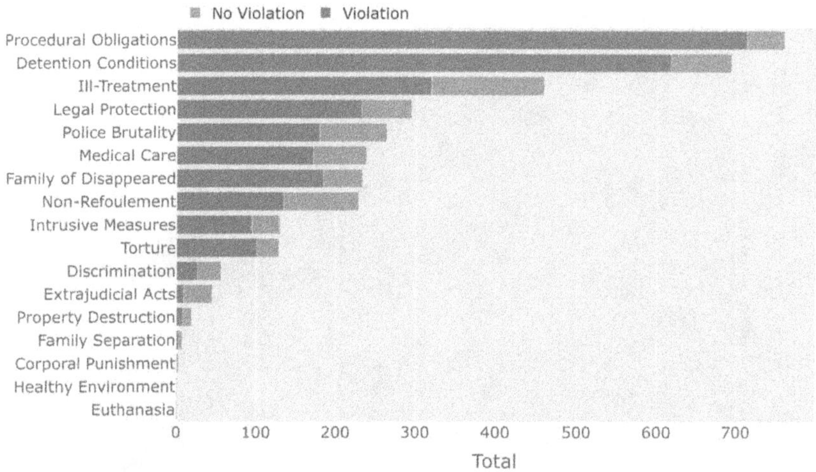

Figure 3.5 Types of obligations (disaggregated)

Table 3.3 further breaks down the information presented in Figure 3.5 and depicts the percentage of each obligation type, separating them as negative and positive obligations.

This analysis demonstrates the scope of the norm by revealing interesting information about the Court's treatment of complaints involving negative and positive obligations. The Court, for example, issued violation decisions for 86% of the claims invoking positive obligations but only for 65% of the claims invoking negative obligations. More than half of the claims invoking negative obligations concern ill-treatment during custody (34%) and police brutality (19%). As for positive obligations, two-thirds of claims pertain to procedural obligations (34%) and failure to provide acceptable detention conditions (31%).

Beyond showing what this norm entails, these findings also showcase why it is more fitting to focus on each obligation separately rather than studying the norm as a single unit. They also reveal that there are clusters of decisions about certain obligations, whereas, about some others, there are only a few decisions. Because of this unevenness, we cannot expect all of these obligations to change at the same time, in the same manner, and with the same magnitude. Finally, tracing separate obligations gives leverage to effectively capture the magnitude of change (i.e., foundational or peripheral change). Despite their recent appearance, positive obligations now take up a sizeable portion of all the complaints concerning the

Table 3.3 *Percentage of claims invoking negative and positive obligations*

Claims invoking negative obligations	Number and percentages of violation decisions	Number and percentages of no violation decision
Ill-treatment during custody	**318 (24%)**	**140 (10%)**
Police brutality	**179 (13%)**	**84 (6%)**
(Non-)Refoulement	134 (10%)	95 (7%)
Intrusive detention measures	95 (7%)	34 (3%)
Torture	100 (7%)	27 (2%)
Discrimination	26 (2%)	30 (2%)
Unacknowledged detention and extrajudicial killings	9 (1%)	36 (3%)
Destruction of property	8 (1%)	11 (1%)
Family separation	3 (0%)	4 (0%)
Corporal punishment	1 (0%)	2 (0%)
Total	**873 (~65%)**	**463 (~35%)**
Claims Invoking Positive Obligations		
Failure to fulfil procedural obligations	**712 (32%)**	**47 (2%)**
Failure to provide acceptable detention conditions	**616 (28%)**	**76 (3%)**
Failure to provide legal protection/remedy	231 (10%)	62 (3%)
Failure to provide necessary medical care	171 (8%)	67 (3%)
Failure to inform relatives of disappeared persons	184 (8%)	49 (2%)
Failure to facilitate euthanasia	0 (0%)	1 (0%)
Failure to provide a healthy environment	0 (0%)	1 (0%)
Total	**1,914 (~86%)**	**303 (~14%)**

norm against torture and inhuman or degrading treatment. As can be seen in Table 3.3 and Figure 3.6, violation decisions concerning positive obligations far surpass the ones for negative obligations (1,914 and 873, respectively). In other words, the Court found states in violation of Article 3 far more often for *inaction* than for action.

The results of this large-scale analysis lead one to the question, why were positive obligations created and used to this extent from the late 1990s onward? The uncharacteristic nature of this period is also confirmed by legal analysis conducted on leading Article 3 jurisprudence. As we will see in Chapters 4 and 5, the Court gradually lowered the minimum thresholds for finding violations since the late 1970s (*peripheral* and *gradual change*), but this trend took an unprecedented leap in the late 1990s. In addition, during the same period, the Court launched positive obligations under Article 3 and transformed the core principles of the norm in a rather swift manner (*core* and *sudden change*). What explains this shift in the late 1990s? I tackle this question in Chapter 6, where I sketch out the conditions that facilitated the new Court's overall audacious tendencies, relying on the theoretical framework presented in the Introduction and Chapter 1.

Measures of Audacity and Forbearance

The results of this analysis also reveal information about the degree to which the Court has been audacious or forbearing over time. The first measure is the willingness to accept *novel claims,* and the second is the overall *propensity* to find a violation. First, I looked at whether the different incarnations of the Court accepted novel claims and how many tries it took for a certain claim to be recognised under Article 3. For this assessment, I focused on the first violation rulings, where the Court recognises a novel claim. This is because such pronouncements require a high degree of judicial audacity. Such rulings also reduce the cost of finding a violation about the same or similar claims in the future, as explained in the Introduction.[49] Figure 3.6 depicts the attitudes of the old Court, the new Court, and the reformed Court toward novel claims.

On the left side, we see the list of claims brought under the prohibition of torture and inhuman or degrading treatment. The blue lines indicate how long it took for a specific claim to be considered to fall under this prohibition. The start of the blue line shows the first year when a particular claim was brought, and the end of the blue line indicates the first year when the Court found a violation with respect to that claim. At first

[49] Ezgi Yildiz et al., "New Norms in Old Regimes: Judicial Strategies for Importing Environmental Norms," *Unpublished Manuscript*, 2022.

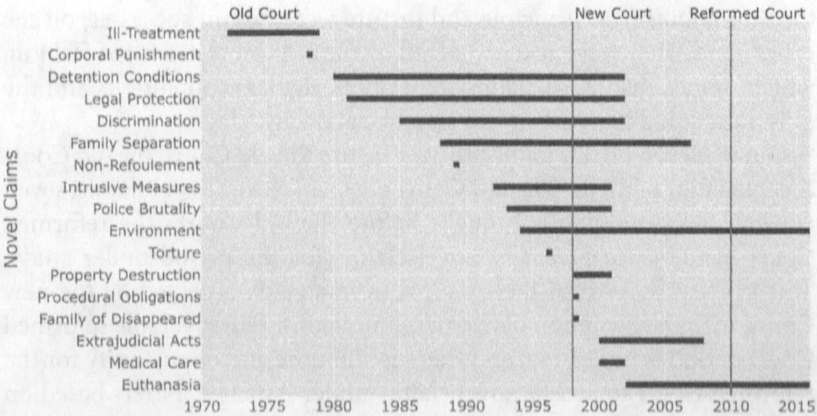

Figure 3.6 Attitudes toward novel claims: period from first claim to first violation ruling

glance, we see a few things. First, the old Court's reception of novel claims was limited. Several blue lines starting during the old Court ended only at the time of the new Court. The new Court, on the other hand, showed a remarkable willingness to accept novel claims. As for the reformed Court, it was confronted with only two novel claims – both carried forward from the new Court period (namely, the obligation to provide a healthy environment and facilitate euthanasia). This is to be expected because, as time progresses, there are not many novel claims left. However, the reformed Court may still appraise and pronounce whether or not these two claims, or others that might be lodged in the future, fall under Article 3.[50]

We also observe that some claims took longer to be accepted. For example, the complaints about detention conditions started in 1980, but the old Court did not find a violation concerning detention conditions until 2001. It was the new Court that recognised unacceptable detention conditions as constituting a violation of Article 3.[51] The claims concerning

[50] There is a pending case before the reformed Court, *Duarte Agostinho and Others* v. *Portugal* and 32 Other States, application no39371/20 (communicated September 7, 2020); for more, see Corina Heri, "The ECtHR's Pending Climate Change Case: What's Ill-Treatment Got to Do with It?," *EJIL: Talk!* (blog), December 22, 2020, www.ejiltalk.org/the-ecthrs-pending-climate-change-case-whats-ill-treatment-got-to-do-with-it/.

[51] *The Greek Case* is a noteworthy exception. The European Commission of Human Rights has considered and found a violation about unacceptable detention conditions. However, since this decision was taken by the Commission, and not the Court itself, it is not included in this particular assessment. The European Commission of Human Rights, Report of 5 November 1969, *Greek Case*, Yearbook XII (1969).

the *non-refoulement* principle and torture were instant successes, on the other hand. They were acknowledged by the old Court in a rapid fashion, which signals that these claims were politically less contentious and the old Court could treat them with selective audacity.

Out of eleven novel claims brought before the old Court, the old Court accepted four of them. The new Court accepted eleven novel claims, seven of which were originally brought before the old Court. The reformed Court has not accepted any novel claims for the period under study. This is because most of these claims were already accepted by the new Court, with the exception of two pending claims. Moreover, the reformed Court period is underway, and there is still time and opportunity for the reformed Court to accept novel claims under Article 3. Purely based on willingness to accept novel claims, the new Court appears to be the most audacious one, while the old Court is selectively audacious. As for the reform Court, it is hard to assess its practices on this front since most of the novel claims were acknowledged by its predecessor, with the exception of two novel claims – namely, the obligation to provide a healthy environment and facilitate euthanasia.

I have also looked at how many repeated claims it took to get a novel claim recognised. Five novel claims were successful on the first try: corporal punishment, *refoulement*, torture, procedural obligations, and state obligations toward the family of the disappeared. Two novel claims (state obligations to provide a healthy environment and to facilitate euthanasia) had only one unsuccessful try each during the period under study. Finally, ten novel claims took more than one attempt to be acknowledged, as outlined in Table 3.4.

As Table 3.4 shows, while most of the claims were acknowledged after a few tries, claims concerning extrajudicial acts (i.e., unacknowledged detention and extrajudicial killings) and discrimination took the most tries. There were seventeen trials before claims about extrajudicial acts were considered to fall under the prohibition of torture and inhuman or degrading treatment, and most of these claims were dismissed due to evidentiary reasons. Similarly, the Court did not find complaints about discrimination to constitute a violation for evidentiary reasons nine out of twelve times. The obligation to provide medical care in detention settings was a distant third when it comes to the number of tries taken before finding the first violation – with four takes, most of which were unsuccessful due to substantive reasons.

When assessing how long it took for a certain claim to be accepted, the quality of applications should also be taken into consideration. Indeed,

Table 3.4 *Prior takes before the acceptance of novel claims*

Novel claims	Number of prior takes	Reasons for finding no violation in prior takes
Extrajudicial acts	**17**	**Substantive, Evidentiary (x16)**
Discrimination	**12**	**Substantive (x3), Evidentiary (x9)**
Medical care	4	Substantive (x3), Evidentiary
Legal protection/remedy	3	Substantive (x3)
Family separation	3	Substantive (x3)
Intrusive detention measures	3	Substantive, Evidentiary (x2)
Detention conditions	2	Substantive, Evidentiary
Police brutality	2	Substantive, Evidentiary
Property destruction	1	Evidentiary
Ill-treatment during custody	1	Substantive

not every application will be of the same quality or be equally convincing. However, since this study strictly focuses on complaints that passed the initial admissibility stage, which weeds out the weakest claims, there should not be striking differences in the quality of claims examined for this study.

When it comes to propensity scores, we see a slightly different picture. Table 3.5 shows that the old Court has a low propensity to find a violation. A higher percentage of rulings were no-violation rulings. It should be noted that the number of cases for the old Court is also relatively low. However, starting with the new Court, we see an upward trend in the propensity to find states in violation, which increases further during the reform Court. Such a trend is expected because it is easier to build on the precedent and continue the progressive trends set in the previous period.

This first-cut analysis of these measures shows some clear differences between the three different incarnations of the Court. The old Court is not audacious across the board when it comes to treating novel claims, as it acknowledges only a select number of them. When it comes to propensity scores, it is mostly forbearing. Therefore, it is apt to characterise the old Court as overall forbearance leaning but selectively audacious, as will be further explained in Chapter 4. The new Court, on the other hand, is uniformly audacious when it comes to novel claims since it accepts nearly all of them. Propensity scores also attest to this as the new Court shows a forty-three-percentage-point increase on the old Court's propensity scores. The sociopolitical conditions that cultivated the new Court's

Table 3.5 *Propensity for finding a violation over time*

Era	Violation count	No violation count	Violation propensity	Difference in % points
Old Court	11	36	30%	–
New Court	893	325	73%	43%
Reformed Court	1,886	415	82%	9%

audacity and how the new Court's audacious attitudes transformed the norm against torture and inhuman and degrading treatment will be discussed in Chapters 5 and 6.

As for the reformed Court, it is harder to read its tendencies at the aggregate level. This is because there is relatively little information about its attitudes toward novel claims since most of these claims were already recognised by the new Court. However, we see that the reformed Court has the highest propensity to find a violation. Although the reformed Court's propensity score is impressive in itself, one can also argue that it comfortably continues the practices of the new Court with only a nine-percentage-point increase. For this reason, I will try to glean more information about the reformed Court's propensity scores by further disaggregating them in Chapter 7.

Conclusion

This chapter has introduced the methodological choices adopted in this book and presented the results of the content analysis carried out on all Article 3 decisions issued between 1967 and 2016. For this analysis, instead of studying norms as unitary phenomena, I have disaggregated them. I have focused on each and every obligation that the norm against torture and inhuman or degrading treatment contains and traced the norm's transformation by taking these separate obligations as a reference. The chapter has mapped out the distinct obligations that this norm entailed and explained why looking at these obligations separately helps us better understand the pace and the magnitude of change. The chapter also introduced some preliminary findings to probe into the dominant tendencies demonstrated during different incarnations of the Court, which range from audacity, selective audacity, selective forbearance, and forbearance. Thus, this chapter has presented an overview before turning to more in-depth analyses of different change episodes in the following chapters.

4

From Compromise to Absolutism? Gradual Transformation under the Old Court's Watch

This chapter traces how the modern understanding of the norm against torture and inhuman or degrading treatment came to be and how it gradually changed over time under the old Court's watch – operating together with the European Commission of Human Rights (the Commission). Taking the Convention drafters' stated intentions as a baseline, I trace the development of the norm through several landmark judgments. I focus on judgments because they present us with two crucial types of information: First, they provide insights into the specific circumstances that led an applicant to seek justice before the Court. Second, they help us glean information about the historical circumstances and the state of the international legal discourse at the time these judgments were written. Judgments that have transformed the norm are either a reflection of or a reaction to the context in which they were pronounced; they help disentangle the historical, political, and legal developments of the time. Each judgment is a milestone that helps us trace the gradual refashioning of the norm against torture and inhuman or degrading treatment. This is why they are especially helpful yardsticks for charting gradual change and identifying the ideal conditions that can facilitate change.

Moreover, I focus on the judgments in which the old Court found at least one violation and, therefore, aim to glean information about how it could muster audacity when it had a limited zone of discretion. I also analyze how the political context and the special nature of the complaints under review influenced the trade-offs the old Court had to make. Such an assessment arguably reveals more information about the dynamics of legal change than an analysis of no-violation instances – where the old Court or the Commission categorically denied the existence of certain obligations under Article 3. This was the case, for example, when the Court denied to acknowledge the obligation not to separate families under Article 3 in *Berrehab* v. *the Netherlands* in 1988 and *Nyberg* v. *Sweden* in 1990.[1]

[1] *Berrehab* v. *the Netherlands*, application no. 10730/84, ECHR (June 21, 1988), *Nyberg* v. *Sweden*, application no. 12574/86, ECHR (August 31, 1990) (struck out of the list).

The Commission took a similar stand when it came to the obligation not to enforce stringent detention conditions in *Kröcher and Möller* v. *Switzerland* in 1981 and *Dohest* v. *Belgium* in 1987 – two other no-violation decisions.[2] These no-violation decisions surely shed light on which obligations fell outside of the norm's scope at a particular point in time. Yet, they do not reveal much about the conditions under which the old Court felt audacious enough to issue progressive decisions with or without trade-offs.

The Genesis of the Prohibition of Torture under the Convention

> No one shall be subjected to torture or to inhuman or degrading treatment or punishment. (Article 3 of the European Convention, 1950).

The Universal Declaration of Human Rights of 1948 was the first human rights document to specifically outlaw torture.[3] The Geneva Conventions of 1949 – composed of four treaties and three additional protocols that laid the foundations of international humanitarian law – was another international treaty including a prohibition of torture. Article 3, common to all four Geneva Conventions, prohibits "violence to life and person, in particular murder of all kinds, mutilation, cruel treatment and torture" and "outrages upon personal dignity, in particular humiliating and degrading treatment" in times of armed conflict.[4]

The European Convention followed suit and prohibited torture and inhuman or degrading treatment under its own Article 3.[5] This article has an open definition and does not list the types of acts falling under it. The

This changed with *Mubilanzila Mayeka and Kaniki Mitunga* v. *Belgium*, application no. 13178/03, ECHR (October 12, 2006), where the Court found that the deportation of an unaccompanied minor amounts to degrading treatment.

2 *Kröcher and Möller* v. *Switzerland*, application no. 84/63/78, European Commission of Human Rights (December 16, 1982). *Dohest* v. *Belgium*, application no. 10448/83, European Commission of Human Rights (May 14, 1987).

3 Walter Kälin, "The Struggle against Torture," *International Review of the Red Cross* 12, no. 324 (1998): 433–44.

4 More specifically, torture and inhuman or degrading treatment are prohibited under Article 12 of the First and Second Conventions, Articles 17 and 87 of the Third Convention, and Article 32 of the Fourth Convention.

5 The European Movement, an independent group, proposed a draft text to the Consultative (today Parliamentary) Assembly. This text served as a basis for the Convention's original text. The members of the European Movement comprised pre-eminent statesmen (several former prime ministers and foreign ministers, and a number of ministers in office) and several other main professional figures of Europe. This body was established at the Congress of Nongovernmental Movements in The Hague on May 8, 1948. Ed Bates, "The Birth of the

Convention itself gives no clues as to the kinds of acts the drafters had in mind when formulating this provision. For that, one must turn to the discussions held during the drafting of the Convention as reflected in the preparatory works.

Seymour Cocks from the British delegation played the most active role in drafting this prohibition.[6] Preferring a closed definition, in a meeting on September 7, 1949, Mr Cocks proposed an amendment that read as follows:

> In particular no person shall be subjected to any form of mutilation or sterilisation, or to any form of torture or beating. Nor shall he be forced to take drugs nor shall they be administered to him without his knowledge and consent. Nor shall he be subjected to imprisonment with such an excess of light, darkness, noise, or silence as to cause mental suffering.[7]

On the following day, Mr Cocks moved his amendment to the Consultative Assembly of the Council of Europe (today's Parliamentary Assembly), where he also delivered a moving speech outlining how torture was perceived in different periods of history. He started with Athens, where torture was seen as an "oriental depravity" and then moved on to practices in the Middle Ages, where torture was a "common instrument of power and authority."[8] He then argued that torture disappeared "with the development of civilisation" in the West, only to reappear with the Third Reich:

> Cases occurred in Greece during the Nazi invasion of naked girls being placed on electric stoves and burnt in order to make them disclose the whereabouts of their friends. There was the deliberate infliction upon women of the bacteria of loathsome diseases. All kinds of ghastly mutilations were perpetrated upon thousands of men and women. (...) I say that to take the straight beautiful bodies of men and women and to maim and mutilate them by torture is a crime against high heaven and the holy spirit

European Convention on Human Rights - and the European Court of Human Rights," in *The European Court of Human Rights Between Law and Politics*, ed. Jonas Christoffersen and Mikael Rask Madsen (New York: Oxford University Press, 2011), 20–22.

6 Sir David Patrick Maxwell-Fyfe and Pierre-Henri Teitgen were the "Convention's two founding fathers," Ed Bates, *The Evolution of the European Convention on Human Rights: From Its Inception to the Creation of a Permanent Court of Human Rights* (Oxford and New York: Oxford University Press, 2010), 76.

7 Council of Europe, European Commission of Human Rights, "Preparatory Work on Article 3 of the European Convention of Human Rights," DH (56) 5 (Strasbourg, May 22, 1956), 2.

8 Ibid., 4.

> of man. I say that it is a sin against the Holy Ghost for which there is no forgiveness. I declare that it is incompatible with civilization.[9]

Sir David Patrick Maxwell-Fyfe took the floor and congratulated Mr Cocks for his moving speech, with which he was in full agreement.[10] André Philip and Pierre-Henri Teitgen from the French delegation seconded the speech.[11] The Assembly then discussed whether and how to include Mr Cocks' proposal in the draft Convention. Mr Teitgen delivered the deciding argument. "It is dangerous," he said, "to want to say more, since the effect of the Convention is thereby limited."[12] Arguing for the benefits of not listing the types of acts to prohibit and allowing the next generation to interpret this prohibition in light of their social circumstances, he called for an open definition.

Following the negotiations, Mr Cocks withdrew his amendment, yet submitted a draft resolution that noted: "[t]he Assembly records its abhorrence at the subjection of any person to any form of mutilation or sterilization or beating."[13] The representatives from Denmark, Sweden, and Norway opposed this on the grounds that sterilization was legally used in their countries. The British delegation also raised an objection, noting that corporal punishment still existed in the United Kingdom.[14] Reaching a consensus on the types of acts that should be covered under this provision proved to be difficult. In the end, Mr Cocks' definitions of torture were not included in the draft text. However, his contribution is crucial for understanding what the drafters had in mind. The fact that Mr Cocks' sentiments were not challenged but supported in principle indicates a form of consensus concerning the dominant understanding of the meaning of torture.[15]

From these proposals and the follow-up discussions, we can deduce how the drafters understood the prohibition of torture. First, the prohibition was written in a reactive manner. The drafters were reacting to the abhorrent events that had recently taken place during the Second World War. Their immediate frame of reference was the Nazi atrocities. They firmly believed that *evil is perpetrated by evil men*, namely the Nazis – who

[9] Ibid.
[10] Ibid.
[11] Ibid., 7.
[12] Ibid.
[13] Ibid., 9.
[14] Ibid., 11–13.
[15] This observation is only limited to torture, as there was no direct discussion on inhuman or degrading treatment.

had brought torture back to Europe. They lost their civility and indulged in this barbaric practice. The Nazi reference also influenced the way they described torture. In the course of the discussions of the Assembly, torture was associated with mutilation, beating, and sterilization as well as subjecting an individual to medical experimentation. These were the very acts that the Nazis perpetrated during the war, another indication that Nazi crimes shaped their viewpoint about the scope of the prohibition at that time.

Second, their understanding of what constituted torture had a religious flavour. To them, torture was a crime against humanity because it was a crime against God. There was also a particular emphasis on maiming and mutilating the body. The torture victim was seen as an object, destroyed and deformed. This formulation revolves around the sacredness of the human body, which has roots in the natural law tradition. One of the foundations of this tradition is that the body and soul are in unity, created in God's own image (*imago Dei*).[16] This understanding promotes "the sacredness of the human personality."[17] It grounds human rights in the sacredness that extends to humans from God.[18]

The religious tone carried over from natural law, which had been the dominant paradigm in legal thinking[19] until the emergence of positive law, whose main premise is that "law is law regardless of its content."[20] In reaction to the atrocities committed during the Second World War, natural law was resurrected,[21] and it influenced the drafting of both the European Convention and the Universal Declaration of Human Rights (the UDHR).[22] Mr Teitgen, one of the forefathers of the Convention, confirms this in his report by describing that the Convention's text was

16 Robert Pasnau, *Thomas Aquinas on Human Nature: A Philosophical Study of Summa Theologiae* (New York: Cambridge University Press, 2002); David Boucher, *The Limits of Ethics in International Relations: Natural Law, Natural Rights, and Human Rights in Transition* (Oxford and New York: Oxford University Press, 2009).

17 Samuel Moyn, *The Last Utopia* (Cambridge, MA: Harvard University Press, 2010), 75.

18 Benjamin Gregg, *Human Rights as Social Construction* (New York: Cambridge University Press, 2011), 14.

19 Moyn, *The Last Utopia*.

20 According to Vincent Andrew, one of the reasons leading to this outcome was the theory of evolution proposed by Darwin, which undermined the great chain of being and the centrality of human nature. For more, see Andrew Vincent, *The Politics of Human Rights* (Oxford and New York: Oxford University Press, 2010), 80.

21 Daniel Mirabella, "The Death and Resurrection of Natural Law," *The Western Australian Jurist* 2, no. 1 (2011): 251.

22 Moyn, *The Last Utopia*, 215.

drafted "in accordance with the principles of natural law, of humanism and of democracy."[23] The connection between natural law and human rights can also be traced to the works of Hersch Lauterpacht, who was the "leading intellectual force" behind the UDHR and, to a great extent, the Convention.[24] According to Lauterpacht, natural law, natural rights, and human rights are cut from the same cloth, and the human rights movement's moral force is grounded in their religious foundations.[25]

The prevailing consensus among scholars is that the return to natural law was a logical reaction to historical events. The destruction generated by the War was attributed to positive (Nazi) law, and the principles of natural law were hailed as an antidote.[26] Referring to the tribunals in the aftermath of the War, David Chandler explains the role of natural law for the global human rights agenda:

> Where the tribunal broke new legal ground was in using natural law to overrule positivist law, to argue that the laws in force at the time in Germany were no defence against the retrospective crime of "waging an aggressive war." This was justified on the grounds that certain acts were held to be such heinous crimes that they were banned by universal principles of humanity. Human rights frameworks were used to undermine positivist law, to cast the winners of the War as moral, not merely militaristic, victors.[27]

The way the drafters conceptualised and defined torture and inhuman or degrading treatment appears to be in line with the theory that human rights discourse underwent a sort of Christianization in the aftermath of the War.[28] Samuel Moyn explains that the European Convention

[23] Bates, *The Evolution of the European Convention on Human Rights*, 2010, 63.

[24] J. Harcourt Barrington, who was involved with drafting the version of the Convention authored by the European Movement, acknowledged "[their] debt to [Lauterpacht] because [they] did quite shamelessly borrow many ideas from his draft Convention on the Rights of Man prepared for the International Law Association in 1948. Hersch Lauterpacht et al., "The Proposed European Court of Human Rights," *Transactions of the Grotius Society* 35 (1949): 25–47.

[25] Hersch Lauterpacht, *An International Bill of the Rights of Man* (New York: Columbia University Press, 1945), 9.

[26] Moyn, *The Last Utopia*, 75.

[27] David Chandler, "The Ideological (Mis)Use of Human Rights," in *Human Rights: Politics and Practice*, ed. Michael Goodhart (Oxford: Oxford University Press, 2009), 118.

[28] There is an ongoing debate about the Christian origins of the European human rights project. For more, see Samuel Moyn, *Christian Human Rights* (Philadelphia: University of Pennsylvania Press, 2015), 4–8; Marco Duranti, *The Conservative Human Rights Revolution: European Identity, Transnational Politics, and the Origins of the European Convention* (Oxford and New York: Oxford University Press, 2017); Aryeh Neier, *The International Human Rights Movement: A History* (Princeton: Princeton University Press, 2012).

and the larger European project had conservative Christian origins.[29] The European human rights project, created to re-stabilise "bourgeois Europe," relied on Christian ethics.[30] Some of the founders, such as Robert Schuman, Paul-Henri Spaak, and Pierre-Henri Teitgen, were avowed Christians. This small group of individuals, mostly men, shaped the European human rights regime and determined which rights to include in the Convention.[31] According to Moyn, the Convention's conservative origins were later forgotten, however.[32] The principles that were introduced as Christian concepts came to define Western European identity during the Cold War.[33] In this process, the content and the spirit of human rights were reinvented, and human rights were secularised.[34]

One reason this transformation was successfully achieved, especially regarding this prohibition, was that it did not include indications as to precisely what constitutes torture and inhuman or degrading treatment. This had two benefits: First, the prohibition – with strong moral aspirations and a weak definition – could appeal to all of the member states signing the treaty.[35] Second, the Commission and the old Court were given an important role in redefining and refashioning the norm in line with changing societal needs. It would be these two institutions that would shape the modern understanding of the norm against torture and its subsequent transformation.

The *Greek Case (1969)* and the Modern Understanding of Torture and Inhuman or Degrading Treatment

> The notion of inhuman treatment covers at least such treatment as deliberately causes severe suffering, mental or physical, which, in the particular situation is

[29] Moyn, *The Last Utopia*, 78–79.

[30] Moyn, *Christian Human Rights*, 170.

[31] Marco Duranti also argues that in comparison to the UN Human Rights Commission, where there were a fair number of women participants, the creation of the European human rights regime was "an overwhelmingly male affair." Duranti, *The Conservative Human Rights Revolution*, 5–6.

[32] Even though the European human rights regime was led by predominantly male Christian Conservatives, they were not the only group shaping the international human rights regime. Politicians and scholars from the Global South and Latin America, some of whom were women, also contributed to the formation of the human rights system currently in place. For more, see Kathryn Sikkink, *Evidence for Hope: Making Human Rights Work in the 21st Century* (Princeton: Princeton University Press, 2017).

[33] Moyn, *The Last Utopia*, 76.

[34] Moyn, *Christian Human Rights*, 173.

[35] Bates, *The Evolution of the European Convention on Human Rights*, 2010, 56.

> unjustifiable. The word "torture" is often used to describe inhuman treatment, which has a purpose, such as the obtaining of information or confessions, or the infliction of punishment, and it is generally an aggravated form of inhuman treatment. Treatment or punishment of an individual may be said to be degrading if it grossly humiliates him before others or drives him to act against his will or conscience.
>
> (The European Commission of Human Rights, Report of November 5, 1969, *Greek Case*, Yearbook XII (1969), p. 186)

The *Greek Case* was by far the most influential decision concerning the prohibition of torture and inhuman or degrading treatment in the early days of Article 3 jurisprudence, and it remains important to this day. Denmark, Sweden, Norway, and the Netherlands brought this case against the military junta that took over the Greek government on April 21, 1967. What provoked this application was the fact that the military junta suspended the constitutional provisions protecting human rights and arrested dissidents with the purpose of preventing a communist takeover.[36] Appalled by the scale of violations committed against the Greek population, the Scandinavian countries and the Netherlands collectively lodged this interstate case.

The European Commission reviewed the complaint for over two years, carrying out a thorough assessment. The Commissioners heard witness accounts of a wide range of physical and psychological ill-treatment and relied on detention reports issued by the International Red Cross. Having systematically analyzed the complaints, the Commission issued its groundbreaking decision. It was the first decision in which an international tribunal decided that a state had practised torture. It also shaped the understanding of what the prohibition of torture and inhuman or degrading treatment entails. Through this case, the Commissioners established a precise definition for "torture" and "inhuman or degrading treatment," and effectively introduced a scale of severity when it comes to identifying them.[37] This distinction served as the basis of the definitions in the Convention against Torture (CAT) – the most specialised international treaty on torture and other ill-treatment and cruel punishment.[38] The Commissioners also specifically identified the types of acts that would

[36] James Becket, "The Greek Case before the European Human Rights Commission," *Human Rights* 1, no. 1 (1970): 91–117.

[37] The *Greek Case*, Year Book of European Convention on Human Rights Vol. 12, 1969 (The Hague: Martinus Nijhoff Publishers, 1971), p. 186.

[38] Magdalena Forowicz, *The Reception of International Law in the European Court of Human Rights* (Oxford and New York: Oxford University Press, 2010), 195.

fall under the prohibition.[39] In the Commission's view, torture included severe beatings (particularly on the head or the genital organs), beating of the feet with a club (*falanga*), food and water deprivation, and mock executions. Additionally, they defined torture as an administrative practice conducted or officially tolerated by public officials for the purpose of extracting information or confession.[40]

It is notable that the definition of torture and inhuman or degrading treatment provided in the *Greek Case* differs significantly from that of the drafters of the Convention. On the surface, the difference could be attributed to the fact that this decision was written by lawyers and judges, whereas the Convention was drafted by politicians and state officials.[41] Upon a closer look, however, the difference is not merely a matter of language. The definition in the *Greek Case* relies on a secular understanding that focuses on the psychology of victims and their feelings (i.e., their subjective experience). It excludes religious rationales for prohibiting torture on moral grounds. Its focus extends beyond the victim's physical integrity to centre on the victim's pain and suffering, whether physical or psychological. Different from natural law, which refers to reason or religious morals to establish why certain acts are wrong, this contemporary understanding relies on empathy to make human rights language more inclusive. Such an approach departs from previous codes of ethics, which were exclusive and applied to only a narrow conception of humanity.[42] For example, Christian ethics, which influenced the natural law tradition, did not concern itself with the rights of groups with different belief systems such as Jews, Muslims, or people deemed racially inferior.[43] Modern human rights language has corrected this pathology to a certain extent.

Several scientific developments preceded and accompanied this shift in legal discourse.[44] First, psychology had matured as a discipline, and

[39] For more, see Professor Metin Basoğlu, ed., *Torture and Its Definition in International Law: An Interdisciplinary Approach* (New York: Oxford University Press, 2017); UN Voluntary Fund for Victims of Torture, "Interpretation of Torture in the Light of the Practice and Jurisprudence of International Bodies," 2011, www.ohchr.org/Documents/Issues/Torture/UNVFVT/Interpretation_torture_2011_EN.pdf.

[40] The *Greek Case*, p. 128.

[41] One should also note that some of the drafters did come from the legal profession as well.

[42] Jack Donnelly, "Normative Versus Taxonomic Humanity: Varieties of Human Dignity in the Western Tradition," *Journal of Human Rights* 14, no. 1 (2015): 1–22.

[43] Paul Gordon Lauren, *The Evolution of International Human Rights: Visions Seen*, 3rd Edition (Philadelphia: University of Pennsylvania Press, 2011), 33.

[44] Mikael Madsen discusses the role of "scientificization" in the development of human rights in Mikael Rask Madsen, "From Cold War Instrument to Supreme European Court: The

studies conducted by psychologists – such as the Milgram shock experiment and later the Stanford prison experiments – became widely known and publicly discussed. While these experiments sparked interest in human psychology, they also confirmed Hannah Arendt's "Report on the Banality of Evil" thesis.[45] After watching Eichmann's trial in 1961, Arendt argued that what led him to commit heinous crimes was not his fanaticism or sociopathic tendencies. It was his inability to make moral judgments about the routines of the job he obsessively followed.[46] Anyone had the capacity to do evil; hence, heinous acts such as torture could be perpetrated by anyone. This view of "evil" is quite different from the conviction of the drafters, who believed that *evil is done by evil men* – such as the Nazis – and it led to a profound change in understanding torture. No longer was it believed that torture and inhuman or degrading treatment occurred only under extraordinary circumstances. Rather, torture and inhuman or degrading treatment could occur in mundane situations and be committed by ordinary people.

Second, the discipline of psychology started to converge with legal studies in the 1960s. Experimental methods became available to investigate legal issues and to understand the psychology of victims.[47] Through the initiative of several émigré lawyers in the US, the field of victimology emerged.[48] Their study of Holocaust victims laid the groundwork for victimology.[49] And, this new approach to victimhood contributed toward a changed discourse on human psychology and human suffering. The reasoning in the *Greek Case* reflected and added to this newly emerging understanding around a secular and victim-focused approach to the prohibition of torture and inhuman or degrading treatment. This approach remains the prevailing paradigm to this day.

European Court of Human Rights at the Crossroads of International and National Law and Politics," *Law and Social Inquiry* 32, no. 1 (2007): 137–59.

[45] S. Alexander Haslam and Stephen Reicher, "Beyond the Banality of Evil: Three Dynamics of an Interactionist Social Psychology of Tyranny," *Personality and Social Psychology Bulletin* 33, no. 5 (2007): 616.

[46] Hannah Arendt, *Eichmann in Jerusalem: A Report on the Banality of Evil*, 1st edition (New York: Penguin Classics, 2006).

[47] June Louin Tapp, "Psychology and the Law: An Overture," *Annual Review of Psychology* 27, no. 1 (1976): 359–404; Andreas Kapardis, *Psychology and Law: A Critical Introduction* (New York: Cambridge University Press, 2010).

[48] Sandra Walklate, *Imagining the Victim of Crime* (New York: Open University Press, 2007), 2.

[49] James Dignan, *Understanding Victims and Restorative Justice* (New York: Open University Press, 2005), 14.

The *Greek Case* decision was also ahead of its time in many ways and, thus, a sort of exception for the European human rights system. At the time, it presented the European human rights regime with a "most severe challenge."[50] It was the height of the Cold War, and the ideological battle between the East and West extended to human rights.[51] At this point, human rights was more a matter of politics than law,[52] and discrediting Greece, a member of the Western bloc, was an audacious move on the part of the Commission.

The Commission could afford to be this audacious for several reasons: First, the Greek military junta represented the very thing that the human rights regime was created to prevent: totalitarian regimes. Second, the decision was part of a concerted attempt in Europe to address the situation in Greece. The Consultative Assembly of the Council of Europe had called on the Greek government to restore its constitutional democracy. It also called on other member states to refer Greece to the European Commission of Human Rights in a resolution.[53] Denmark, Norway, Sweden, and the Netherlands responded to that call and filed identical complaints. These countries did not harbour ulterior motives – no ethnic ties, territorial, or commercial interests. Their responses represented a common European concern about the developments in Greece.[54] Third, the damage could be controlled to a certain extent. The case was never referred to the Court. Hence, the only decision about this matter was given by the Commission – a quasi-judicial body. The Commission's report was directly sent to the Committee of Ministers. The Committee of Ministers sent the report to Greece together with proposals for a friendly settlement in the spirit of legal diplomacy.[55]

For these reasons, the Commission could afford to give such an audacious ruling without risking a full-blown political pushback from member states. The *Greek Case* still generated a significant impact on the way the norm against torture and inhuman or degrading treatment was understood at the time and is understood today. Arguably, the *Greek Case* represents the modern take on the prohibition of torture and inhuman or

[50] Becket, "The Greek Case before the European Human Rights Commission," 93.
[51] Vincent, *The Politics of Human Rights*, 122.
[52] Mikael Rask Madsen, "Protracted Institutionalization of the Strasbourg Court: From Legal Diplomacy to Integrationist Jurisprudence," in *The European Court of Human Rights between Law and Politics*, ed. Jonas Christoffersen and Mikael Rask Madsen (New York: Oxford University Press, 2011), 49.
[53] Parliamentary Assembly, *Resolution 346* (June 23, 1967).
[54] Becket, "The Greek Case before the European Human Rights Commission."
[55] Bates, *The Evolution of the European Convention on Human Rights*, 268.

degrading treatment. Since this 1969 decision, the norm against torture and inhuman or degrading treatment has continued to expand its reach and encompass increasingly high standards of treatment.

The Old Court Setting the Bar after the *Greek Case*

In this section, I will examine two cases that greatly contributed to the transformation of the European jurisprudence on torture prohibition: *Ireland* v. *the United Kingdom* and *Tyrer* v. *the United Kingdom*. Although both complaints were brought against the United Kingdom and both judgments were issued the same year, the Court treated them in significantly different ways. While the former is a cautious forbearing judgment, the latter is one of the most audacious judgments in the entire jurisprudence. Why was this the case?

To explain the Court's varying attitudes in these two rulings, we need to revisit the framework introduced in Chapter 1, which expects that the width of discretionary space largely determines the Court's forbearing or audacious tendencies. In particular, when the Court's zone of discretion is limited, it may be more inclined to be deferent to national interests (e.g., national security concerns) and less willing to hold states accountable for resource-intensive positive obligations or the abuses committed by private individuals. The Court could selectively be audacious, however, especially when addressing issues with lower stakes. That is one of the reasons why the old Court was forbearing when deciding *Ireland* v. *the United Kingdom*, but it could be more audacious when dealing with *Tyrer* v. *the United Kingdom* – a case with lower stakes, involving clear evidence of societal trends in favor of a progressive approach.

Case #1: Ireland *v.* the United Kingdom *(1978) and the Five Techniques*

> The Court considers in fact that, whilst there exists on the one hand violence which is to be condemned both on moral grounds and also in most cases under the domestic law of the Contracting States but which does not fall within Article 3 of the Convention, it appears on the other hand that it was the intention that the Convention, with its distinction between "torture" and "inhuman or degrading treatment," should by the first of these terms attach a special stigma to deliberate inhuman treatment causing very serious and cruel suffering.
>
> (*Ireland* v. *the United Kingdom*, application no. 5310/71, ECHR (January 18, 1978), §167)

Ireland v. *the United Kingdom* was a landmark decision that set a high bar for identifying torture and inhuman or degrading treatment in the context of emergency situations. As such, it had significant ramifications far beyond the context from which it arose in Northern Ireland.[56] It also showcased the implications of according courts with only narrow discretionary space, as was the case for the old Court. Indeed, the old Court was more cautious about emergency situations where the responding state would feel threatened. Therefore, it carefully balanced states' national security concerns with its mandate to safeguard the protection of rights.

Ireland v. *the United Kingdom* typifies the old Court's mission to balance national security and human rights. It was decided amid an atmosphere of fear in Europe. The late 1960s and 1970s witnessed much upheaval in Western Europe, including left-wing (Marxist-Leninist) terrorism spread by organizations such as the Red Army Faction (RAF) in Western Germany; the Italian Red Brigade; the French Action Direct; and the Belgian Communist Combatant Cells.[57] Soon after, right-wing (or neo-fascist) terrorist networks emerged,[58] and, although their activities remained sporadic in Europe, they added to the instability created by the left-wing terrorist groups.[59] Violent ethnic nationalist groups such as the ETA (Basque Country and Freedom),[60] the IRA (Provisional Irish Republican Army),[61] and the PKK (Kurdistan Workers' Party) were also highly active.[62]

Ireland v. *the United Kingdom* arose from the specific context of "the troubles in Northern Ireland," during which over 1,100 people

[56] Deirdre Donahue, "Human Rights in Northern Ireland: Ireland v. the United Kingdom," *Boston College International and Comparative Law Review* 3, no. 2 (1980): 377–432.

[57] Stefan M. Aubrey, *The New Dimension of International Terrorism* (Zurich: VDF Hochschulverlag AG, 2004), 45.

[58] Ehud Sprinzak, "Right-Wing Terrorism in a Comparative Perspective: The Case of Split Delegitimization," *Terrorism and Political Violence* 7, no. 1 (1995): 25.

[59] Aubrey, *The New Dimension of International Terrorism*, 45.

[60] Robert P. Clark, "Patterns of ETA Violence, 1968–1980," in *Political Violence and Terror: Motifs and Motivations*, ed. Peter H. Merkl (Berkeley: University of California Press, 1986), 135.

[61] Adrian Guelke, "Loyalist and Republican Perceptions of the Northern Ireland Conflict: The UDA and Provisional IRA," in *Political Violence and Terror: Motifs and Motivations*, ed. Peter H. Merkl (Berkeley: University of California Press, 1986), 98.

[62] This conflict has taken more than 30,000 lives since 1984. Svante E. Cornell, "The Kurdish Question in Turkish Politics," in *Dangerous Neighborhood: Contemporary Issues in Turkey's Foreign Relations*, ed. Michael Radu (Oxon and New York: Routledge, 2003), 123; Ersel Aydinli, "Between Security and Liberalization: Decoding Turkey's Struggle with the PKK," *Security Dialogue* 33, no. 2 (2002): 209–25."

had been killed and over 11,500 people injured.[63] This entrenched conflict was sparked by intercommunal violence between the long-divided Protestant and Catholic communities. The Protestants (termed Loyalists or Unionists) constituted nearly two-thirds of the population, with Catholics (known as Republicans or Nationalists) making up the remainder. The Catholic minority had the active support of the IRA. Economic, social, political, and religious differences between these two communities resulted in violent clashes and an upsurge in terrorist activities by the IRA.[64] In an attempt to control the situation, the British authorities in Northern Ireland took to the extrajudicial detention or internment of terrorist suspects, especially suspected members of the IRA and, by association, the Catholic community. The British government saw the IRA operatives as a direct threat to law and order, while viewing Protestant terrorism that targeted the Catholic community (rather than the state itself) as less serious. This affected public discourse as well. While the IRA operatives were portrayed as "terrorists" or "enemies," the Protestant terrorists were considered "criminals" or "hooligans."[65] In this respect, the two groups were treated differently.

"The troubles in Northern Ireland" provided an opportunity to put Article 15 to the test. Ireland submitted the first derogation request in 1957, and the grounds of their request were evaluated in the *Lawless* v. *Ireland* case in 1961. Gerald Richard Lawless, a member of the IRA, complained that the Irish authorities had detained him for five months without bringing him before a judge. Ireland countered that their emergency legislation justified this practice. In its decision, the Court found that Ireland's declaration of public emergency was justified given that there was "a secret army [of IRA operatives] engaged in unconstitutional activities and using violence to attain its purposes," and that there was a "steady and alarming increase in terrorist activities."[66] The Court added that these activities went beyond the territories of the Republic of Ireland and thus posed a threat to the country's relationship with its neighbour. Ireland was thus not in breach of its obligations under the Convention.[67]

Then came *Ireland* v. *United Kingdom*. Ireland lodged a complaint that questioned the legality of the United Kingdom's internment of terrorist

63 *Ireland* v. *the United Kingdom*, application no. 5310/71, ECHR (January 18, 1978).
64 *Ireland* v. *the United Kingdom*, § 13–33.
65 Ibid., § 63.
66 *Lawless* v. *Ireland (No.3)*, application no. 332/57, ECHR (July 1, 1961) §28.
67 Ibid., § 30.

suspects and complained about their treatment. The complaint particularly concerned the extrajudicial arrest, detention, and internment of suspected terrorists in Northern Ireland between August 1971 and December 1975. This case offered another opportunity to discuss the extent of states' derogation rights. In its 1978 decision, the Court granted the British authorities in Northern Ireland the same derogation right as they had done to Ireland. The Court emphasised that it is up to the member states to determine whether there is indeed a public emergency and what is necessary to overcome it. It reminded them that the Court's role is *subsidiary* and that national judges are in a better position to assess the situation as well as the necessity of the measures to reverse it.[68] In this respect, the Court effectively deferred to the decision of the British authorities and did not find detaining suspects without trial a violation in this instant.

The treatment of the detainees, however, fell outside of this derogation request. The Court reviewed the complaint and found that the United Kingdom committed a violation. More specifically, the Court identified the interrogation methods known as the "five techniques" as constituting inhuman or degrading treatment but not torture: *wall-standing* (forcing detainees to remain in stress positions for long stretches of time); *hooding* (covering the detainees' heads with a dark-coloured bag at all times except during interrogations); *subjection to noise* (playing continuous loud and hissing noise); *deprivation of sleep* (not allowing detainees to sleep); and *deprivation of food and drink* (not offering a sufficient diet). However, two years earlier, when carrying out an initial review of the case, the European Commission had identified these five techniques as torture – modern versions of the techniques used to extract information in previous times. In *Ireland* v. *the United Kingdom,* the Court did not share the Commission's view. It confirmed that these techniques were systematically used to extract information and confession, condemning them on moral grounds. But it did not find them sufficiently brutal to generate suffering as intense and cruel as the word "torture" implies.[69] In doing so, the Court set a high bar for identifying and finding torture.

The judgment was a controversial compromise intended to propitiate the United Kingdom. Judges Zekia, O'Donoghue, Evrigenis, and Matscher criticised the decision in their separate opinions. Civil society groups, as well as the UN Committee against Torture and Special Rapporteur on Torture, later

[68] Ibid., § 207.
[69] Ibid., § 167.

made statements arguing that these techniques should have been classified as torture.[70] Most criticised the judgment for being decided in a way that exonerated the United Kingdom from the stigma of torture and compared it to the very different outcome of the *Greek Case*. According to Michael O'Boyle, former Deputy Registrar at the Court, the reason the Court did not classify these acts as torture – as it had in the *Greek Case* – was due to the difference in the type of regime under consideration. Unlike Greece, the United Kingdom was not a military dictatorship but "an accepted democratic country faced with an armed uprising."[71]

This high bar left a legacy, as discussed in the introductory chapter. Little did the judges know at the time that the George W. Bush administration would use this very case as a legal basis to distinguish torture from other forms of ill-treatment to justify their War on Terror policies in the aftermath of 9/11.[72] In 2002, the US Department of Justice wrote the infamous Torture Memos, where they used the euphemism "enhanced interrogation methods" to carve out large exceptions to the torture definition.[73] They defined torture as an act causing extreme pain that one would associate with organ failure or even death.[74] They deliberately made the target small and high. Anything not falling within these narrow terms was considered a valid interrogation method. However, as we will see in Chapter 5, the European Court would reverse this compromise made in *Ireland* v. *the United Kingdom* later on and attempt to amend its unintended consequences in future cases.

Case #2: Tyrer *v.* the United Kingdom *(1978) and the Living Instrument Principle*

> The Court must also recall that the Convention is a living instrument which, as the Commission rightly stressed, must be interpreted in the light of

[70] Nigel Rodley and Matt Pollard, *The Treatment of Prisoners under International Law* (New York: Oxford University Press, 2009), 101–5.

[71] Michael O'Boyle, "Torture and Emergency Powers under the European Convention on Human Rights: Ireland v. the United Kingdom," *American Journal of International Law* 71 (1977): 689.

[72] For more, see Karen J. Greenberg, ed., *The Torture Debate in America* (Cambridge and New York: Cambridge University Press, 2006), 362.

[73] This memorandum is known as the Yoo-Bybee memorandum, as it was drafted by John Yoo, then Deputy Assistant Attorney General of the US, and signed in by Jay S. Bybee, then the head of Office of Legal Counsel of the US Department of Justice.

[74] Memorandum for Alberto R. Gonzales Council to the Present (August 1, 2002) – Washington D.C. 20530, p. 28–29.

> present-day conditions. In the case now before it, the Court cannot but be influenced by the developments and commonly accepted standards in the penal policy of the member States of the Council of Europe in this field.
>
> (*Tyrer* v. *the United Kingdom*, application no. 5856/72, ECHR (April 25, 1978), §31)

Tyrer v. *the United Kingdom* differs from the *Greek Case* and *Ireland* v. *the United Kingdom* not only because it was not an interstate complaint but also because its stakes were lower. It concerned a fifteen-year-old boy, Anthony Tyrer, who had been subjected to judicial corporal punishment (i.e., corporal punishment ordered by a court of law). Tyrer lodged this case with the support of the National Council for Civil Liberties (today, Liberty) – an NGO based in London.[75] Upon assessing the complaint, the Court held that the punishment did not cause serious or lasting physical damage. Yet, it also found that the treatment objectified Tyrer, impaired his dignity and physical integrity, and constituted degrading treatment.[76]

At first glance, this may appear as a straightforward and simple finding, but *Tyrer* has exercised significant influence on later jurisprudence. *Tyrer* represents a drastic change in the type of acts covered under Article 3. As explained in earlier in this chapter, corporal punishment had been discussed during the drafting of the Convention, but the British delegation raised objections against listing it as a prohibited act under Article 3. When the drafters learned that corporal punishment was legally used in the United Kingdom at the time, they dropped the idea of including it. But twenty-nine years later, the Court declared judicial corporal punishment a violation of Article 3. The *Tyrer* judgment thus represents a change from the dominant mindset at the time of the drafting of the Convention and a break from prior conceptualizations of the prohibition.

Tyrer also heralded the progressive interpretation that would be used to refine the prohibition in future cases. Here, in this case, the Court introduced "the living instrument principle," which essentially means that the Convention principles are to be interpreted in light of evolving human rights standards, improved ethical codes, and social and scientific changes.[77] Reviewing *Tyrer* in this spirit, the Court found that applying

[75] *Tyrer* v. *the United Kingdom*, application no. 5856/72, ECHR (April 25, 1978), §33. This was an early example of participation from civil society in human rights litigation, which became a more frequent practice later on.

[76] *Tyrer* v. *the United Kingdom*, §33.

[77] George Letsas, "Strasbourg's Interpretive Ethic: Lessons for the International Lawyer," *European Journal of International Law* 21, no. 3 (2010): 527.

judicial corporal punishment amounted to degrading treatment. But even beyond the specifics of this case, it also signalled something bigger – henceforth, the Court may adopt higher standards when assessing complaints regarding torture and other forms of ill-treatment.

The sitting British judge, Sir Gerald Fitzmaurice, criticised the decision in his separate opinion. Acknowledging that he himself was subjected to corporal punishment, Judge Fitzmaurice claimed that the decision ran the risk of being a penal reform.[78] Although *Tyrer* spurred some debates in the United Kingdom, it did not immediately lead to any real penal reform. The United Kingdom government introduced changes following another corporal punishment case, *Campbell and Cosans* v. *the United Kingdom* (1982).[79] Following that case, the United Kingdom introduced the Education Act (No. 2) in 1986, which abolished corporal punishment in British public schools.[80]

A number of changes made a ruling like *Tyrer* possible in 1978, despite the risk of criticism like that raised by Judge Fitzmaurice. First, forbearance was beginning to pay off. The Court's cautious approach gave member states the signal that it was willing to operate at a lower sovereignty cost. As a result, by the 1970s, the number of member states subscribing to the Court's jurisdiction had increased, and the Court began to have more authority. Second, the *détente* period (1969–1979) allowed some breathing room for human rights. The 1975 Helsinki Accords brought the Western and Eastern blocs closer and reduced tensions between them. The Accords generated political and sociological changes that transformed the international human rights agenda in Europe and beyond.[81] The Helsinki Declaration, which came out of the Accords, also formally acknowledged the international human rights agenda as a post-Second World War "historical reality."[82]

Although the Helsinki Declaration was merely a nonbinding declaration of intent, it shaped the relationship between the East and the West. It encouraged transnational contact between civil society organizations,

78 *Tyrer* v. *the United Kingdom* (separate opinion of Judge Sir Gerald Fitzmaurice), §14.

79 *Campbell and Cosans* v. *the United Kingdom*, application no. 7511/76;7743/76, ECHR (25 February 1982).

80 Barry Phillips, "The Case for Corporal Punishment in the United Kingdom. Beaten into Submission in Europe?," *International and Comparative Law Quarterly* 43, no. 1 (1994): 156.

81 Daniel C. Thomas, *The Helsinki Effect: International Norms, Human Rights, and the Demise of Communism* (Princeton: Princeton University Press, 2001).

82 G. John Ikenberry, *After Victory: Institutions, Strategic Restraint, and the Rebuilding of Order after Major Wars* (Princeton: Princeton University Press, 2001), 227.

activists, journalists, diplomats, and politicians on both sides.[83] The emergence of a transnational network of activists across ideological blocs worked toward increasing awareness about human rights in the East and the West alike.[84] The Helsinki Accords in particular paved the way for the transformation of European societies and the European integration project,[85] which would become interwoven with a heightened interest in human rights.[86]

Tyrer channelled the spirit of this moment by showing that the European Court could be the leader of the rights revolution in Europe. The specific traits of this case also made it easy for the Court to assume this role. This complaint's central concern – judicial corporal punishment – was not a matter of high politics or national security, and it was only still practised in the United Kingdom.[87] Because the trend in Europe had long been against judicial corporal punishment, finding corporal punishment incompatible with the prohibition of torture and inhuman or degrading treatment was not likely to raise red flags or scare other member states away. Europe was ready to eradicate judicial corporal punishment.

Despite its progressive spirit, the *Tyrer* decision was limited in some respects. The Court did not stick to this resolve about corporal punishment throughout. The fact that the punishment was ordered by a court (i.e., the state) was the reason the European Court could view this treatment contrary to Article 3. For example, the same Court found that corporal punishment ordered by a headmaster did not constitute a violation of Article 3 in *Costello-Roberts* v. *the United Kingdom* in 1993.[88] The main

[83] Sarah B. Snyder, *Human Rights Activism and the End of the Cold War: A Transnational History of the Helsinki Network* (Cambridge: Cambridge University Press, 2011), 8.

[84] According to scholars such as Daniel Thomas and Sarah Snyder, this brought the end of the Cold War. Snyder, *Human Rights Activism and the End of the Cold War*, 2. For more on the influence of the Helsinki Final Act on the demise of communism in the region, see Thomas, *The Helsinki Effect*.

[85] Mikael Rask Madsen, "International Human Rights and the Transformation of European Society: From 'Free Europe' to the Europe of Human Rights," in *Law and the Formation of Modern Europe: Perspectives from the Historical Sociology of Law*, ed. Mikael Rask Madsen and Chris Thornhill (Cambridge University Press, 2014), 259.

[86] The Copenhagen criteria introduced in 1993 stipulated respecting human rights and the rule of law as a condition for membership – attesting to the constitutive role of human rights for the European project. Christos Kassimeris and Lina Tsoumpanou, "The Impact of the European Convention on the Protection of Human Rights and Fundamental Freedoms on Turkey's EU Candidacy," *The International Journal of Human Rights* 12, no. 3 (2008): 332. See also Andrew Williams, *EU Human Rights Policies: A Study in Irony*, Oxford Studies in European Law (Oxford and New York: Oxford University Press, 2004).

[87] Phillips, "The Case for Corporal Punishment in the United Kingdom," 156.

[88] *Costello-Roberts* v. *the United Kingdom*, application no. 13134/87, ECHR (March 25, 1993).

differense between these two cases was that while in *Tyrer* the punishment was ordered by the state (i.e., a vertical violation), in *Costello-Roberts*, it was ordered by a private individual (i.e., a horizontal violation).[89] It appears that the old Court was not entirely ready to acknowledge horizontal violations – violations perpetrated by private individuals, as we see in the case of Nahide.

What Comes after *Tyrer*? The Old Court's Cautious Audacity in *Soering*

> In the Court's view, having regard to the very long period of time spent on death row in such extreme conditions, with the ever-present and mounting anguish of awaiting execution of the death penalty, and to the personal circumstances of the applicant, especially his age and mental state at the time of the offence, the applicant's extradition to the United States would expose him to a real risk of treatment going beyond the threshold set by Article 3.
>
> (*Soering* v. *United Kingdom*, application no. 14038/88, ECHR (July 7, 1989), §111)

Although the living instrument principle equipped the Court with the ability to lower the thresholds to find violations, the Court referred to this principle only once more in the context of Article 3. In 1989, the Court issued *Soering* v. *United Kingdom*, where it recognised the *non-refoulement* principle under Article 3. Specifically, the Court argued that extraditing a fugitive to another state where he may be subject to torture "would hardly be compatible with the underlying values of the Convention, that 'common heritage of political traditions, ideals, freedom, and the rule of law' to which the preamble refers."[90] The Court also acknowledged that "the death row phenomenon" – the emotional distress felt by prisoners waiting to be executed – is a form of inhuman treatment. It then found that extraditing Jens Soering to the United States, where he would experience the death row phenomenon, would violate Article 3. In so doing, the Court departed from the Commission's earlier decision about the same case, where the Commission did not find a violation of Article 3.[91]

In arriving at this conclusion, the Court relied on the UN Convention on Torture, which specifically states, "no State Party shall … extradite a

[89] Michael K. Addo and Nicholas Grief, "Does Article 3 of The European Convention on Human Rights Enshrine Absolute Rights?," *European Journal of International Law* 9, no. 3 (1998): 518.

[90] *Soering* v. *United Kingdom*, application no. 14038/88, ECHR (7 July 1989), §88.

[91] Ibid., §76–78.

person where there are substantial grounds for believing that he would be in danger of being subjected to torture." But what provided the Court with the judicial courage to arrive at such a conclusion was the existence of a new protocol to the Convention: Protocol 6 prohibiting capital punishment in times of peace, adopted by the Committee of Ministers in 1982.[92] The Protocol was signed by sixteen member states at the time when *Soering* was under review. The signatories were Austria, Belgium, Denmark, Finland, France, Germany, Greece, Iceland, Italy, Luxembourg, the Netherlands, Norway, Portugal, Spain, Sweden, and Switzerland. The countries that did not sign Protocol 6 were in the minority – Cyprus, Ireland, Liechtenstein, Malta, the United Kingdom, and Turkey. The Court rightly interpreted this development as the majority of the Council of Europe member states intending to abolish the death penalty and justified its decision about death row constituting a violation of Article 3 based on this interpretation.[93]

Amnesty International intervened in this case and argued that considering the Western European countries' evolving standards, the death penalty in itself should be considered a form of inhuman or degrading treatment.[94] The Court did not go as far as agreeing with Amnesty's claim and prohibiting the death penalty itself, however. Instead, the Court underlined that capital punishment is permitted under Article 2 of the Convention, which reads as follows: "Everyone's right to life shall be protected by law. No one shall be deprived of his life intentionally save in the execution of a sentence of a court following his conviction of a crime for which this penalty is provided by law." The Court reasoned that the original drafters could not possibly have intended a general prohibition of the death penalty. It stressed that Article 3 should be in harmony with Article 2 instead of nullifying it.[95] Therefore, the death penalty would not breach Article 3, even though the Convention is interpreted as a living document and even though capital punishment is not in congruity with "regional standards of justice."[96]

This decision did not prohibit capital punishment,[97] but at least ensured that Jens Soering would not receive the death penalty upon his extradition

[92] Ibid., §104.
[93] Ibid., §103.
[94] Ibid., §101.
[95] Ibid., §103.
[96] Ibid., §102.
[97] This would change later when the Court ruled that evolving state practice indicated that the death penalty is prohibited in Europe. See *Al-Saadoon and Mufdhi* v. *the United Kingdom*, application no. 61498/08, ECHR (March 2, 2010).

to the United States.[98] Beyond *Soering*, the Court's decision about the speculative ill-treatment of a fugitive fortified the basis of the principle that the prohibition of torture is absolute.[99] The old Court would reiterate this conviction in 1996 in *Chahal* v. *the United Kingdom*, where it established that torture and ill-treatment are prohibited regardless of the victim's conduct.[100] These two decisions played a part in the norm's gradual transformation under the old Court's watch.

Indeed, the old Court had progressive instincts, yet it could not always act on them. The old Court's narrow discretionary space did not leave it much room to engage in audacity; instead, the old Court often felt the need to offer compromises when it came to cases involving national security concerns (as seen in *Ireland* v. *the United Kingdom*) or violations committed by private individuals (as seen in *Costello-Roberts* v. *the United Kingdom*). Despite such hesitations, the old Court made a colossal contribution to the norm's evolution, planting the seeds of progress by introducing the living instrument principle. As we see in Chapter 5, the new Court would take this principle to an even higher level and certify the absoluteness of the prohibition of torture, which cannot be justified even in self-defence.

Conclusion

This chapter has provided an overview of how the modern understanding of the norm against torture and inhuman and degrading treatment came to be and discussed its subsequent gradual transformation. Taking the Convention drafters' stated intentions as a baseline, it has traced the development of the norm through several landmark judgments. Relying on legal analysis, I have noted that the bounds of the norm against torture were initially limited to appease member states during the time of the old Court. The old Court could expand the norm only when it was safe to do so – when the stakes were low and there was an emerging consensus around an issue. This constraint influenced the way the norm against torture and inhuman or degrading treatment developed in the early days of the European human rights regime. Chapter 5 offers an account of the norm's transformation during the time of the new Court, which came to enjoy a wider discretionary space.

98 Susan Marks, "Yes, Virginia, Extradition May Breach the European Convention of Human Rights," *The Cambridge Law Journal* 49, no. 2 (1990): 197.

99 Addo and Grief, "Does Article 3 of The European Convention on Human Rights Enshrine Absolute Rights?," 522.

100 *Chahal* v. *United Kingdom*, application no. 22414/93, ECHR[GC] (November 15, 1996), §79.

5

New Court, New Thresholds, New Obligations

This chapter reviews the transformation of the norm against torture and inhuman or degrading treatment during the new Court by focusing on key moments and key obligations. In the earlier years of its tenure, the new Court issued a series of important rulings that fundamentally transformed the norm against torture and inhuman or degrading treatment. First, taking the living instrument principle introduced in *Tyrer* v. *the United Kingdom* to heart, the new Court began lowering the bar for what constituted a violation. In so doing, the new Court reversed the compromises that the old Court made, especially regarding the member states' national security concerns. This also meant that the new Court, compared to the old Court, had a drastically higher rate of finding states in violation, as explained in Chapter 3.

Second, unlike the old Court, the new Court also showed a willingness to recognise a series of novel claims – some of which were resource-intensive positive obligations and some concerned violations perpetrated by private actors. The reason the new Court could deviate from the practices of the old Court was that it could enjoy a wider discretionary space and therefore felt less compelled to offer trade-offs to states and resort to forbearance. When the new Court took over, this prohibition began to cover a wide range of new obligations. These included, for example, offering a legal remedy to the victims of domestic violence and child abuse or providing sufficient medical care to inmates, elderly care patients, and detained irregular migrants.[1] This chapter lists the achievements of the new Court, and it highlights how its approach differs from the stand taken by the old Court.

[1] For a comprehensive account of the doctrinal developments under Article 3, see Natasa Mavronicola, *Torture, Inhumanity and Degradation under Article 3 of the ECHR: Absolute Rights and Absolute Wrongs* (Oxford and New York: Hart Publishing, 2021); Laurens Lavrysen and Natasa Mavronicola, *Coercive Human Rights: Positive Duties to Mobilise the Criminal Law under the ECHR* (London: Hart Publishing, 2020).

Lowered Thresholds for Torture

While the old Court used the living instrument principle only twice in the context of Article 3, the new Court resorted to the living instrument principle immediately after its inception in the 1999 *Selmouni* v. *France* judgment. Ahmed Selmouni brought up this case and complained that he had been tortured while in police custody. The French government objected to this characterization, arguing that similar acts had not been considered torture in previous case law. They referred specifically to *Ireland* v. *the United Kingdom,* in which, as we have seen in Chapter 4, the old Court declared specific intense interrogation methods were inhuman and degrading treatment – but not torture.[2] The Court found that Selmouni suffered various forms of ill-treatment that caused him physical and mental pain and suffering, characterizing this treatment as torture because the mistreatment was *intentional* for the purpose of extracting a confession.[3] In response to the French objection, the Court declared that certain acts that had been defined as *inhuman and degrading treatment* in the past could be defined as *torture* in the future, emphasizing the need for increasingly high standards when reviewing claims about breaches of fundamental rights.[4]

This progressive spirit did not end with *Selmouni.* The Court continued to lower the thresholds for torture when interpreting Article 3 in the years that followed. For example, in 2005, in *Nevmerzhitsky* v. *Ukraine*, the Court decided not to focus solely on the intent of the perpetrators when classifying an act as torture. It found that force-feeding an inmate on hunger strike amounts to torture based on the severity of the treatment and the suffering it caused and not on whether the government had intended to inflict the pain.[5] The Ukrainian government had not been able to demonstrate that its force-feeding of Nevmerzhitsky was medically necessary, but it was also clear that they had not force-fed the inmate for the purpose of extracting information or a confession either.[6] Setting aside the issue of

[2] The case concerned the treatment of detainees linked to the Irish Republican Army (IRA) in Northern Ireland. The allegations included the "five techniques": wall standing, hooding, subjection to noise, deprivation of sleep, and deprivation of food and drinks. The Court found that these acts amounted to only inhuman and degrading treatment in 1978.

[3] *Selmouni* v. *France*, application no. 25803/94, ECHR[GC] (July 28, 1999) §98.

[4] *Selmouni* v. *France*, §101.

[5] In response to the applicant's resistance, he was handcuffed and forced to swallow the tube to transfer food. *Nevmerzhitsky* v. *Ukraine*, application no. 54825/00, ECHR (April 5, 2005) §90.

[6] Ibid., §96.

whether the suffering caused was intentional or not, the Court decided the treatment constituted torture.

The standard used in *Nevmerzhitsky* was very different from what had been established not only in prior jurisprudence, but also in the definition of torture under the Convention against Torture (CAT). The intentionality of the treatment to extract information or to punish had consistently been considered the decisive element in identifying torture.[7] So, why did the Court suddenly relax this standard in *Nevmerzhitsky*? An experienced judge, whom I interviewed at the Court, explained to me that proving intent is difficult, but such difficulty should not disqualify the complaint. Although a clear intention will always be a decisive factor, when it is difficult to establish, then the Court's decision will turn on the severity of the treatment.[8] The introduction of this new twofold standard enabled the new Court to classify *Nevmerzhitsky* as torture. It was an audacious move, and afterward, more and more violent acts could be characterised as torture whether or not the intent was proven.[9]

Lowered Thresholds for Inhuman or Degrading Treatment

The definitions of what constitutes inhuman or degrading treatment also substantially changed in the late 1990s.[10] One of the most telling examples of this transformation is the changing view around whether unacceptable detention conditions constitute a form of inhuman or degrading treatment. As Antonio Cassese explains, "the conditions of prison detention," including solitary confinement, deficiencies in medical treatment of detainees, or life imprisonment, were not initially considered Article 3 violations.[11] With the exception of the *Greek Case*, where the Commission found unacceptable detention conditions to be a violation, complaints in relation to detention conditions or intrusive detention measures were

[7] For a comprehensive doctrinal assessment of the definition of torture, see Ergün Cakal, "Assessing (and Making Sense of) Severity: Conceptualising and Contextualising Torture's Core," *Nordic Journal of International Law* 91, no. 2 (2022): 284–309.

[8] Interview 8.

[9] Manfred Nowak and Elizabeth McArthur, "The Distinction between Torture and Cruel, Inhuman and Degrading Treatment," *Torture* 16, no. 3 (2006): 150.

[10] For an assessment of the Court's approach to vulnerability, see Corina Heri, *Responsive Human Rights: Vulnerability, Ill-Treatment and the ECtHR* (Oxford: Hart Publishing, 2021).

[11] Antonio Cassese, "The Prohibition on Torture and Inhuman or Degrading Treatment or Punishment," in *Human Dimension of International Law: Selected Papers of Antonio Cassese*, ed. Paola Gaeta and Salvatore Zappala (New York: Oxford University Press, 2008), 302.

disregarded during the time of the old Court. This hesitation was mostly because ensuring acceptable detention conditions, a form of positive obligation, was resource-intensive. It required states to dedicate funds to improve the living conditions in detention centres. In that sense, the obligation to provide acceptable detention conditions had a resemblance to those deriving from social and economic rights, which called for states to take progressive measures to guarantee the enjoyment of rights.

The old Court did not view Convention rights through the lens of positive obligations at the time. It had a quite limited view of what constituted inhuman or degrading treatment. For example, in *B.* v. *the United Kingdom* (1981), the applicant complained about his detention conditions in Broadmoor Hospital, where he had been receiving medical treatment for paranoid schizophrenia. Specifically, he claimed that the cells were overcrowded, they lacked adequate sanitary facilities, and that he had no privacy.[12] He expressed a constant fear of being attacked by other patients due to the lack of privacy and overcrowding.[13] Upon reviewing the evidence presented, the Commission dismissed the applicant's allegations. The Commission found them "exaggerations" and argued as follows:

> The Commission notes, firstly, that the applicant has a tendency to *exaggerate* the inadequacy of conditions in Broadmoor Hospital partly because of his uncooperative and *negative attitude towards the institution* where he considered he should never have been detained.
>
> Nevertheless, certain of the applicant's complaints have some basis, particularly that concerning overcrowding. There is no doubt that there was deplorable overcrowding in the dormitory accommodation in which the applicant slept from February 1974 to December 1976. Particularly unpleasant must have been the dormitories in Kent and Cornwall Houses between February and August 1974. This serious overcrowding is borne out by official reports of the Parliamentary Estimates Committee and the Butler Committee. Moreover, although major improvements have been carried out by the time of the [Commission's] Delegates visit to Broadmoor in July 1977, *the dormitory accommodation still appeared cramped and bleak. However, by that time the applicant had been located to a single room.* (…)
>
> As regards the applicant's complaints about sanitary conditions, contrary to the applicant's assertions, there were toilet facilities in Kent and Cornwall Houses. It is true, however, that there were no such facilities in the small dormitory on Ward II of Dorset House during the applicant's

[12] *B.* v. *the United Kingdom*, application no. 6870/75, European Commission of Human Rights (October 7, 1981) §5. The rest of the complaint under Article 3 concerned the applicant's employment and the medical treatment that he went through.

[13] *B.* v. *the United Kingdom*, § 174.

> stay there from October 1974 to about the late summer of 1975. There were only chamber pots and a commode. The toilet, which was subsequently installed, appears not to have been screened by a curtain at first. Moreover, it was accepted by hospital staff during the Delegates' visit in July 1977 that, outside the dormitories, the sanitary conditions, washing facilities and toilets were less than satisfactory. *It appears that the applicant unduly and obsessively magnified his complaint concerning the absence of toilet paper.*[14]

Brushing off the allegations in this manner, the Commission concluded that the facilities' conditions were "extremely unsatisfactory," but did not find a violation.[15]

Let us examine the way in which the Commission constructed its reasoning in *B.* v. *the United Kingdom*. First, the Commission did not fully engage with how the conditions affected the psychology of the applicant, who was already suffering from a mental condition. In so doing, it downplayed his legitimate complaints. Second, the Commission found it sufficient that the applicant was moved to a single room by the time of the official visit of the delegation, although he had to struggle in an overcrowded cell for two and a half years before the move.[16] Cassese rightfully criticises this decision, arguing that the applicant's relocation to the single room at the time of the official visit could "in no way reduce the importance of, let alone cancel, the previous conditions of overcrowding."[17] He then adds, "[o]ne is left with the feeling that the Commission deliberately avoided passing judgment on whether or not overcrowding – to the extent that the applicant had suffered from it for a long period of time – amounted to inhuman treatment."[18] As Cassese observes, the decision was evasive in that the Commission simply avoided addressing whether unacceptable detention conditions could violate Article 3. The dissenting opinion of Commissioners Opsahl and Tenekides reflected the shape of things to come. They proposed that "there are no watertight distinctions between social and civil rights" and "a modern welfare state cannot use compulsion in social and mental care – or crime control – without at the same time taking the responsibility for a sufficient follow-up."[19] They argued further

[14] (Emphasis added) *B.* v. *the United Kingdom*, § 175–78.

[15] Ibid., § 180.

[16] Cassese, "The Prohibition on Torture and Inhuman or Degrading Treatment or Punishment," 304.

[17] Ibid.

[18] Ibid.

[19] *B.* v. *the United Kingdom* (Mr. Opsahl and Mr. Tenekides, dissenting opinion).

that the detainee's rights "to live in acceptable conditions and be treated for illness" could fall under Article 3.[20]

The vision the Commissioners Opsahl and Tenekides expressed in 1981 would be fully realised twenty years later when the Court issued the *Dougoz* v. *Greece* judgment.[21] The applicant, a refugee awaiting expulsion from Greece due to drug-related offences, complained about his detention conditions. He claimed that his cell was overcrowded to the point that some detainees had to sleep in the corridor and that they were not given beds or mattresses. He further argued that the cell was unhygienic and lacked sufficient sanitary facilities, natural light, and fresh air.[22]

This complaint was received differently from *B.* v. *United Kingdom* in a number of ways. First, the Court granted credibility to the applicant's claim. It emphasised that the government did not deny his allegations concerning the lack of beds and bedding.[23] Second, referring to the *Greek Case*, the Court argued, "conditions of detention may sometimes amount to inhuman or degrading treatment."[24] Third, the Court relied on the European Committee for the Prevention of Torture (CPT) reports concerning the detention centres at issue. These reports highlighted that "the cellular accommodation and detention regime in that place were quite unsuitable for a period in excess of a few days, the occupancy levels being grossly excessive and the sanitary facilities appalling."[25] Finally, the Court concluded that the detention conditions, particularly "the serious overcrowding and absence of sleeping facilities, combined with the inordinate length of the period during which he was detained in such conditions" are in violation of Article 3.[26]

In *Dougoz,* the Court established that condemning detainees to live in unacceptable conditions could amount to degrading treatment. In doing so, it effectively expanded the scope of Article 3. More symbolically, this decision showed how the minimum threshold of severity required to invoke Article 3 had decreased over time. Issues that the Commission did not consider to be serious enough in *B* v. *the United Kingdom* were viewed as constituting degrading treatment twenty years later in *Dougoz.*

[20] Ibid.
[21] *Dougoz* v. *Greece*, application no. 40907/98, ECHR (March 6, 2001).
[22] Ibid., §20.
[23] Ibid., §45.
[24] Ibid., §46.
[25] Ibid.
[26] Ibid., §48.

This trend, surely, is not isolated or limited to the norm against torture and inhuman or degrading treatment. Several other scholars have noted a tendency to apply higher standards over time for human rights in general. Margaret Keck and Kathryn Sikkink, for example, describe this phenomenon as "raising the bar,"[27] while Christopher J. Fariss refers to it as "the changing standard of accountability."[28] In essence, all refer to the same phenomenon: Courts and other human rights institutions have applied increasingly higher standards when assessing human rights violations. But as we see in this book, this trend might have occasional slowdowns or even reversals.

Against the Ticking Time Bomb Scenario: The Prohibition of Torture Is Absolute

To conclude the story about lowering thresholds, I now turn to one last important case, which reversed the compromise that had been made in *Ireland* v. *the United Kingdom* and underscored the absolute nature of the prohibition against torture: *Gäfgen* v. *Germany*. Issued only one year after the decision concerning Nahide (*Opuz* v. *Turkey*), *Gäfgen* certainly shares its forward-looking vision. While in Nahide's case, the Court audaciously found Turkey in violation for not taking measures to protect her from her abusive husband, in *Gäfgen*, the Court found that even threatening a suspect with torture is a form of inhuman treatment. These two decisions shook the prior understandings around the prohibition of torture. While the former reaffirmed that states could be held accountable for violations committed by private actors, the latter certified that torture can never be justified.

Gäfgen v. *Germany (2010)*

> In this connection, the Court accepts the motivation for the police officers' conduct and that they acted in an attempt to save a child's life. However, it is necessary to underline that, having regard to the provision of Article 3 and to its long-established case-law, the prohibition on ill treatment of a person applies irrespective of the conduct of the victim or the motivation of the authorities. Torture, inhuman or degrading treatment cannot be inflicted even in circumstances where the life of an individual is at risk.
>
> (*Gäfgen* v. *Germany*, application no. 22978/05, ECHR[GC] (June 1, 2010), §107)

[27] Margaret E. Keck and Kathryn Sikkink, *Activists beyond Borders: Advocacy Networks in International Politics* (Ithaca and London: Cornell University Press, 1998).

[28] Christopher J. Fariss, "Respect for Human Rights Has Improved over Time: Modeling the Changing Standard of Accountability," *American Political Science Review* 108, no. 2 (2014): 297–318.

Only three years after the new Court's creation in 1998, the world would be shaken by the terrorist attacks of September 11, 2001. Amid the anxiety that arose after 9/11, the new Court – just like the old Court – was called to strike a balance between protecting rights and respecting national security laws and measures. European societies, in full solidarity with the United States, condemned the terrorist attacks. This solidarity was perhaps most famously expressed in *Le Monde*'s headline, "We are all Americans now."[29] European countries were quick in identifying transnational terrorism as a threat to international security, but they did not feel as threatened as the Americans, whose national psyche was scarred by 9/11.[30] It was only after the Madrid train bombings of 2004 and the London attacks of 2005 that Europe's vulnerability became clear too.[31] Realizing that the threat could lie well within the borders of Europe, Europeans took measures at both the national and the EU levels.[32] Several European states developed counter-terrorism strategies, including intrusive anti-terror laws and stringent border control regimes that monitor migratory networks.[33] The EU mirrored these policies. Europol (the law enforcement body of the EU) increased its authority,[34] and FRONTEX (a new border management agency that monitors migration and external borders) was established in 2004.[35]

In addition, there was a series of attempts to declare emergency laws.[36] For example, under the Anti-Terrorism, Crime and Security Act of 2001, the United Kingdom requested derogation from its obligations under

[29] Karin Von Hippel, "Introduction: Europe Confronts Terrorism," in *Europe Confronts Terrorism*, ed. Karin Von Hippel (Basingstoke and New York: Palgrave Macmillan, 2005), 1.

[30] Vinca LaFleur, "A View from America: Tactical Unity, Strategic Divide," in *Europe Confronts Terrorism*, ed. Karin Von Hippel (Basingstoke and New York: Palgrave Macmillan, 2005), 196.

[31] Von Hippel, "Introduction: Europe Confronts Terrorism," 4.

[32] Jörg Monar, "Common Threat and Common Response? The European Union's Counter-Terrorism Strategy and Its Problems," *Government and Opposition* 42, no. 3 (2007): 296; Doron Zimmermann, "The European Union and Post-9/11 Counterterrorism: A Reappraisal," *Studies in Conflict and Terrorism* 29, no. 2 (2006): 139.

[33] Peter Mandaville, "Muslim Transnational Identity and State Responses in Europe and the UK after 9/11: Political Community, Ideology and Authority," *Journal of Ethnic and Migration Studies* 35, no. 3 (2009): 503.

[34] Coolsaet Rik, "EU Counterterrorism Strategy: Value Added or Chimera?," *International Affairs* 86, no. 4 (2010): 862.

[35] Neal Andrew W., "Securitization and Risk at the EU Border: The Origins of FRONTEX," *JCMS: Journal of Common Market Studies* 47, no. 2 (2009): 338–43.

[36] This picture changed in 2015 following a series of terror attacks, which targeted France in particular and resulted in the deaths of 148 people. In January 2015, gunmen affiliated with Al-Qaeda attacked the offices of the satirical magazine Charlie Hebdo and a Jewish kosher

Article 5 of the Convention (which provides protection against arbitrary detention or imprisonment without a fair trial), claiming that there was a "public emergency threatening the life of the nation."[37] However, in 2005, after the House of Lords found the "indefinite administrative detention of foreign national terrorism suspects to be incompatible with the Convention" (*Belmarsh* case), the government withdrew its derogation claim.[38] Other anti-terror laws introduced in several other European countries have restricted freedom of assembly, the right to liberty and security, and the right to privacy – sometimes targeting specific national, ethnic, and religious groups.[39]

In this new context, the work of domestic courts and the European Court has become even more essential. They have assumed the important mission of holding the line against excesses of executive and legislative branches in the fight against terrorism.[40] Fully aware of this responsibility, the Court has taken on the daunting task of carefully balancing the member states' security interests with its mandate to uphold the Convention principles. *Gäfgen* v. *Germany* serves as an expression of this determination. In *Gäfgen,* the Court established that even threatening to torture a suspect may amount to a violation under Article 3.[41] Although *Gäfgen* is not perfectly emblematic of complaints arising from the fight against terrorism, it helped to flesh out the principles that can be applied to them.

store. Then on November 13, 2015, a group of terrorists affiliated with the so-called Islamic State of Iraq and Syria (ISIS) carried out a coordinated attack in Paris, killing 130 people. While suicide bombers carried out an attack at the Stade de France stadium, heavily armed men simultaneously opened fire at the Bataclan concert hall and several restaurants and bars. These attacks elevated the threat perception in France and beyond. On November 14, Francois Hollande, former President of France, described the attacks as an "act of war" and declared a state of emergency, which remained in force until November 1, 2017.

37 Joint Committee on Human Rights (House of Lords, House of Commons), "Counter-Terrorism Policy and Human Rights (Seventeenth Report): Bringing Human Rights Back In – Human Rights Joint Committee" (London, March 25, 2010), https://publications.parliament.uk/pa/jt200910/jtselect/jtrights/86/8607.htm.

38 Joint Committee on Human Rights (House of Lords, House of Commons), §25.

39 Daniel Moeckli, *Human Rights and Non-Discrimination in the "War on Terror"* (Oxford and New York: Oxford University Press, 2008).

40 Colin Warbrick, "The European Response to Terrorism in an Age of Human Rights," *European Journal of International Law* 15, no. 5 (2004): 1017.

41 Steven Greer, "Is the Prohibition against Torture, Cruel, Inhuman and Degrading Treatment Really 'Absolute' in International Human Rights Law?," *Human Rights Law Review* 15, no. 1 (2015): 101; Stijn Smet, "Conflicts between Absolute Rights: A Reply to Steven Greer," *Human Rights Law Review* 13, no. 3 (2013): 496; Natasa Mavronicola, "Is the Prohibition against Torture and Cruel, Inhuman and Degrading Treatment Absolute in International Human Rights Law? A Reply to Steven Greer," *Human Rights Law Review* 17, no. 3 (2017): 481; 489.

Magnus Gäfgen complained about the ill-treatment he suffered while being interrogated about a boy he had kidnapped. At the time of the interrogation, neither the police nor the boy's family knew that the applicant had already killed the boy. In order to extract information about the boy's whereabouts without resorting to physical force, police threatened the applicant. Following a ten-minute interrogation under the threat of ill-treatment, he disclosed the information that the interrogators sought. According to the Court, this constituted a violation of Article 3. The threat of torture was the decisive factor in this decision. The applicant, who had previously refused to reveal any information, did so only following the interrogators' threats. The Court reasoned thus: "the real and immediate threats of deliberate and imminent ill-treatment to which the applicant was subjected during his interrogation must be regarded as having caused him considerable fear, anguish, and mental suffering."[42] It noted that the use of threat was not "a spontaneous act but was premeditated and calculated in a deliberate and intentional manner."[43] The Court, therefore, deemed this experience as having amounted to inhuman treatment.[44]

By doing so, the Court underlined that even in circumstances where the lives of persons are at risk, ill-treatment could not be justified.[45] The Court emphasised that "the prohibition on ill-treatment of a person applies irrespective of the conduct of the victim or the motivation of the authorities."[46] What is also interesting to note is that the Court reached this conclusion even without requiring a medical report showing the long-term impact on the applicant. The message was loud and clear: the prohibition of torture is absolute.[47] This approach effectively contradicted

[42] *Gäfgen* v. *Germany*, application no. 22978/05, ECHR[GC] (June 1, 2010), §103.

[43] Ibid., § 104.

[44] Ibid., § 108.

[45] Ibid., § 107.

[46] Ibid.

[47] The principle that the prohibition of torture is absolute, regardless of the victim's conduct, was first iterated in *Chahal* v. *the United Kingdom*, application no. 22414/93, ECHR[GC] (November 15, 1996). It should be noted, however, that the true nature of this absoluteness has been subject to a debate today – known as *the Gäfgen debate*. According to Steven Greer, when evaluating the Gäfgen case, the Court neglected the real victim's (the child who was abducted) right not to be tortured. He further underlines that the state also had an obligation to protect the boy from being tortured and murdered by Mr Gäfgen. In doing so, Greer points to a conflict between two absolute rights. Therefore, he finds the requirement that no exception to this prohibition "can be accepted, defended, justified, or tolerated in any circumstances whatever," problematic. To resolve this moral dilemma, Stijn Smet proposes the following: in such cases of conflict between absolute rights, a negative right (the right to be free from torture) should outweigh a positive right (the right

the arguments for necessity invoked to justify pressuring a (terror) suspect in order to extract information to save others in "ticking bomb" like scenarios.[48] It also reversed the *Ireland* v. *the United Kingdom* compromise by underlining the prohibition of torture is absolute, and it cannot be taken lightly or justified even for the purpose of saving lives or in the name of national security.

The Dawn of Positive Obligations

Nearly a decade before acknowledging the Turkish government's obligation to protect Nahide from her abusive husband, the Court began laying down other positive obligations that enhance the protections offered under the prohibition of torture and ill-treatment. The innovation of positive obligations is an example of sudden change because they entered the picture in the late 1990s within a short span of time and in rapid succession. As we may remember from Chapter 1, there are five main positive obligations identified.[49] These are the obligations to provide legal protection and remedy, to inform the relatives of disappeared persons, to provide acceptable detention conditions, to provide necessary medical care, and to carry out effective investigations.

Although these obligations are wide-ranging in coverage, they have some common denominators. That is to say, the Court embraced positive obligations that share one of two characteristics: either they are semantically linked to the prohibition of torture and ill-treatment, or they have an auxiliary value – strengthening the degree of protection Article 3 provides.

First, these obligations are logically linked to the prohibition's core meaning (i.e., its central concern).[50] In the case of the norm against torture,

to be protected from torture perpetrated by state agents or private parties). Moreover, Natasa Mavronicola argues that the absoluteness of the prohibition refers to its "legal non-displaceability" and not the fact that there cannot be any "circumstances in which some might defend or even tolerate torture [and inhuman or degrading treatment]." Greer, "Is the Prohibition against Torture, Cruel, Inhuman and Degrading Treatment Really 'Absolute' in International Human Rights Law?," 101; Stijn Smet, "Conflicts between Absolute Rights," 496; Mavronicola, "Is the Prohibition against Torture and Cruel, Inhuman and Degrading Treatment Absolute in International Human Rights Law?," 481.

48 For a comprehensive assessment of this argument, see Fritz Allhoff, *Terrorism, Ticking Time-Bombs, and Torture* (Chicago: The University of Chicago Press, 2012).

49 There are also two unsuccessful obligations: the obligation to facilitate euthanasia and the obligation to provide a healthy environment.

50 For a discussion on a norm's core meanings, see Nicole Deitelhoff and Lisbeth Zimmermann, "Things We Lost in the Fire: How Different Types of Contestation Affect

this is the victim's mental or physical suffering or impaired dignity. This is no surprise, because this prohibition was initially only concerned with the pain and suffering caused by the treatment or punishment of prisoners, criminals, or terrorist suspects in detention. This reference was kept for positive obligations, too. This is how, for example, the Court established Nahide's victimhood in *Opuz* v. *Turkey*. In *Opuz*, the victim's case was argued as follows: "[the victim] had been subjected to violence, injury, and death threats several times but the authorities were negligent towards her situation, which caused her *pain and fear*."[51] The decision centred on the pain she had to endure due to the authorities' negligence. That is, Nahide's treatment could be categorised as a form of inhuman or degrading treatment based on the pain and suffering that the government's *inaction* generated.

As a matter of fact, the Court employed a similar logic when recognizing negative obligations that are not traditionally associated with the prohibition of torture. For example, the Court began considering the destruction of property, homes, or livelihood under Article 3 using a similar logic. This issue was brought to the Court's attention in the context of the Kurdish conflict in Turkey in the 1990s. The Court found the Turkish security forces' destruction of homes and property – as a counterterrorism tactic – a violation in *Selçuk and Asker* v. *Turkey* in 1998 for the first time.[52] Ordinarily, destruction of homes or property would not be associated with Article 3, but with Article 8 (right to respect for private and family life), or Article 1 of Protocol 1 (protection of property). However, the Court began acknowledging the destruction of homes and livelihood as Article 3 violations, not due to the actual loss of property, but rather due to the destruction's effect on the victim's psychology and the extreme distress and hardship it generates.

Second, in addition to appealing to the core meaning, another trait that positive obligations share is their auxiliary protection value. This is how procedural obligations are created and justified, for example. The Court first recognised states' procedural obligations under Article 3 in *Assenov and Others* v. *Bulgaria* in 1998.[53] The case concerns the

the Robustness of International Norms," *International Studies Review* 22, no. 1 (2020): 51–76; Nicole Deitelhoff and Lisbeth Zimmermann, "Norms under Challenge: Unpacking the Dynamics of Norm Robustness," *Journal of Global Security Studies* 4, no. 1 (2019): 2–17.

[51] *Opuz* v. *Turkey*, application no. 33401/02, ECHR (June 9, 2009) § 154.

[52] *Selçuk and Asker* v. *Turkey*, application no. 12/1997/796/998–999, ECHR (April 24, 1998).

[53] *Assenov and Others* v. *Bulgaria*, application no. 90/1997/874/1086, ECHR (October 28, 1998).

Bulgarian police's ill-treatment of Anton Assenov, a teenage boy of Roma origin.[54] The Assenov family complained both about Anton's ill-treatment and the domestic authorities' failure to carry out a prompt and impartial investigation. Upon reviewing the complaint, the Court could not find sufficient evidence to ensure the injuries Anton sustained were due to police violence, but it did not stop there. Instead of dismissing Anton's complaint, the Court found the Bulgarian government in violation for not carrying out an effective investigation.[55] Specifically, it argued that Articles 1 and 3, read together, would require "by implication that there should be an effective official investigation. (…) If this were not the case, the general legal prohibition of torture and inhuman and degrading treatment and punishment, despite its fundamental importance, would be ineffective in practice and it would be possible in some cases for agents of the State to abuse the rights of those within their control with virtual impunity."[56] Hence, the Court emphasised that the prohibition of torture and ill-treatment cannot be fully realised without effective investigations and that procedural obligations offer a supplementary layer of protection.

While the Court laid out the legal foundations of procedural obligations under Article 3 in *Assenov*, consolidating this obligation was not necessarily a straightforward affair. Two years after *Assenov*, the Court retreated from its strong position in that case. In *Ilhan* v. *Turkey* (2000), it proposed that finding a procedural violation under Article 2 (right to life) would be justified as the provision entails the obligation to protect the right to life.[57] Nevertheless, this would not always be the case for Article 3, the Court argued. Since Article 3 is defined in substantive terms, it would not include an innate procedural obligation. The Court then qualified this statement, arguing that it may find a procedural breach if the circumstances require it.[58] To back up its argument, the Court pointed out that there is already a separate article concerning effective remedy in the Convention, Article 13.[59] According to Article 13, "[e]veryone whose rights and freedoms as set forth in this Convention are violated shall have an effective remedy before a national authority notwithstanding that the

[54] *Assenov and Others* v. *Bulgaria*, §8–10.
[55] Ibid., §106.
[56] Ibid., §102.
[57] *Ilhan* v. *Turkey*, application no. 22277/93, ECHR [GC] (June 27, 2000).
[58] *Ilhan* v. *Turkey*, §92.
[59] Ibid.

violation has been committed by persons acting in an official capacity." Victims could seek redress and procedural safeguards relying on this article, the Court argued, and it showed its hesitation to establish procedural obligations under Article 3 in *Ilhan*.[60]

This position had supporters. For example, the former British Judge Nicholas Bratza was an ardent critic of establishing separate procedural obligations under Article 3. In his separate opinion in *Poltoratskiy* v. *Ukraine*, Judge Bratza supported the reasoning presented in *Ilhan*. He stated that the complaint concerning effective investigations should have been examined under Article 13 instead of "the so-called 'procedural aspects' of Article 3."[61] Similarly, in *Kuznetsov* v. *Ukraine* (2003), Judge Bratza dissented and expressed that "[his] preference would have been to examine the complaint concerning the lack of effective official investigation into the applicant's allegations of ill-treatment under Article 13 of the Convention instead of Article 3."[62] As Judge Bratza emphasised in his dissenting opinions, addressing states' procedural obligations was a matter of preference at the time.

The Court thus initially oscillated between reviewing procedural violations under Article 3 and declining to do so, instead referring to Article 13. For example, in *Çakıcı* v. *Turkey* (1999), the Court found it would not be necessary to find a separate procedural violation under Article 3, as the alleged deficiencies in the investigation would be covered under Article 13.[63] Yet, in *Labita* v. *Italy*, it followed the *Assenov* line of reasoning and decided that there was a procedural breach due to the ineffectiveness of the investigation conducted.[64] After a series of inconsistent decisions, the Court settled on the existence of procedural obligations in Article 3 and gave them more recognition by coining the phrase "the procedural limb of Article 3."[65] Subsequently, a new

60 Ibid., §92.

61 *Poltoratskiy* v. *Ukraine*, application no. 38812/97, ECHR (April 29, 2003), (Nicholas Bratza, separate opinion).

62 *Kuznetsov* v. *Ukraine*, application no. 39042/97, ECHR (April 29, 2003), (Nicholas Bratza, partly dissenting opinion).

63 *Çakıcı* v. *Turkey*, application no. 23657/94, ECHR[GC] (July 8, 1999) §93. See also *Berktay c. Turquie*, application no. 22493/93, ECHR (March 1, 2001); *Denizci and Others* v. *Cyprus*, application nos. 25316–25321/94 and 27207/95, ECHR (May 23, 2001);

64 *Labita* v. *Italy*, application no. 26772/95, ECHR[GC] (April 6, 2000) §133–136. See also *Sevtap Veznedaroglu* v. *Turkey*, application no. 32357/96, ECHR (April 11, 2000); *Dikme* v. *Turkey*, application no. 20869/92, ECHR (July 11, 2000).

65 The practice of looking into a "procedural limb" under Article 3 was first introduced in the following cases: *Balogh* v. *Hungry*, application no. 47940/99, ECHR (July 20, 2004);

practice of looking at the violations under both *substantive* and *procedural* limbs of Article 3 began.[66]

This is to say, procedural obligations under Article 3 were first recognised in 1998 and consolidated around the mid-2000s in a relatively swift manner. Today procedural obligations are no longer questioned. Moreover, the Court referred to procedural obligations, and in particular, the duty to investigate, as a type of "detachable obligation" that is "capable of binding" states separately.[67] It appears that states' procedural obligations are on their way to turning into autonomous obligations separate from the substantive elements under Article 3,[68] and they are widely invoked, as we saw in Chapter 3. They are the single most invoked obligations under Article 3, to be exact.

Procedural obligations were, of course, not the only example of positive obligations. All in the same year, 1998, the Court recognised the obligation to provide legal protection in *A* v. *the United Kingdom* (a case concerning domestic abuse of a minor);[69] the obligation to inform the family

Khashiyev and Akayeva v. *Russia*, application nos. 57942/00 and 57945/00, ECHR (February 24, 2005); *Akkum and Others* v. *Turkey*, application no. 21894/93, ECHR (March 24, 2005); *Süheyla Aydin* v. *Turkey*, application no. 25660/94, ECHR (May 24, 2005). The phrase was used for the first time in a partly dissenting opinion written by Judges Rozakis, Bonello, and Straznicka in *Calvelli and Ciglio* v. *Italy* (2002). There, the dissenting judges referred to the "procedural limb of the protection of the right to life." Therefore, the term first was first employed in the context of Article 2 and then travelled to Article 3, in *Balogh* v. *Hungary* (2004), where the Court referred to the procedural limb of Article 3 for the first time.

66 See, for example, *Bekos and Koutropoulos* v. *Greece*, application no. 15250/02, ECHR (December 13, 2005); *Danelia* v. *Georgia*, application no. 68622/01, ECHR (October 17, 2006); *Affaire Melinte c. Roumanie*, application no. 43247/02, ECHR (November 9, 2006); *Akpinar and Altun* v. *Turkey*, application no. 56760/00, ECHR (February 27, 2007); *Gök and Güler* v. *Turkey*, application no. 74307/01, ECHR (July 28, 2009); *Premininy* v. *Russia*, application no. 44973/04, ECHR (February 10, 2011).

67 While this characterization concern only Article 2 (right to life), it has implications for Article 3 claims. *Varnava and Others* v. *Turkey*, application nos. 16064/90, 16065/90, 16066/90, 16068/90, 16069/90, 16070/90, 16071/90, 16072/90, 16073/90, ECHR[GC] (September 18, 2009), §138. This issue was first raised in *Šilih* v. *Slovenia*, application no. 71463/01, ECHR[GC] (April 9, 2009) §159. This same logic was applied in *Association 21 December 1989 and Others* v. *Romania*, application no. 33810/07, ECHR (May 24, 2011), where the Court established that "although [procedural obligation] is triggered by the acts concerning the substantive aspects of Article 2, it can give rise to a finding of a separate and independent 'interference'" (§116).

68 *Šilih* v. *Slovenia* (Joint Dissenting Opinion of Judge Bratza and Türmen), §9. See also Lucy Colter and Can Yeginsu, "Inquests and the 'Detachable' Article 2 Obligation: In Re McCaughey," *Judicial Review* 16, no. 3 (2011): 293.

69 *A* v. *the United Kingdom*, application no. 100/1997/884/1096, ECHR (September 23, 1998).

of disappeared persons in *Kurt* v. *Turkey* (a case concerning an enforced disappearance);[70] and the obligation to refrain from destroying home and property for the first time in *Selçuk and Asker* v. *Turkey* (a case concerning counterterrorism operation in the southeast of Turkey).[71] As epitomes of sudden change, these positive obligations assumed a taken-for-granted status not long after their initial acknowledgement.[72]

Limits of Progress under the New Court

This rapid, progressive jurisprudential trend had its limits, too. For example, one area in which the Court showed inhibition was to recognise the systematic nature of some discriminatory policies that violate Article 3, as I have argued elsewhere.[73] While the Court was willing to recognise that isolated instances of discrimination against minorities may amount to a violation of Article 3, it was less willing to accept the systemic nature of targeted discriminatory policies or the racial motivations behind gross human rights violations.[74] For example, in *Ahmet Özkan and Others* v. *Turkey*, a case concerning Turkish forces' raid on a remote village in the southeast of Turkey and the treatment of detained villagers, the Court found that the Turkish government violated Article 3.[75] However, the Court declined to consider the punitive purposes of this operation and its targeted nature.

Similarly, in *Anguelova* v. *Bulgaria*,[76] a case concerning the ill-treatment of a person of Roma origins and failure to provide them with an effective remedy,[77] the Court did not situate this individual incident in "the broader

[70] *Kurt* v. *Turkey*, application no. 15/1997/799/1002, ECHR (May 25, 1998).
[71] *Selçuk and Asker* v. *Turkey*.
[72] One year before, the European Commission confirmed the states' obligation to provide medical care in *P.M* v. *Hungary* (a case concerning the treatment of a life-sentence prisoner). *P.M.* v. *Hungary*, application no. 23636/94, European Commission of Human Rights (September 9, 1998).
[73] Ezgi Yildiz, "A Court with Many Faces: Judicial Characters and Modes of Norm Development in the European Court of Human Rights," *European Journal of International Law* 31, no. 1 (August 7, 2020): 86. This was also revealed in an interview with a lawyer who brought cases before the European Court. Interview 35.
[74] Dia Anagnostou, "The Strasbourg Court, Democracy and the Protection of Marginalised Individuals and Minorities," in *The European Court of Human Rights and the Rights of Marginalised Individuals and Minorities in National Context*, ed. Dia Anagnostou and Evangelia Psychogiopoulou (Leiden, Boston: Brill Nijhoff, 2010), 1–26.
[75] *Ahmet Özkan and Others* v. *Turkey*, application no. 21689/93, ECHR (April 6, 2004).
[76] *Anguelova* v. *Bulgaria*, application no. 38361/97, ECHR (June 13, 2002).
[77] Ibid., §3.

context of systematic racism and hostility which law-enforcement bodies in Bulgaria had repeatedly displayed," as the applicant requested.[78] This decision, however, sparked one of the sharpest dissenting opinions of the Convention system's history. Judge Bonello came down on the majority decision, with which he partly disagreed:

> I consider it particularly disturbing that the Court, in over fifty years of pertinacious judicial scrutiny, has not, to date, found one single instance of violation of the right to life (Article 2) or the right not to be subjected to torture or to other degrading or inhuman treatment or punishment (Article 3) induced by the race, colour or place of origin of the victim. Leafing through the annals of the Court, an uninformed observer would be justified to conclude that, for over fifty years democratic Europe has been exempted from any suspicion of racism, intolerance or xenophobia. The Europe projected by the Court's case-law is that of an exemplary haven of ethnic fraternity, in which peoples of the most diverse origin coalesce without distress, prejudice or recrimination. The present case energises that delusion.
>
> Frequently and regularly, the Court acknowledges that members of vulnerable minorities are deprived of life or subjected to appalling treatment in violation of Article 3; but not once has the Court found that this happens to be linked to their ethnicity. Kurds, coloureds, Muslims, Roma and others are again and again killed, tortured or maimed, but the Court is not persuaded that their race, colour, nationality or place of origin has anything to do with it. Misfortunes punctually visit disadvantaged minority groups, but only as the result of well-disposed coincidence.[79]

In *Nachova and Others* v. *Bulgaria*,[80] the next case complaining about police violence against the Roma, the Court once again faced the question of whether the alleged acts were motivated by racist attitudes toward the Roma.[81] This time, the applicants complained that military police shot and killed their relatives, and they brought a witness statement confirming that one of the officers shouted, "You damn Gypsies" at the victims.[82] The European Roma Rights Centre (ERRC), Interights, and the Open Society Justice Initiative (OSJI) intervened as third parties on the side of the applicants.[83] They made the case for shifting the burden of proof to

[78] Ibid., §164.
[79] Ibid. (Partly dissenting opinion of Judge Bonnello), §2–3.
[80] *Nachova and Others* v. *Bulgaria*, application no. 43577/98 and 43579/98, ECHR[GC] (July 6, 2005).
[81] Ibid., §2.
[82] Ibid., §153.
[83] Ibid., §138–43.

the responding government and criticised the Court's strict standards when reviewing claims concerning systemic racism.[84] Regardless, the Court found that the "statement is in itself an insufficient basis for concluding that the respondent State is liable for a racist killing."[85] It further added that "[i]t is true that a number of organizations, including intergovernmental bodies, have expressed concern regarding the occurrence of such incidents. However, the Court cannot lose sight of the fact that its sole concern is to ascertain whether in the case at hand the killing of [the victims] was motivated by racism."[86] Finally, the Court held that it was not possible to establish whether "racist attitudes" were a factor in the alleged acts and, therefore, could not find a substantive violation.[87] But it found a procedural violation and delegated the responsibility of establishing racist motivations behind "hate-induced violations" to the national authorities.[88]

The Court's reluctance to acknowledge the racial dimension behind the complaints related to police violence against the Roma came to a halt in *Stoica* v. *Romania*, where the Court found the imposition of discriminatory measures constituted a violation of Article 3 in conjunction with Article 14 (protection from discrimination).[89] The case was represented by the ERRC and the Roma Center for Social Intervention and Studies ("the Romani CRISS").[90] The applicant, who was of Roma origin, came with a similar complaint – namely, ill-treatment by the police and the failure to investigate his allegations. The applicant also claimed that "the impugned events and the flaws in the investigation had been motivated by racial prejudice," relying on Article 3 in conjunction with Article 14.[91]

Seeing the persistent attempts of the victims and the civil society organizations,[92] the Court followed a different approach in this case. It found the responding government in violation after making a strong statement on racial violence and states' responsibility to fight racism:

[84] Ibid., §140–41.
[85] Ibid., §153.
[86] Ibid., §155.
[87] Ibid., §158.
[88] Ibid., §164.
[89] *Stoica* v. *Romania*, application no. 42722/02, ECHR (March 4, 2008).
[90] Ibid., §2.
[91] Ibid., §3.
[92] James A. Goldston, "The Struggle for Roma Rights: Arguments That Have Worked," *Human Rights Quarterly* 32, no. 2 (2010): 311–25; James A. Goldston, "Public Interest Litigation in Central and Eastern Europe: Roots, Prospects, and Challenges," *Human Rights Quarterly* 28, no. 2 (2006): 492–527.

> Racial violence is a particular affront to human dignity and, in view of its perilous consequences, requires from the authorities special vigilance and a vigorous reaction. It is for this reason that the authorities must use all available means to combat racism and racist violence, thereby reinforcing democracy's vision of a society in which diversity is not perceived as a threat but as a source of its enrichment.[93]

This achievement is a significant jurisprudential leap, yet it has not been a straightforward success story. What is more, *Stoica* is not the final word on the racist motivation behind discriminatory policies. There are other cases that have continued to test the Court's willingness to recognise the systematic nature of some discriminatory policies that are in violation of Article 3.[94] At the moment of writing this book, this topic has not been fully resolved within the European human rights regime.[95]

Conclusion

This chapter has explored how the new Court, immediately after its creation in 1998, enforced increasingly lower thresholds for severity to find a violation under the prohibition of torture and inhuman or degrading treatment and introduced several key positive obligations. I have explained that with a few audacious rulings, the new Court reversed the compromises that the old Court made, especially regarding the member states' national security concerns. Different from the old Court, its audacity was across the board. The new Court accepted almost all the novel claims brought before it – even those concerned with resource-intensive positive obligations and the violations perpetrated by private actors. Having described the achievements of the new Court, I have also discussed the areas where this progress was slower. In particular, I have looked at the Court's treatment of claims arising from systemic racist policies. The following chapter explains why the norm's fundamental transformation transpired rapidly and smoothly in the late 1990s, detailing what was peculiar about this period.

93 Ibid., §117.

94 See, for example, *V.C.* v. *Slovakia*, application no. 18968/07, ECHR (November 8, 2011), *X.* v. *Turkey*, application no. 24626/09, ECHR (October 9, 2012), *Identoba and Others* v. *Georgia*, application no. 73235/12, ECHR (May 12, 2015).

95 For a discussion of discrimination based on sexual orientation, see Paul James Johnson and Silvia Falcetta, "Sexual Orientation Discrimination and Article 3 of the European Convention on Human Rights: Developing the Protection of Sexual Minorities," *European Law Review*, April 2018, 167–85. https://eprints.whiterose.ac.uk/127012/.

6

Change Unopposed

The Court's Embrace of Positive Obligations

This chapter explains why and how states' positive obligations deriving from the prohibition of torture and inhuman or degrading treatment emerged rapidly in the late 1990s and the early 2000s, using the theoretical framework presented in the Introduction and Chapter 3. This change episode deserves such close attention because this was not an insignificant instance with little to no consequences. Rather, the introduction of positive obligations fundamentally reshaped what this prohibition entails. What is also interesting to observe is that, despite its wide practical implications, this change went through without any noticeable opposition and was quickly internalised. What explains this?

The idea of positive obligations was conceived long after the time when the European Convention was drafted and adopted. It goes without saying that the drafters of the European Convention did not have positive obligations in mind when formulating Article 3. Positive obligations differ from the types of obligations they discussed, which included primarily physical ill-treatment and torture, as explained in Chapter 4. Positive obligations are resource-intensive obligations, and they require states to undertake measures that go beyond simply noninterfering or refraining from violating rights.[1] Instead, they call for active state involvement in fulfilling rights and protecting vulnerable groups against acts perpetrated by state agents or private actors.

For example, this is what the Court has established in *A* v. *the United Kingdom*, where the Court found that the United Kingdom failed to protect a minor from his step-father's physical abuse and thus violated its positive duties.[2] While positive obligations bring forth a protective shield for the victims, as we see in this example, they are certainly not boundless.[3]

[1] Steven Greer, "The Interpretation of the European Convention on Human Rights: Universal Principle or Margin of Appreciation?," *UCL Human Rights Review* 3 (2010): 5.

[2] *A* v. *the United Kingdom*, application no. 25599/94, ECHR (September 23, 1998).

[3] Natasa Mavronicola, *Torture, Inhumanity and Degradation under Article 3 of the ECHR: Absolute Rights and Absolute Wrongs* (Oxford and New York: Hart Publishing, 2021), 128.

The European Court leaves states some margin in fulfilling them.[4] As Natasa Mavronicola explains, the logic behind these obligations is not that states have to guarantee that torture and ill-treatment will never occur; rather, it simply means that states should adopt effective legal frameworks and "reasonable" and "adequate" measures.[5] While these obligations' definition and applicatory scope continue to be fleshed out in the case law, their existence is not questioned, and they are not contested. They are now part and parcel of the European (and international) anti-torture jurisprudence.

Despite their significance and prevalence, as we saw in Chapter 3, positive obligations were not put in place via a formal amendment procedure; instead, the European Court introduced them by means of several important rulings.[6] Their rapid introduction via the Court's jurisprudence was a judicial innovation that brought about a foundational change in the way the norm against torture and inhuman or degrading treatment is understood and applied. In this chapter, we will discover the legal reasons and the sociopolitical drivers behind the creation of positive obligations. In what follows, I will first explain why we need positive obligations by drawing from expert interviews I carried out in and around the Court. I will then turn to discussing why these obligations came to the surface in the late 1990s and the early 2000s by relying on the results of my large-N analysis of the Court's jurisprudence, insights from interviews, and secondary sources.

Legal Reasons behind Positive Obligations

The introduction of positive obligations under Article 3 was one of the subjects that I discussed with my interlocutors. I talked to seventeen judges, eight Registry officials, and eleven lawyers and representatives working for various civil society organizations. No matter their background, all thirty-six interviewees agreed that positive obligations have served to enhance human rights protection in practice. Some told me that their creation was logical and necessary.[7] Others told me that the Court was motivated by the conviction that human rights protection should be holistic without and any blind spots.[8] Without positive obligations,

4 Ignacio de la Rasilla del Moral, "The Increasingly Marginal Appreciation of the Margin-of-Appreciation Doctrine," *German Law Journal* 7, no. 6 (2006): 611–23.

5 Mavronicola, *Torture, Inhumanity and Degradation under Article 3 of the ECHR*, 152.

6 Sandra Krahenmann, "Positive Obligations in Human Rights Treaties" (Geneva, Graduate Institute of International and Development Studies, 2012), 20.

7 Interview 16; Interview 27; Interview 28; Interview 32.

8 Interview 2; Interview 5; Interview 7; Interview 9; Interview 32; Interview 33.

said one judge from a Western European country, "we would have a partial picture about what rights imply and how they can be violated."[9] Another judge with a similar background acknowledged that positive obligations helped "bridge the arbitrary distinction" between political and civil rights on one side and social rights on the other.[10] Other judges insisted that we need positive obligations to make the Convention "more meaningful and effective and not simply a declaration,"[11] and to "create the conditions for people to enjoy their rights."[12] Indeed, positive obligations serve such a supplementary function, as seen in the cases of obligations to provide legal protection and to carry out an effective investigation discussed in Chapter 5. They facilitate the successful realization of negative obligations, and they create suitable conditions for individuals to enjoy their rights and seek redress when these rights are violated. Therefore, some positive obligations can be considered as the preconditions or natural extensions of negative obligations, as one former judge told me.[13]

Despite their recent appearance, positive obligations are now an integral part of the European human rights regime and not the subject of any visible contestation. As one judge from a Western European country expressed, "it is difficult to imagine human rights protection today without the concept of positive obligations, in much the same way as it is difficult to imagine the eradication of discrimination without the use of affirmative action."[14] A human rights lawyer working for an international civil society organization explained their value in the most succinct way: "positive obligations are one of those very useful concept laws which allows human rights lawyers to make creative arguments, which now helps to push the boundaries for protection that is offered and essentially change the way things operate."[15]

When asked about the legal sources of positive obligations, the majority of the judges interviewed pointed to the Convention itself. Three judges argued that positive obligations are derived from the evolutive interpretation of Article 3,[16] while four other judges explained their

[9] Interview 2.
[10] Interview 9.
[11] Interview 11.
[12] Interview 16.
[13] Ibid.
[14] Interview 10.
[15] Interview 28.
[16] Interview 5; Interview 6; Interview 15.

development as rooted in a reading of Article 3 together with Article 1.[17] Article 1 obliges state parties to ensure all the Convention rights are protected within their jurisdiction; indeed, the Court often relies on Article 1 when prescribing positive obligations.[18] The logic here is that Article 1 lays down a horizontal obligation requiring member states to secure all the other obligations under the Convention.[19] It obliges states to take appropriate steps and adopt a proactive approach to protect the Convention rights.[20] These steps may include preventing violations, protecting victims, or providing effective remedies, which is what most of the positive obligations require.[21]

The legal logic underpinning positive obligations can be illustrated with an example. When establishing the Turkish government's responsibility to protect Nahide from her husband's abuse, the Court read Article 1 and Article 3 together. Engaging these two provisions at the same time, the Court pronounced that states should enact measures to protect individuals from inhuman or degrading treatment, even if such treatment is committed by private actors. The Court also emphasised that such protection is especially required for children and other vulnerable groups, such as victims of domestic violence.[22]

While this overview explains the legal reasons, it does not reveal the conditions that made the inception of positive obligations possible: Why were such obligations all swiftly brought to light in the late 1990s? To provide an answer to this question, I turn to the framework of analysis discussed in the Introduction and Chapter 1.

The framework is composed of one necessary condition and three contributing factors. The framework advances that, for courts to engage in audacious interpretations, they need a wide discretionary space and little to no interference or negative feedback from states. There are also three other contributing factors that facilitate audacious behaviour. These are changes in societal trends, the principles or precedents introduced in other legal instruments or by other legal bodies, and civil society campaigns. Let us now examine how these sociopolitical factors simultaneously aligned in the late 1990s.

17 Interview 4; Interview 7; Interview 8; Interview 10.
18 Article 1 reads as follows: "The High Contracting Parties shall secure to everyone within their jurisdiction the rights and freedoms defined in Section I of this Convention."
19 Interview 4.
20 Interview 10.
21 Interview 4; Interview 8; Interview 10.
22 *Opuz* v. *Turkey*, application. no. 33401/02, ECHR (June 9, 2009), §159.

Sociopolitical Reasons behind Positive Obligations

I The Inception of the New Court with a Wider Discretionary Space

According to my framework, the creation of the new Court was the most important factor in bringing positive obligations to bear on the norm against torture and inhuman or degrading treatment. With the structural reorganization initiated by Protocol 11, the old Court was remodelled into the *de facto* Supreme Court of Europe and began to stand on firmer ground. For the first time, the Court enjoyed high levels of authority and autonomy without the need to compromise on either. Having secured this status, the new Court could now adopt an even more progressive approach without confronting resistance from member states. The new Court had an unprecedented willingness to accept novel claims and tended to find states in violation at a greater rate compared to the old Court, as the analysis presented in Chapter 3 showed.

In this chapter, I present additional evidence from my large-N analysis explaining why the institutional transformation of the Court was the necessary condition. I argue that the critical event that enabled this institutional transformation was the adoption of Protocol 11 in 1994 and its entry into force in 1998.[23] Hence, from its inception in 1994 and onward, Protocol 11 signaled to both the old Court and the European Commission of Human Rights (the Commission) that the new structure of the European human rights regime would be different.

Let us imagine a scenario in which Protocol 11 had never been adopted or enforced, with the Commission remaining a quasi-judicial filtering mechanism and the Court a part-time judicial body without compulsory jurisdiction. In so doing, we will see that, without Protocol 11, the foundational change that occurred in the late 1990s would not have been straightforward or maybe even possible.

First, consider the role of the Commission as a gatekeeper.[24] The Commission followed stringent criteria when declaring cases admissible and referring them to the Court (see Figure 6.1). The percentage of inadmissibility decisions fell after the adoption of Protocol 11 in 1994, which

[23] Laura García-Montoya and James Mahoney, "Critical Event Analysis in Case Study Research," *Sociological Methods and Research* (2020) https://doi.org/10.1177/004912412092620.

[24] Karen J. Alter, "The Evolution of International Law and Courts," in *The Oxford Handbook of Historical Institutionalism*, ed. Orfeo Fioretos, Tulia G. Falleti, and Adam Sheingate (Oxford University Press, 2016), 600.

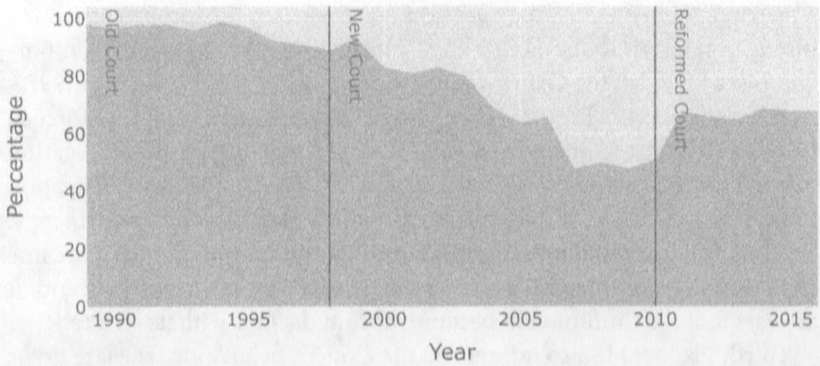

Figure 6.1 Inadmissibility decisions as a percentage of all cases lodged under Article 3

intensified when the Protocol went into force in 1998. In 1993, 96% of the cases brought under Article 3 were declared inadmissible by the Commission, and in 1998 this number decreased to 89%. The new Court had significantly lower rates of inadmissibility decisions. The inadmissibility rate is below 70% on average; in 2007 and 2009, only 48% of cases were declared inadmissible. The rate of inadmissibility decisions is not an insignificant detail. It indicates an interpretive body's willingness to review complaints that meet technical requirements for admissibility.[25]

While admissibility screening is a useful tool to weed out unfounded applications, when applied too strictly, it may also discard well-founded complaints. Recent research shows that some of the cases declared inadmissible by the European Court are, in fact, legally valid claims.[26] Looking at the difference between the admissibility screening done by the Commission, we can deduce that the new Court is more permissive than the Commission. It is also plausible to assume that if Protocol 11 had not abolished the Commission in 1998, the Commission would have continued to apply stricter standards for admissibility decisions – perhaps finding some of the complaints concerning positive obligations inadmissible.

[25] European Court of Human Rights, "Practical Guide on Admissibility Criteria," available at www.echr.coe.int/documents/admissibility_guide_eng.pdf.

[26] See, for example, Janneke Gerards, "Inadmissibility Decisions of the European Court of Human Rights: A Critique of the Lack of Reasoning," *Human Rights Law Review* 14, no. 1 (2014): 148–58.

Second, and relatedly, the data also demonstrates the importance of the timing of referrals to the Court. The Commission referred to all the important cases in which the Court would establish positive obligations in 1997 – after the adoption of Protocol 11 in 1994 but just before its entry into force in 1998. The list of cases includes *A* v. *the United Kingdom* (positive obligation to provide legal protection/remedy), *Kurt* v. *Turkey* (positive obligation to inform the family of disappeared persons), and *Assenov and Others* v. *Bulgaria* (obligation to investigate). From 1994 and onward, once it became clear that the Commission's role as the gatekeeper was nearing its end, it appears that the Commission became more audacious with its referrals.

Third, Protocol 11 also influenced the Court's behaviour. The late 1990s were not the first time the Court reviewed complaints invoking positive obligations. Figure 6.2 portrays violation (above) and no violation (below) rulings concerning claims invoking positive obligations during the period under study.[27] At first look, we see that the complaints concerning the violation of states' positive obligations under Article 3 had come before the Commission and the old Court earlier, in the late 1970s and the early 1980s. Yet, the Commission and the old Court did not consider these complaints as constituting violations of, or falling under, Article 3. The second cluster of complaints came afterward in the late 1990s, and there we see some violation decisions, which increased at a higher rate around the mid-2000s. This implies that the Commission and the old Court were, at first, categorically against positive obligation claims and this orientation changed in the period after 1998.

We can assess the old Court's approach to positive obligations under Article 3 in the period before 1998 qualitatively by looking at some of its judgments involving positive obligation claims. For example, in *Guzzardi* v. *Italy* (1980), the applicant complained about his living conditions in Asinara, an island where the applicant was obliged to reside for three years by a court order. This island was inhabited mostly by prison staff and their families.[28] In addition to limited movement and work opportunities, the applicant had to live in a building, which he described to be "dilapidated"

[27] Some of the no-violation decisions in the late 1970s and early 1980s were only given by the Commission. That is, the Commission passed a judgment and never referred it to the Court. For example, in *Bonnechaux* v. *Switzerland*, the Commission did not find the applications' complaint about detention conditions and failure to provide medical care to constitute a violation. *Bonnechaux* v. *Switzerland*, application no. 8824/78, European Commission of Human Rights (December 5, 1978). However, the case was not referred to the Court.

[28] *Guzzardi* v. *Italy*, application no. 7367/76 ECHR (November 6, 1980)

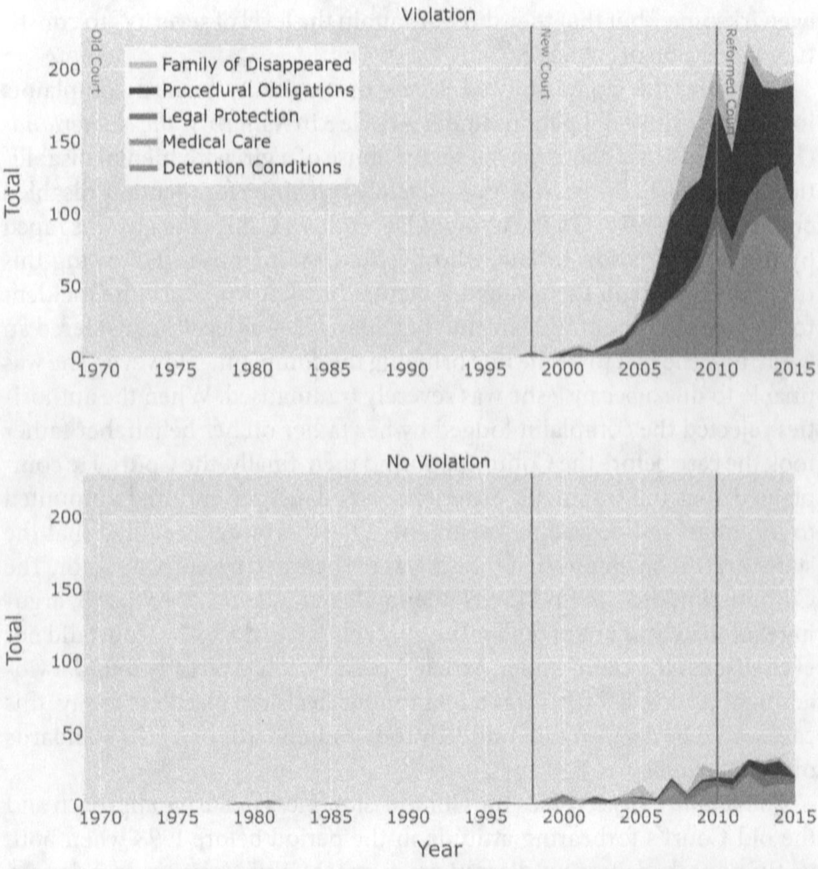

Figure 6.2 Distribution of violation and no violation rulings invoking positive obligations

and "almost uninhabitable."[29] At another point, the applicant complained about the substandard "health and sanitary conditions in the inhabited zones."[30] The Commission found that the applicant's claims did not fall under Article 3, and the Court agreed.[31] Without elaborating further, the Court unanimously found that the living conditions were "unpleasant or

[29] Ibid., §31.
[30] Ibid., §42.
[31] Ibid., §50.

even irksome," but that they did not "attain the level of severity" to constitute a violation of Article 3.[32]

Similarly, the Court showed a lack of sensitivity toward complaints invoking positive obligations under Article 3 in *X and Y* v. *the Netherlands* (1985).[33] This case concerns the sexual abuse of a girl with mental disabilities. The girl had been living in a privately run home for mentally disabled children since 1970. On the night of December 14, 1977, the girl was raped by the director's son-in-law, who lived on the premises. Following this traumatic incident, the girl had a mental breakdown. Since the incident took place after the girl's sixteenth birthday, she was legally considered an adult, and she had to be the one bringing the complaint. However, she was unable to do so because she was severely traumatised. When the authorities rejected the complaint lodged by her father on her behalf, her father took the case before the Commission and then, finally, the Court. He complained that the traumatic experience his daughter endured amounted to inhuman and degrading treatment.[34] Furthermore, he added that the state was responsible even if the act was perpetrated by a private actor. The Commission did not find the Netherlands in violation of Article 3, arguing that there was not much for the government to do.[35] The Court did not even discuss the claim under Article 3 because it had already found a violation of Article 8.[36] This was a unanimous decision. Needless to say, this case would be decided differently by today's standards or by the standards of the late 1990s.

The *X and Y case* typifies the Commission's less inclusive approach and the old Court's forbearing attitude in the period before 1998 when both institutions had narrow discretionary space. This decision is coloured by two trends associated with the Commission and the old Court: unwillingness to find a violation for abuse perpetrated by private actors and to impose resource-intensive positive obligations on states. From these trends, we can reasonably conclude that the old Court and the Commission would not have had the audacity to bring out several positive obligations in rapid succession in 1998, as the new Court did. This, however, does not imply that the old Court and the Commission would have never introduced positive obligations. They may well have, but it would probably have taken them much longer. It is also likely that the change

[32] Ibid., §107.
[33] *X and Y* v. *the Netherlands*, application no. 8978/80, ECHR (March 26, 1985).
[34] Ibid., §33.
[35] Ibid., §33.
[36] Ibid., §34.

they would have generated might have been less consequential. Due to their overriding preference for forbearance, they would have introduced fewer positive obligations of a less controversial nature. This would include, for example, procedural obligations or obligations to provide acceptable detention conditions.

In Sections II, III, and IV, I will turn to other contributing factors outlined in the framework, namely norm change's congruity with changing societal trends, legal principles promoted by other instruments or institutions, and civil society campaigns.

II Congruity of Positive Obligations with Societal Trends in the Aftermath of Eastward Expansion

The late 1990s was a transformative moment due to the alignment of several sociopolitical factors.[37] A wave of human rights euphoria coalesced in the post–Cold War period that lasted until the advent of the War on Terror.[38] That euphoria had two main drivers: One was the increasing number of countries that were either liberal democracies or perceived as transitioning to democracy. To belong to this group, states had to make explicit commitments to human rights. Even illiberal countries were gradually acquiescing to the international human rights regime. The other driver was the proliferation of human rights in two directions: the introduction of new rights and legal instruments and the unprecedented salience of the human rights discourse. New legal rights were introduced through legislation or judicial decisions at the domestic and international levels. In this regard, the UN played a key role by introducing new mandates for special procedures or establishing new treaty bodies.[39] The implications of this proliferation went beyond the human rights community as human rights language gained more traction in public discourse, with the emergence of new rights (e.g., right to water or right to clean environment)[40] and new

[37] Michael P. Scharf, "Seizing the 'Grotian Moment': Accelerated Formation of Customary International Law in Times of Fundamental Change," *Cornell International Law Journal* 43 no. 3 (2010): 439–69.

[38] Tim Dunne and Marianne Hanson, "Human Rights in International Relations," in *Human Rights: Politics and Practice*, ed. Michael Goodhart, 3rd edition (Oxford: Oxford University Press, 2016), 61–76.

[39] Jack Donnelly, *Universal Human Rights in Theory and Practice* (Ithaca: Cornell University Press, 2013).

[40] Nina Reiners, *Transnational Lawmaking Coalitions for Human Rights* (Cambridge and New York: Cambridge University Press, 2021); Madeline Baer, *Stemming the Tide: Human Rights and Water Policy in a Neoliberal World* (Oxford University Press, 2017); John H.

rights movements (e.g., those concerning sexual minorities or persons with disabilities).[41]

At the regional level, following the Eastward expansion (i.e., accession of formerly communist countries to the European human rights regime), European societies were primed and ready to bridge the gap between negative and positive obligations in the late 1990s.[42] "Timing was ripe," as one judge explained.[43] The introduction of positive obligations was the natural next step in Western Europe, where the rule of law standards were already well-established, according to one human rights activist.[44] Positive obligations would serve a supplementary function in protecting rights and upholding the rule of law in Western Europe. Yet, these obligations were even more necessary for Eastern European countries that had to be introduced to a strong rule of law tradition.[45] One judge from an Eastern European country divulged that having just gone through a regime change, Eastern European countries needed to be introduced to positive obligations.[46] Another judge from the same region even claimed that positive obligations appeared to be "the only solution to change the mentality of the [Eastern European] states."[47] These obligations would teach them how to establish a holistic and effective human rights protection system by, for example, directing them to take appropriate steps to prevent continuous violations and to provide effective remedies to the victims.

According to another judge, positive obligations were proposed to patch up Europe's increasingly diversified social fabric after the Eastward expansion.[48] Upon welcoming new member states, the Court started reviewing cases coming from both well-established democracies and those still in transition. Positive obligations were ideal tools to strengthen the rule of law tradition in both old and new members alike.[49] A judge

Knox and Ramin Pejan, eds., *The Human Right to a Healthy Environment* (Cambridge: Cambridge University Press, 2018).

41 Bob Clifford, "Introduction: Fighting for New Rights," in *The International Struggle for New Human Rights*, ed. Bob Clifford (Philadelphia: University of Pennsylvania Press, 2011), 1–13.

42 Interview 27; Interview 7.

43 Interview 9.

44 Interview 27.

45 Robert Harmsen, "The European Convention on Human Rights after Enlargement," *The International Journal of Human Rights* 5, no. 4 (2010): 33.

46 Interview 11.

47 Interview 13.

48 Ibid.

49 Interview 16.

from a Western European country explained the essentiality of positive obligations as follows:

> Again, this is a process of evolution. You must also, however, remember that the early and mid-1990s saw the Convention being signed by many Central and East European countries which had previously been within the Soviet Bloc. The Court was suddenly faced with several countries which, even if they had abandoned torture or inhuman or degrading treatment as a direct tool, still had a deficient legal and administrative system which did not enable the proper investigation of instances of inhuman or degrading treatment, or where such treatment was endemic in certain institutions like asylums and care homes. This, if not solidified, must certainly have precipitated the development of positive obligations in this field.[50]

In a similar vein, another judge confirmed that the Court launched positive obligations in response to pervasive problems such as appalling conditions at detention centres, elderly care homes, or mental institutions in new member states.[51]

To better understand this exigency argument, let us examine the logic behind the creation of procedural obligations, which were discussed in Chapter 5. According to my interlocutors, procedural obligations are necessary to hold domestic authorities fully accountable and to teach the importance of due diligence. Procedural obligations help address evidentiary problems embedded in the majority of the complaints brought under Article 3. Since the Court does not carry out its own investigations and must rely on the findings presented by the parties involved, any procedural deficiency could have a serious consequence.[52] As one judge told me, it is an arduous effort to prove whether substantive violations indeed took place.[53] When the responding states fail to supply the Court with relevant medical reports, detention records, or any other documents that could be relied upon as proof, the victims cannot substantiate their claims.[54] This puts the victims at a disadvantage and prevents the Court from arriving at a conclusion with certainty. States' failures to help the Court establish facts do a disservice to the victims. Therefore, by invoking procedural obligations, the Court may at least find violations for not duly investigating or not providing effective remedies.

[50] Interview 10.
[51] Interview 11.
[52] Interview 15.
[53] Interview 12.
[54] Ibid.

A look at the jurisprudence also shows that this development was directly informed by emerging social needs in European societies, especially in the aftermath of Eastward expansion. My analysis of the case law reveals that the majority of the violation rulings concern countries such as Turkey and Russia – where the Court had already identified the lack of effective investigation as a systematic problem in its previous case law.[55] This list includes several formerly communist Eastern European countries such as Ukraine, Romania, Bulgaria, and Moldova, where domestic legal and administrative systems have clear deficiencies that prevent proper investigations, as one judge underlined.[56]

The Court was not alone in promoting procedural obligations and due diligence. Political bodies of the Council of Europe aided the Court in this mission. The Parliamentary Assembly of the Council of Europe expressed its support by commending the Court "for the extensive case law it has developed on impunity, in particular by imposing on member states the positive obligation to investigate serious human rights violations and to hold their perpetrators to account."[57] Similarly, the Committee of Ministers highlighted the importance of following procedural steps to fully realise the obligations deriving from the Convention. The Committee emphasised that the obligation to implement judgments may go beyond simply paying compensation to the victims (just satisfaction). It may also require "in exceptional circumstances the re-examination of a case or a reopening of proceedings."[58]

Moreover, the Committee relied on the Court's case law when defining the duty to investigate in its *Guidelines on Eradicating Impunity for Serious Human Rights Violations*. According to these guidelines, "States are under a procedural obligation arising under Article 3 of the Convention to carry out an effective investigation into credible claims that a person has been seriously ill-treated, or when the authorities have reasonable grounds to suspect that such treatment has occurred."[59] It is not insignificant

55 Interview 20.

56 Interview 10.

57 Parliamentary Assembly of the Council of Europe, State of Human Rights in Europe: The Need to Eradicate Impunity, *Resolution 1675(2009)*, available at http://assembly.coe.int/nw/xml/XRef/Xref-XML2HTML-EN.asp?fileid=17756&lang=en.

58 Committee of Ministers of the Council of Europe, on the Re-examination or Reopening of Certain Cases at Domestic Level Following Judgments of the European Court of Human Rights, *Recommendation No. R(2000)2* (January 19, 2000), available at https://search.coe.int/cm/Pages/result_details.aspx?ObjectID=09000016805e2f06

59 Committee of Ministers of the Council of Europe, Guidelines of the Committee of Ministers of the Council of Europe on Eradicating Impunity for Serious Human Rights

that both the Parliamentary Assembly and the Committee of Ministers encouraged the Court to develop positive obligations. The fact that they took up the promotion of positive obligations also attests to the claim that this was indeed in line with the emerging needs of European societies, also acknowledged by the political institutions of the Council of Europe.

III Legal Principles and Jurisprudence in Support of Positive Obligations

When introducing positive obligations, the Court did not need to put up too much of a fight. The ideational foundations of positive obligations were already established by voices within academia and the human rights community before the Court ventured into progressively introducing them under Article 3. Philosopher Henry Shue opposed the separation of negative and positive rights, arguing that the distinction between these two groups of rights is built upon false premises.[60] According to Shue, negative rights (rights to security) include a positive dimension, namely prevention.[61] Correspondingly, the fulfilment of positive rights (rights to subsistence) requires correlative duties, such as the full guarantee of security.[62] Similarly, Philip Alston and Gerard Quinn dispute this dichotomy by arguing that some civil and political rights, such as the right to a fair trial, cannot be realised without state involvement.[63]

This idea reverberated within the UN, too. Asbjorn Eide, the former Special Rapporteur on the Right to Adequate Food as a Human Right, fleshed out the connection between negative and positive obligations. He introduced a tripartite typology to categorise obligations in his 1987 *Right to Food as a Human Right* report, which included obligations to respect, protect, and fulfil.[64] Eide's typology intended to abolish the dichotomy of positive and negative rights, and show that the protection of rights

Violations, *CM/Del/Dec(2011)1110/4.8-app5/* (March 30, 2011), available at https://search.coe.int/cm/Pages/result_details.aspx?ObjectId=09000016805cd111

60 Henry Shue, *Basic Rights: Subsistence, Affluence, and U.S. Foreign Policy* (Princeton: Princeton University Press, 1st edition, 1980, 2nd edition, 1996).

61 Shue, 39.

62 Ibid., 37.

63 Philip Alston and Gerard Quinn, "The Nature and Scope of States Parties' Obligations under the International Covenant on Economic, Social and Cultural Rights," *Human Rights Quarterly* 9, no. 2 (1987): 184.

64 Ida Elisabeth Koch, *Human Rights as Indivisible Rights: The Protection of Socio-Economic Demands under the European Convention on Human Rights* (Leiden and Boston: Martinus Nijhoff Publishers, 2009), 14.

requires not only noninterference but also specific measures designed to ensure rights' complete fulfilment. This idea was also invoked in several UN instruments. For example, Article 2 of the Convention against Torture (CAT), which entered into force in 1987, obliged each state party "to take effective legislative, administrative, judicial or other measures to prevent acts of torture in any territory under its jurisdiction."[65] Similarly, the Human Rights Committee's General Comment No 31, adopted in 2004, stated that refraining from violating rights is not sufficient.[66] States must also protect individuals from acts perpetrated by private persons or entities. Finally, the UN General Assembly underlined the need for state obligations to respect and "take appropriate legislative and administrative and other appropriate measures to prevent violations" in Resolution 60/147 – *Basic Principles and Guidelines on the Rights to a Remedy and Reparations for Victims of Gross Violations.*[67]

Other international tribunals and legal instruments also played their part in acknowledging and promoting positive obligations. The UN Human Rights Committee was the first judicial body to refer to states' obligation to investigate in *Bleier* v. *Uruguay* in 1982.[68] The Committee said, "the State party has the duty to investigate in good faith all allegations of violation of the Covenant made against it and its authorities."[69] Six years later, the Inter-American Court of Human Rights issued the *Velasquez Rodriguez* ruling, highlighting state obligations to "prevent, investigate, and punish any violation of the rights recognised by the convention."[70] Thus, in its first-ever judgment, the Inter-American Court of Human Rights lodged the duty to investigate and inform the family of disappeared persons.

Traces of the main logic behind positive obligations, and the duty to investigate in particular, can also be found in Article 12 of the CAT and in 1992 General Comment 20 on Article 7. Article 12 obliges each state party to "ensure that its competent authorities proceed to a prompt and

[65] UN General Assembly, *Convention against Torture and Other Cruel, Inhuman or Degrading Treatment or Punishment*, 10 December 1984, United Nations, Treaty Series, vol. 1465, p. 85.

[66] UN Human Rights Committee (HRC), "General Comment No. 31 [80], The Nature of the General Legal Obligation Imposed on States Parties to the Covenant," CCPR/C/21/Rev.1/Add.13 § (2004).

[67] UN General Assembly, "Basic Principles and Guidelines on the Right to a Remedy and Reparation for Victims of Gross Violations of International Human Rights Law and Serious Violations of International Humanitarian Law," Resolution 60/147 (2005).

[68] *Bleier* v. *Uruguay*, Communication No. R. 7/30 (March 29, 1982).

[69] Ibid., §13,3.

[70] *Velasquez Rodriguez*, Judgment of July 29, 1988, IACtHR (Ser. C) No. 4 (1988), § 166.

impartial investigation, wherever there is reasonable ground to believe that an act of torture has been committed in any territory under its jurisdiction."[71] General Comment 20 states, "Article 7 should be read in conjunction with article 2, paragraph 3, of the Covenant. (…) Complaints must be investigated promptly and impartially by competent authorities so as to make the remedy effective."[72] Hence, when the Court began systematically prescribing positive obligations, the idea did not sound alien or out of the ordinary. Positive obligations were quickly internalised, and their recent addition to the European human rights system went almost unnoticed.[73] The African Commission followed suit and recognised positive obligations in the *Ogoniland Case* in 2001.[74]

The existing legal principles concerning positive obligations also prepared the grounds for the *Opuz* v. *Turkey* judgment, where the Court found Turkey in violation of Article 3 for not taking the necessary steps to protect Nahide from domestic violence.[75] The Court specifically referred to the Convention on the Elimination of All Forms of Discrimination against Women (CEDAW) and the CEDAW Committee's General Recommendation no. 19, which prohibits gender-based violence. In addition, the Court invoked the relevant jurisprudence of the CEDAW Committee as well as the Inter-American Court and Commission. The Court then turned to the UN General Assembly Declaration on the Elimination of Violence against Women (1993). Invoking this declaration, the Court expressed that states have an obligation to "exercise due diligence to prevent, investigate, and…punish acts of violence against women, whether those acts are perpetrated by the State or private persons."[76]

Finally, the Court cited the Committee of Ministers' 2002 Recommendation.[77] This recommendation requires the Council of Europe

[71] UN General Assembly, *Convention against Torture.*

[72] UN Human Rights Committee (HRC), *CCPR General Comment No. 20: Article 7 (Prohibition of Torture, or Other Cruel, Inhuman or Degrading Treatment or Punishment)*, March 10, 1992.

[73] Interview 16.

[74] *Social and Economic Rights Action Center (SERAC) and Center for Economic and Social Rights (CESR)* v. *Nigeria*, communication no. 155/96, African Commission on Human and People's Rights (May 27, 2002).

[75] *Opuz* v. *Turkey*, § 72–91.

[76] Ibid., § 76–79.

[77] Committee of Ministers of the Council of Europe, *Recommendation Rec(2002)5* (April 30, 2002).

member states to "classify all forms of violence within the family as criminal offences and envisage the possibility of taking measures in order, *inter alia*, to enable the judiciary to adopt interim measures aimed at protecting victims, to ban the perpetrator from contacting, communicating with or approaching the victim, or residing in or entering defined areas."[78] Building upon this strong international legal framework, the Court found the Turkish government's unwillingness or inability to protect Nahide to be a violation of Article 3. In so doing, the Court brought victims of domestic violence in Europe under the protection of the prohibition of torture.

As we see in Nahide's case, an ample supply of legal principles and precedents existed prior to and during the time when the Court acknowledged various positive obligations under Article 3. This arguably facilitated the process and granted the Court legitimacy to launch such a foundational change. In this regard, one judge spoke to me about the importance of the CAT in propelling the Court's progressive interpretation.[79] Another judge said: "I have no doubt that the European Convention for the Prevention of Torture and Inhuman or Degrading Treatment or Punishment, and the Committee for the Prevention of Torture (CPT) (….) were important catalysts in this delicate process of norm evolution."[80] They added that the Court often relies on the CPT's reports as evidence.[81] A former judge confirmed this and maintained that the CPT reports make up for the Court's inability to carry out fact-finding.[82] Another judge divulged that if the CPT and other UN mechanisms had not ventured into new fields, judges would not be aware of the existence of new developments.[83]

Similarly, a judge from Western Europe underscored the importance of hard and soft law materials regarding the prohibition of torture and ill-treatment. They explained that "European prison rules, first introduced in the 1990s and renewed in 2007, for example, had an impact on the way such things are viewed."[84] They emphasised that "the Minimum Standards of the Treatment of Prisoners were introduced" in this period too.[85] They then ventured into arguing that "in the 1990s, a lot of these materials were created

[78] *Opuz* v. *Turkey*, § 82.
[79] Interview 1.
[80] Interview 10
[81] Ibid.
[82] Interview 16.
[83] Interview 11.
[84] Interview 15.
[85] Ibid.

and discussed, and this had an impact on the interpretation. We have an interpretative rule that says that we have to interpret the Convention in harmony with the international trends."[86] In their view, these instruments were decisive in changing the way the norm against torture and inhuman or degrading treatment was understood in the 1990s.

IV Active Promotion by Civil Society Groups

In the late 1990s and 2000s, civil society organizations operating in Europe used strategic litigation to bring various issues to light.[87] This list includes gross human rights violations perpetrated during counterterrorism operations in the southeast of Turkey and in Chechnya, or racial discrimination against the Roma in Central and Eastern Europe.[88] Civil society participation has been extremely important in highlighting large-scale and concealed violations that take place with impunity.[89] Different civil society groups have been actively involved in court proceedings by providing legal representation and advice to the individual applicants, or by submitting *amicus curiae* briefs. Interights, Amnesty International, the Open Society Justice Initiative (OSJI), the European Roma Rights Center (ERRC), and the Kurdish Human Rights Project (KHRP) played a particularly prominent role in drawing public attention to Article 3 violations.

In addition to addressing such urgent questions, several of these organizations have slowly worked on bringing out positive obligations and developing legal standards around them. Believing that rights cannot be fully realised without positive obligations, they have pushed for the adoption of positive obligations from different angles.[90] For example, the Geneva-based Association for the Prevention of Torture (APT) has been active in preserving already established international standards and advocated preventive measures.[91] Interights, a defunct London-based NGO, had been an adamant supporter of preventing violence against women, believing that "rights that are implemented best are the rights for men."[92] In

[86] Ibid.

[87] Laura Van den Eynde, "An Empirical Look at the Amicus Curiae Practice of Human Rights NGOs before the European Court of Human Rights," *Netherlands Quarterly of Human Rights* 31, no. 3 (2013): 279–80.

[88] Interview 16; Interview 34; Interview 35; Interview 36.

[89] Loveday Hodson, *NGOs and the Struggle for Human Rights in Europe* (Oxford and Portland: Hart Publishing, 2011), 8.

[90] Interview 27; Interview 28; Interview 31; Interview 32.

[91] Interview 31.

[92] Interview 27.

order to realise this objective, Interights submitted third-party observations in support of Nahide's claims and called for providing legal protection for vulnerable groups such as domestic violence or rape victims in *Opuz v. Turkey*. Meanwhile, the OSJI has worked to alleviate the treatment of Roma people in Central and Eastern Europe. They highlighted the need for measures to eradicate systemic discrimination and extensive remedies for the victims.[93] Redress and Liberty have focused on a large selection of issues, including anti-terror legislation, excessive use of force, violence against women and the LGBT community, and the development of rules in custodial settings.[94]

These organizations have benefited from three working methods: specialization, transfer of issue area expertise, and utilization of standards developed in other legal regimes (cross-fertilization). They have developed thematic or country-based specializations over the years, which made them more attuned to the deterioration of international standards or human rights situations in domestic contexts. For example, Interights would be the leading organization dedicated to ending violence against women, whereas the OSJI would pay closer attention to discrimination, and Amnesty International would follow up on the cases of enforced disappearances or grave human rights violations.[95]

Transfer of expertise was another asset that helped civil society organizations increase the collective impact of their work. By transferring their expertise and skills to another issue or region, they have readily developed working strategies to address human rights violations. For example, European human rights groups first developed their expertise in the systemic mistreatment of communities throughout "the Troubles in Northern Ireland" in the 1970s. Then, this expertise was transferred to cases about the Kurdish conflict in Turkey and the Chechen conflict in Russia, as human rights lawyers who had worked for these causes disclosed in interviews with me.[96] The lawyers who represented the Northern Irish cases also offered advice to Kurdish and Chechen victims. They became part of the same litigation network, either providing legal representation to the victims or training local lawyers.

Finally, to bolster their arguments, civil society organizations have often relied upon existing principles in other treaties or standards

[93] Interview 28.
[94] Interview 32.
[95] Interview 26; Interview 27; Interview 28.
[96] Interview 34; Interview 35; Interview 36.

developed domestically or internationally.[97] This is a strategy intended to legitimise their arguments and to enlighten the Court about principles that might be of assistance when interpreting a provision. This leads to another unexpected but welcome outcome. When such organizations refer to the existing or emergent principles or standards developed by the jurisprudence of other courts, it helps disseminate those principles across different legal regimes. Cross-referencing human rights jurisprudence harmonises international standards and strengthens human rights protections across the board.[98] In this regard, civil society organizations act as pollinating bees that help diffuse legal principles.

Kurt v. *Turkey* – where the Court first acknowledged states' positive obligation toward the relatives of disappeared persons – illustrates how these key working methods helped them promote positive obligations. Koçeri Kurt, the victim's mother, brought the complaint, alleging that state authorities had been implicated in her son's disappearance.[99] It might be unusual to hear that such a complaint would fall under Article 3. It might sound even more unusual to extend the victimhood status to the relatives of a disappeared person under this prohibition.

However, this was the way the Inter-American Court of Human Rights and the UN Human Rights Committee approached enforced disappearance cases prior to *Kurt*. For example, in *Velasquez Rodriguez* v. *Honduras*, which concerned a large number of disappearances in Honduras in the early 1980s, the Inter-American Court underscored the need for an "effective search for the truth by the government."[100] Later on, in the case of *Bamaca Velasquez* v. *Guatemala*, the Inter-American Court established that the victim and his relatives had a right to obtain information about "the violations and the corresponding responsibilities from the competent state organs," and that states have a duty to investigate and prosecute.[101] The UN Human Rights Committee applied a similar logic in the *Mariam, Philippe, Auguste and Thomas Sankara* v. *Burkina-Faso* – a case about Thomas Sankara, the assassinated President of Burkina Faso. Sankara's wife brought the case before the Committee. The case concerned the events that took place during the 1987 *coup d'état* in Ouagadougou. The Committee concluded that "the family of a man killed in disputed

[97] Interview 31; Interview 32; Interview 33.

[98] Ezgi Yildiz et al., "New Norms in Old Regimes: Judicial Strategies for Importing Environmental Norms," *Unpublished Manuscript*, 2022.

[99] *Kurt* v. *Turkey*, § 14–18.

[100] *Velasquez Rodriguez* v. *Honduras*, § 177.

[101] *Bamaca Velasquez* v. *Guatemala*, Ser. C No. 91, IACtHR (2002) § 75.

circumstances have suffered and continue to suffer because they still do not know the circumstances surrounding the death of Thomas Sankara or the precise location where his remains were officially buried. Thomas Sankara's family has the right to know the circumstances of his death."[102]

Relying on this jurisprudence, Koçeri Kurt lodged her complaint before the European Court. She was represented by Françoise Hampson and Aisling Reidy, lawyers affiliated with the Kurdish Human Rights Project (KHRP) – a London-based NGO that engaged in strategic litigation to highlight human rights violations in the Kurdish conflict in the 1990s and early 2000s. The KHRP was established by Kerim Yıldız,[103] who is a lawyer of Kurdish origins. He had the idea of establishing the KHRP when he was a student at the University of Essex, and he shared this idea with his professor Kevin Boyle, who was a Northern-Irish human rights activist and a barrister. With the support of the late Boyle, the KHRP was established and came into the network of professors and activist lawyers working in Essex and London. Yıldız then connected the KHRP with the Diyarbakir Human Rights Association (DHRA), a local NGO based in the primarily Kurdish-populated city of Diyarbakır. The DHRA would help this network by not only monitoring human rights violations in the region but also by referring select exemplary cases to the KHRP.[104]

The Essex-KHRP-DHRA triangle acted as a strategic litigation network.[105] They used the Court as a forum to raise awareness about the gross violations committed by the Turkish government during counter-terrorism operations in the southeast of Turkey. The network had local and international partners. The DHRA (a domestic NGO) cooperated with the KHRP (a London-based NGO) and a network of activist lawyers in Essex and London. This triangle ceased to exist when the KHRP was closed. However, some of the lawyers and academics working for the KHRP established the European Human Rights Advocacy Centre (EHRAC), based at Middlesex University in London. The EHRAC began working in partnership with Memorial, an NGO based in Moscow. The EHRAC-Memorial partnership focused on bringing cases against Russia

[102] *Mariam, Philippe, Auguste and Thomas Sankara* v. *Burkina-Faso*, communication no. 1159/2003, U.N. Doc. CCPR/C/86/D/1159/2003 (2006) §12.2

[103] Not related to the author of this book.

[104] Interview 35.

[105] This strategic litigation network carried the characteristics of activist networks that Margaret E. Keck and Kathryn Sikkink describe in their seminal work. Margaret E. Keck and Kathryn Sikkink, *Activists Beyond Borders: Advocacy Networks in International Politics* (Ithaca and London: Cornell University Press, 1998).

and advocating for the implementation of court decisions. The EHRAC also assisted lawyers in Russia, particularly in the South Caucasus, and concentrated its efforts on strengthening the capacity of local NGOs.[106]

The Essex-KHRP-DHRA triangle – a network specialised in flagging the systematic violations committed against the Kurdish population in Turkey – helped Koçeri Kurt successfully present her complaint before the European human rights system. The case was brought before the Commission by Professors Kevin Boyle and Françoise Hampson in 1994 and then referred to the Court in 1997.[107] This time, Professor Françoise Hampson, Aisling Reidy, Osman Baydemir, and Kerim Yıldız represented Koçeri Kurt. When preparing this case, the legal counsel relied on legal principles developed in the context of similar gross human violations in Latin America. In particular, they urged the Court to consider this matter in line with the jurisprudence of the Inter-American Court and the UN Human Rights Committee and to recognise Koçeri Kurt's own victimhood under Article 3.[108] They argued that "the next-of-kin of disappeared persons must also be considered victims of, *inter alia*, ill-treatment."[109] State authorities had been responsible for her son's disappearance, which caused her extreme suffering. State authorities' failure to investigate her allegations and provide her with reliable information exacerbated her distress and anguish. Thus, the government was directly responsible for not only her son's disappearance but also for the suffering she endured as a result.[110]

Upon reviewing the case, the Court could not find evidence to rule that the applicant's son had been a victim of ill-treatment.[111] It could establish, however, that the authorities had failed to conduct an effective investigation and provide the necessary information regarding the circumstances surrounding her son's disappearance.[112] More importantly, the Court found the applicant to be "the mother of the victim of a human rights violation and herself the victim of the authorities' complacency in the face

[106] For more, see European Human Rights Advocacy Center (EHRAC) www.mdx.ac.uk/our-research/centres/ehrac. Similarly, the Russian Justice Initiative, registered as an NGO in Utrecht, cooperated with the Nazran-based organization Pravovaia Initsiativa and the Moscow-based Legal Assistance-Astreya to bring cases concerning violations in the North Caucasus.

[107] *Koçeri Kurt* v. *Turkey*, application no. 24276/94, European Commission of Human Rights (December 5, 1996), §2.

[108] *Kurt* v. *Turkey*, § 84.

[109] Ibid., §130.

[110] Ibid.

[111] Ibid., §107–116.

[112] Ibid., §133–34.

of her anguish and distress."[113] Thereby, the Court determined that states have a positive obligation to inform the relatives of disappeared persons, which was first introduced by the Inter-American Court – a development dubbed as "Latin-Americanization of the European system."[114]

Transnational human rights groups had an important role in establishing this obligation and in documenting Koçeri Kurt's victimhood. The KHRP legally represented the applicant, and the DHRA provided her with the initial help and (possibly) referred her case to the KHRP.[115] When the national authorities dismissed her requests for further information regarding the detention of her son, she sought help at the DHRA, where she submitted a statement explaining the circumstances surrounding her son's disappearance.[116] This statement was later presented before the Commission as evidence.[117] The Commission found that the statement, which the DHRA provided, had evidentiary value and used it to corroborate the applicant's testimony.[118] Finally, Amnesty International submitted an *amicus curiae* brief and furnished the Court with further observations in relation to the existing legal principles concerning enforced disappearances.[119]

The *Kurt* ruling generated a momentous change: introducing states' obligation to duly investigate and inform the relatives of victims. More importantly, it extended the victim status to the relatives of the disappeared persons.[120] This ruling opened the door for other victims like Koçeri Kurt, who could seek remedies for the suffering they endure due to the disappearance of their family members.

This precedent also helped activists bring complaints over the European governments' involvement with the CIA's extraordinary rendition operations. The first of these was *El-Masri* v. *The Former Yugoslav Republic of Macedonia*.[121] Khaled El-Masri's rendition story was an illustration of one

[113] Ibid., §134.
[114] Christina M. Cerna, "The Inter-American System for the Protection of Human Rights," *Florida Journal of International Law* 16, no. 1 (2004): 202.
[115] Interview 34; Interview 35; Interview 36.
[116] *Kurt* v. *Turkey*, §17.
[117] Ibid., §34.
[118] Ibid., §50.
[119] Ibid., §71.
[120] Interview 16. The Court would limit this status only to close family members in subsequent case law. See, for example, *Çakıcı* v. *Turkey*, application no. 23657/94, ECHR [GC] (July 8, 1999).
[121] *El-Masri* v. *The Former Yugoslav Republic of Macedonia*, application no. 39630/09, ECHR [GC] (December 13, 2012).

of the darkest War on Terror practices. He was kidnapped in Macedonia, where he was held incommunicado and ill-treated, then handed over to the CIA agents who transferred him to a secret detention facility in Afghanistan, where he was tortured. He spent more than four months in a small cell, not knowing where he was and what his fate would be, until they released him somewhere near the Albanian border. El-Masri's case, which was represented by lawyers affiliated with the OSJI, immediately became high-profile.[122] The UN Office of the High Commissioner for Human Rights (OHCHR), Interights, Redress, the International Commission of Jurists, and Amnesty International all intervened in the written procedure as third parties.[123] They advocated for the society's right to know the truth about secret detention and rendition program, by relying on the principle set in *Kurt* v. *Turkey*.[124] These appeals clearly resonated with the reformed Court, which then argued that the case was highly significant "not only for the applicant and his family but also for other victims of similar crimes and the general public, who had the right to know what had happened."[125]

Let us remember that this major legal victory was only possible due to a collaborative international effort that we first saw in *Kurt* and then in *El-Masri*.[126] Several specialised civil society organizations brought together their expertise and invoked existing and emerging legal principles. This strategy was replicated in various other cases. For example, in *Assenov and Others*, the European Roma Rights Center and Amnesty International called for the Court's acknowledgment of procedural obligations.[127] Interights intervened in *M. C.* v. *Bulgaria* to highlight states' obligation to provide legal protection to rape victims.[128] In each case, careful arguments were made so that the Court would have a chance to develop positive obligations and bring new groups of victims under the protection of Article 3. Civil society organizations' increased participation

[122] Ibid., §2.
[123] Ibid., §10.
[124] Ibid., §179.
[125] Ibid., §191.
[126] The *El-Masri* decision strikes a different tone than *Kurt* v. *Turkey*, as it has a much broader application and scope. It concerns not only the relatives of the disappeared persons but also society at large. In so doing, it effectively extends the application of the principle set in *Kurt* and refines its morphology. Yet, it was the *Kurt* ruling that changed the existing paradigms by making it possible to bring a claim on behalf of the relatives of disappeared persons in the first place.
[127] *Assenov and Others* v. *Bulgaria*, application no. 90/1997/874/1086, ECHR (October 28, 1998).
[128] *M.C.* v. *Bulgaria*, application no. 39272/98, ECHR (December 4, 2003).

not only provided hope for victims like Koçeri Kurt and Khaled El-Masri, but also helped normalise the sudden appearance of positive obligations in international jurisprudence.

Conclusion

This chapter has explained why the norm against torture and inhuman and degrading treatment dramatically expanded in the period after 1998. Relying on the framework of analysis explained in the Introduction and Chapter 1, it has assessed the conditions that made the Court audacious enough to effectuate these resource-intensive obligations. First, the new Court, as a full-time court with compulsory jurisdiction, came to enjoy a wide discretionary space. This attribute conferred it with more judicial courage to issue audacious rulings across the board and recognise a range of important positive obligations under Article 3. Second, there was a growing need for positive obligations in European societies, especially in the aftermath of the Eastward enlargement. Positive obligations were necessary for both the Western and Eastern European countries alike. They served a supplementary role for rights protection in Western Europe and played a crucial role in inducting Eastern European countries into a rule of law tradition. Last but not least, creating positive obligations was less likely to raise eyebrows because they were already established in the jurisprudence of other courts and were actively promoted by civil society groups.

7

Legal Change in Times of Backlash

Standards change over time, and the manner in which they change may take many forms. International courts play an important role in transforming norms, as I have argued in this book. They are ideally placed to refashion existing norms, adapting them to changing times and societal needs. I have shown how this change process takes place within the European human rights system. In particular, I have demonstrated how the European Court refined the norm against torture and inhuman or degrading treatment over a period of nearly five decades. My analysis of the norm's transformation in the late 1990s might leave the reader with the impression that change is only about progressive norm expansion. Yet, this book is not meant to be solely about progress or about the 1990s. Rather, my approach is meant to capture the conditions under which the Court is likely to be audacious while also telling us why progressive change is hindered – or even reversed – when these conditions change and forbearance prevails.

Forces of progressive and regressive legal change are two sides of the same coin. The dramatic progress of the 1990s was followed by stagnation and removal of certain protections, as we will see in this chapter. Member states' negative feedback was an important factor in this not-so-subtle shift. Unlike the new Court, the reformed Court's lifetime has been dominated by reform talks and widespread negative feedback. Drawing from the framework presented in the Introduction and further explained in Chapter 1, I argue that this atmosphere has contributed to the selective forbearance we observe at the reformed Court today.

Brief History of the Reform Process

In 2010, the Council of Europe kicked off a series of High-Level Conferences to discuss how to restructure the European human rights regime and address the Court's growing caseload problem. These meetings were organised at the initiative of the Swiss, Turkish, British, Belgian, and Danish Chairmanships of the Council of Europe. These governments not only spearheaded the conversations around reforming the Court, but also provided draft declarations and shaped the substantive contents to be discussed. Indeed, these reform proposals reflected these governments' visions for the Court.

The first of these, the 2010 Interlaken Declaration, identified the Court's backlog and unenforced judgments as threats to the European human rights regime's efficiency.[1] The İzmir Declaration, issued the following year, highlighted that national authorities should take on larger responsibilities to protect rights at the national level – also known as the subsidiarity principle.[2] The idea behind this suggestion was that ensuring rights protection at the national level would prevent the Court from being overwhelmed with applications. This message was repeated in the Brighton Declaration in 2012. The member states invited the Court "to give great prominence" to the principles of subsidiarity and margin of appreciation and to apply them consistently.[3] Similarly, the 2015 Brussels Declaration "invite[d] the Court to remain vigilant in upholding the States Parties' margin of appreciation,"[4] while the 2018 Copenhagen Declaration emphasised that national authorities have a larger role in protecting rights, introducing preventive measures, and providing effective remedies.[5]

In order to understand the collective message channeled through these declarations, let us briefly revisit what the principle of subsidiarity and the margin of appreciation doctrine mean. These two concepts, both developed by the Court itself, are directly related to the extent of the Court's power over domestic authorities.[6] The principle of subsidiarity means that national authorities have a greater responsibility in safeguarding rights

1 High-Level Conference on the Future of the European Court of Human Rights, "Interlaken Declaration" (2010), www.echr.coe.int/Documents/2010_Interlaken_FinalDeclaration_ENG.pdf.

2 High-Level Conference on the Future of the European Court of Human Rights, "Izmir Declaration" (2011), www.echr.coe.int/Documents/2011_Izmir_FinalDeclaration_ENG.pdf.

3 High-Level Conference on the Future of the European Court of Human Rights, "Brighton Declaration" (April 19–20, 2012), www.echr.coe.int/Documents/Brussels_Declaration_ENG.pdf.

4 High-Level Conference on the Future of the European Court of Human Rights, "Brussels Declaration" (2015), www.echr.coe.int/Documents/Brussels_Declaration_ENG.pdf.

5 High-Level Conference on the Future of the European Court of Human Rights, "Copenhagen Declaration" (2018), www.echr.coe.int/Documents/Copenhagen_Declaration_ENG.pdf.

6 For more, see Andreas Føllesdal, "Subsidiarity and International Human-Rights Courts: Respecting Self-Governance and Protecting Human Rights – Or Neither?," *Law and Contemporary Problems* 79, no. 2 (2016): 147–63.

and offering remedies,[7] with the European Court's role seen as supplementary and limited to providing supranational review.[8] Similarly, the margin of appreciation doctrine grants national authorities the discretion to identify appropriate measures necessary to address and remedy violations.[9] Like the subsidiarity principle, it views the European Court's role as auxiliary and allows states leeway when it comes to fulfilling their obligations under the Convention.

While all of the declarations requested "enhanced subsidiarity" – whereby the primacy of the domestic authorities' role is re-emphasised – the Brighton and Copenhagen Declarations, in particular, ventured into prescribing how the Court should operate.[10] In this regard, these two declarations reflected the discontent of the United Kingdom and Denmark, the organisers of the High-level Conferences in Brighton and Copenhagen.[11] The United Kingdom's reform vision carried a strong anti-immigration flavour. David Cameron, the then Prime Minister, announced the news of the reform at the Parliamentary Assembly of the Council of Europe by stating, "the time is right to ask some serious questions about how the Court is working." He then added that the Court should not "see itself as an immigration tribunal … [and] undermine its own reputation by going over national decisions where it does not need to."[12] The Danish

[7] The Court described the nature of this principle in the *Belgian Linguistic* case as follows: "[The Court] cannot assume the role of the competent national authorities, for it would thereby lose sight of the subsidiary nature of the international machinery of collective enforcement established by the Convention. The national authorities remain free to choose the measures which they consider appropriate in those matters which are governed by the Convention. Review by the Court concerns only the conformity of these measures with the Convention." *Belgian Linguistic Case*, application no. 1474/62;1677/62; 1691/62; 1769/63; 1994/63; 2126/64, ECHR (July 23, 1968), §10.

[8] Laurence R. Helfer, "Redesigning the European Court of Human Rights: Embeddedness as a Deep Structural Principle of the European Human Rights Regime," *European Journal of International Law* 19, no. 1 (2008): 128.

[9] Philip Leach, *Taking a Case to the European Court of Human Rights*, New Edition, 4th edition (Oxford and New York: Oxford University Press, 2017), 161–62 at 5.11.

[10] Helen Fenwick, "Enhanced Subsidiarity and a Dialogic Approach – Or Appeasement in Recent Cases on Criminal Justice, Public Order and Counter-Terrorism at Strasbourg against the UK?," in *The UK and European Human Rights: A Strained Relationship?*, ed. Katja S. Ziegler, Elizabeth Wicks, and Loveday Hodson (Oxford and Portland: Bloomsbury Publishing, 2015), 196.

[11] Lize R. Glas, "From Interlaken to Copenhagen: What Has Become of the Proposals Aiming to Reform the Functioning of the European Court of Human Rights?," *Human Rights Law Review* 20, no. 1 (2020): 121–51.

[12] David Cameron, Speech on the European Court of Human Rights. Parliamentary Assembly of the Council of Europe (January 25, 2012), available at www.gov.uk/government/speeches/speech-on-the-european-court-of-human-rights.

government shared similar concerns about immigration and deportation cases. Lars Løkke Rasmussen, then the Danish Prime Minister, stated that "In Denmark… we have a critical debate about the expansive interpretation by the European Court of Human Rights, in particular on the question of the deportation of foreign criminals. It does not resonate with the general public understanding of human rights when hardcore criminals cannot be deported."[13] As Mikael Madsen establishes in his study, Danish criticism was mostly for domestic consumption and driven by the right-wing Danish government in power at the time.[14]

Such sentiments were by no means only shared by the governments of the United Kingdom and Denmark. They also widely resonated in Switzerland, Italy, and Russia, for example. The Swiss People's Party (a right-wing populist party that received the most votes in the 2019 federal election) depicts the Court as a threat to the Swiss legal order.[15] This harsh reaction is fueled by the party's fear of a Court ruling against some of its popular initiatives, such as banning the construction of minarets and deporting criminals.[16] The party attempted to bypass the Court by putting forward a proposal that would put domestic law above International Law. Despite their efforts, this initiative was ultimately rejected by the Swiss people on November 25, 2018.[17] The Italian Constitutional Court, on the other hand, declared in a 2015 ruling that the Italian Constitution is "axiologically dominant" over the European Convention and that domestic judges should favour an interpretation that is compatible with the Italian Constitution.[18]

13 Jacques Hartmann, "A Danish Crusade for the Reform of the European Court of Human Rights," *EJIL: Talk!* (blog), November 14, 2017, www.ejiltalk.org/a-danish-crusade-for-the-reform-of-the-european-court-of-human-rights/.

14 Mikael Rask Madsen, "Two-Level Politics and the Backlash against International Courts: Evidence from the Politicisation of the European Court of Human Rights," *The British Journal of Politics and International Relations* 22, no. 4 (2020): 729.

15 Tilmann Altwicker, "Switzerland: The Substitute Constitution in Times of Popular Dissent," in *Criticism of the European Court of Human Rights: Shifting the Convention System: Counter-Dynamics at the National and EU Level*, ed. Patricia Popelier, Koen Lemmens, and Sarah Lambrecht (Cambridge: Intersentia, 2016), 395, http://edoc.unibas.ch/43279/.

16 Ibid., 400.

17 John Revil, Swiss Reject Proposal to Put Domestic Law above International Rules. *Reuters* (November 25, 2018), available at www.reuters.com/article/us-swiss-treaties/swiss-reject-proposal-to-put-domestic-law-above-international-rules-idUSKCN1NU05T.

18 Sabato Raffaele, "Judicial Dialogue: The Experience of Italy," in *Judicial Dialogue and Human Rights*, ed. Amrei Müller and Hege Elisabeth Kjos (New York: Cambridge University Press, 2017), 275.

In a similar fashion, the Russian Constitutional Court successfully established the Russian Constitution's supremacy over the European Convention before Russia's recent expulsion from the Council of Europe. With a 2015 judgment, the Russian Constitutional Court granted itself the right to review whether the European Court judgments are aligned with the Russian Constitution.[19] This move was to counter what Russian President Putin viewed as the "politicization" of European Court rulings and the perceived discrimination against Russia.[20] Courtney Hillebrecht, who documents a series of strategies that Russia used to undermine the Court's authority, argues that this decision endowed "the Russian Constitutional Court and the Russian government with the ability to opt out of particular ECtHR decisions."[21]

These overlapping grievances expressed by the Court's long-time allies, such as the United Kingdom, Denmark, Switzerland, and Italy, as well as newcomers like Russia, shaped the discussions at the High-Level Conferences. The reform proposals expressed in these meetings showed that improving the Court's functions and addressing the case backlog were not member states' only concerns. In particular, the Brighton and Copenhagen Declarations articulated a renewed vision for the Court by emphasizing the principle of subsidiarity and the margin of appreciation doctrine. The draft versions of both of these declarations, which contained even more direct language on weakening the Court's autonomy and review powers, were leaked before their final versions.[22] The harsh tone in the leaked documents sent a strong signal and amplified the message that the Court should show deference to national authorities that are better placed to protect rights and offer remedies. This effectively implied that the Court should refrain from issuing rulings with wider policy implications, especially when it comes to politically salient issues,

[19] Aaron Matta and Armen Mazmanyan, "Russia: In Quest for a European Identity," in *Criticism of the European Court of Human Rights: Shifting the Convention System: Counter-Dynamics at the National and EU Level*, ed. Patricia Popelier, Sarah Lambrecht, and Koen Lemmens (Cambridge: Intersentia, 2016), 481.

[20] Ibid., 496. Political crises such as the war with Ukraine and Georgia and the annexation of Crimea led to a sour relationship between the Council of Europe members and the isolated Russia.

[21] Courtney Hillebrecht, *Saving the International Justice Regime: Beyond Backlash against International Courts* (Cambridge and New York: Cambridge University Press, 2021), 138.

[22] Laurence Helfer, "The Burdens and Benefits of Brighton," *ESIL Reflections* 1, no. 1 (2012): 1–6; Alice Donald and Philip Leach, "A Wolf in Sheep's Clothing: Why the Draft Copenhagen Declaration Must Be Rewritten," *EJIL: Talk!* (blog), February 21, 2018, www.ejiltalk.org/a-wolf-in-sheeps-clothing-why-the-draft-copenhagen-declaration-must-be-rewritten/.

such as the right of refugees, asylum seekers, or any other politically undesired groups.

Some scholars have interpreted member states' reliance on these two principles as an appeal to the Court to adopt a more conservative and state-friendly position.[23] The language used in these declarations certainly attests to that. For example, the Copenhagen Declaration clearly identifies the role of the Court as "provid[ing] a safeguard for violations that have not been remedied at national level and authoritatively interpret[ing] the Convention in accordance with relevant norms and principles of public international law, and, in particular, in the light of the Vienna Convention on the Law of Treaties (VCLT), giving appropriate consideration to present-day conditions."[24] It is rather telling that member states favour an interpretive method that has only a minor part in the Court's history,[25] instead of *the living instrument principle* developed by the Court itself in *Tyrer* v. *the United Kingdom.*[26] The living instrument principle, namely that rights should be interpreted in light of present-day conditions, is more readily associated with expansive interpretation. Despite sounding like a technical suggestion, this plea to be more loyal to the intentions of the drafters and the treaty text itself has sent strong signals to the Court and informed its interpretive preferences to a great extent, as I argue here.

In addition to the calls for forbearance made throughout the High-Level Conferences, most visibly in the Brighton and Copenhagen Declarations, various countries have criticised the Court over specific judgments that they deemed to be politically motivated. For example, the United Kingdom questioned the legitimacy of the European Court's judgments on prisoners' voting rights.[27] *Hirst (No.2)* v. *the United Kingdom* and *Greens and MT* v. *the United Kingdom* infuriated the government, particularly the then Prime Minister David Cameron.[28] The House of

[23] See for example, Oddný Mjöll Arnardóttir, "The Brighton Aftermath and the Changing Role of the European Court of Human Rights," *Journal of International Dispute Settlement* 9, no. 2 (2017), 3.

[24] High-Level Conference on the Future of the European Court of Human Rights, Copenhagen Declaration.

[25] George Letsas, "Strasbourg's Interpretive Ethic: Lessons for the International Lawyer," *European Journal of International Law* 21, no. 3 (2010): 513.

[26] *Tyrer* v. *the United Kingdom*, application no. 5856/72, ECHR (April 25, 1978).

[27] Kanstantsin Dzehtsiarou and Alan Greene, "Legitimacy and the Future of the European Court of Human Rights: Critical Perspectives from Academia and Practitioners," *German Law Journal*. 12, no. 10 (2011): 1710.

[28] Owen Bowcott, "Prisoners 'Damn Well Shouldn't' Be Able to Vote, Says David Cameron," *The Guardian*, December 13, 2013, available at: www.theguardian.com/politics/2013/dec/13/prisone Prisoners 'Damn Well Shouldn't' rs-right-to-vote-david-cameron.

Commons and the Supreme Court backed his position. While the House of Commons voted overwhelmingly in favour of keeping the blanket ban on February 10, 2011,[29] the Supreme Court passed a judgment on October 16, 2013, upholding the blanket ban on inmates' voting rights.[30] Similarly, the government of Russia vehemently objected to the *Yukos* judgment (*Oao Neftyanaya Kompaniya Yukos* v. *Russia*), in which the Court awarded Yukos (a Russian oil company) shareholders nearly 1.9 billion euros – the largest award in the Court's history.[31] The Constitutional Court of Russia defied this judgment, pronouncing: "Russia was not bound to enforce the ECtHR decision on the award of pecuniary compensation to the company's ex-shareholders, as it would violate the Constitution of the Russian Federation."[32] Last but not least, the government of Turkey challenged the Court's 2014 *Cyprus* v. *Turkey* ruling, where the Court ordered the Turkish government to pay 90 million euros to the government of Cyprus.[33] Ahmet Davutoğlu, then Foreign Minister of Turkey, firmly reported that "in terms of the grounds of this ruling, its method and the fact that it is considering a country that Turkey does not recognise as a counterparty, we see no necessity to make this payment."[34] Turkey has not paid the requested amount to this day, despite the reminders sent from the Committee of Ministers.[35]

[29] House of Commons, Hansard Debate, February 10, 2011, C. 502. The motion to keep the current ban was supported by 234 parliamentarians and opposed by 22.

[30] *R (on the application of Chester) (Appellant)* v. *Secretary of State for Justice (Respondent) and McGeoch (AP) (Appellant)* v. *The Lord President of the Council and another (Respondents) (Scotland)*, UKSC 63 (October 16, 2013).

[31] The exact amount is EUR 1,866,104,634. *Oao Neftyanaya Kompaniya Yukos* v. *Russia*, application no. 14902/04, ECHR (July 31, 2014).

[32] Iryna Marchuk and Marina Aksenova, "The Tale of Yukos and of the Russian Constitutional Court's Rebellion against the European Court of Human Right," *Osservatorio Costituzionale, Associazione Italiana Dei Costituzionalisti (AIC)*, 2017, 1–2. See also Marina Aksenova and Iryna Marchuk, "Reinventing or Rediscovering International Law? The Russian Constitutional Court's Uneasy Dialogue with the European Court of Human Rights," *International Journal of Constitutional Law* 16, no. 4 (2018): 1322–46.

[33] The ECtHR ordered Turkey to pay 30,000,000 euros to compensate for the non-pecuniary damage suffered by the relatives of the missing persons and 60,000,000 euros for the enclaved Greek-Cypriot residents of the Karpas peninsula. *Cyprus* v. *Turkey*, application no. 25781/94, ECHR[GC] (May 12, 2014).

[34] Tulay Karadeniz and Ece Toksabay, "Turkey to Ignore Court Order to Pay Compensation to Cyprus," *Reuters*, May 13, 2014, available at www.reuters.com/article/us-turkey-cyprus-davutoglu/turkey-to-ignore-court-order-to-pay-compensation-to-cyprus-idUSBREA4C0AX20140513.

[35] PACE Committee on Legal Affairs and Human Rights, The Implementation of the Judgments of the European Court of Human Rights, *Doc. 15123* (July 15, 2020), 18–19.

The Influence of the Reform Process on the Court

Various scholars explored the ways in which the Court has responded to this widespread negative feedback and political pushback, which only some identify as a full-blown backlash.[36] For example, Mikael Madsen observes a significant increase in the percentage of rulings that refer to subsidiarity or margin of appreciation in the period between 2005 and 2015.[37] Başak Çall focuses on the differential treatment in the case law and argues that the Court reserves stricter review for authoritarian and authoritarian-leaning states.[38] Similarly, Øyvind Stiansen and Erik Voeten find that the Court has increasingly shown greater deference to consolidated Western European democracies in its recent jurisprudence.[39]

Such a varied impact, or bifurcated approach, is to be expected.[40] As established in the literature, international courts are often financially and politically supported by Western states,[41] as is the case for the European Court.[42] Hence, the negative feedback from this support base is more likely to be taken into account by the Court.[43] However, as explained in

[36] For distinguishing backlash from political pushback see, Mikael Rask Madsen, Pola Cebulak, and Micha Wiebusch, "Backlash against International Courts: Explaining the Forms and Patterns of Resistance to International Courts," *International Journal of Law in Context* 14, no. 2 (2018): 197–220. For an argument that the recent reform process did not hamper the Court's authority, see Alec Stone Sweet, Wayne Sandholtz, and Mads Andenas, "The Failure to Destroy the Authority of the European Court of Human Rights: 2010–2018," *The Law and Practice of International Courts and Tribunals* 21, no. 2 (2022): 244–77.

[37] Mikael Rask Madsen, "Rebalancing European Human Rights: Has the Brighton Declaration Engendered a New Deal on Human Rights in Europe?," *Journal of International Dispute Settlement* 9, no. 2 (2018): 199–222. Janneke Gerards does not find qualitative evidence that such references are accompanied by less strict standards of review. For more, see Janneke Gerards, "Margin of Appreciation and Incrementalism in the Case Law of the European Court of Human Rights," *Human Rights Law Review* 18, no. 3 (2018): 495–515.

[38] Başak Çalı, "Coping with Crisis: Whither the Variable Geomety in the Jurisprudence of the European Court of Human Rights," *Wisconsin International Law Journal* 35, no. 2 (2018): 237–76; Başak Çalı, "Autocratic Strategies and the European Court of Human Rights," *European Convention on Human Rights Law Review* 2, no. 1 (March 10, 2021): 11–19.

[39] Øyvind Stiansen and Erik Voeten, "Backlash and Judicial Restraint: Evidence from the European Court of Human Rights," *International Studies Quarterly* 64, no. 4 (2020): 770–84."

[40] Laurence R. Helfer and Clare Ryan, "LGBT Rights as Mega-Politics: Litigating before the ECtHR," Duke Law School Public Law & Legal Theory Series No. 2021–32, January 15, 2022, 30, https://doi.org/10.2139/ssrn.3867604.

[41] Hillebrecht, *Saving the International Justice Regime*, 40–41.

[42] Laurence R. Helfer and Erik Voeten, "Walking Back Human Rights in Europe?," *European Journal of International Law* 31, no. 3 (2020): 825.

[43] Stiansen and Voeten, "Backlash and Judicial Restraint," 770.

this book, issue characteristics matter, too. The reformed Court is likely to choose selective forbearance when dealing with politically salient issues, such as immigrants and refugees, and some resource-intensive positive obligations regardless of the regime type of the responding state.

The extent to which this reform process, as well as the widespread negative feedback, influenced the reformed Court and undermined its authority has also been a subject of academic debate. For example, Larry Helfer and Erik Voeten identify regressive trends, which became dominant at the Court, especially in the 2012 post-Brighton period.[44] Through an analysis of judicial dissents, they establish that some of the judges themselves believe that the Grand Chamber has overturned previously progressive rulings.[45] They argue that this trend may be due to two reasons. First, the Court may be responding to political signals and criticisms of its previously expansive rulings, similar to what I argue here. Second, the Court may be following the right-restrictive trends at the domestic level.[46] They point out the fact that there is now a growing number of European countries that favour more limited human rights protections accorded to "politically unpopular groups," such as refugees and asylum seekers, terrorist suspects, and nontraditional families.[47] Alec Stone Sweet, Wayne Sandholtz, and Mads Andenas disagree with this analysis, arguing that there are no clear regressive trends and that the efforts to "rein" the Court have failed.[48] They maintain that the Court's authority remains intact because it is protected by the rules governing treaty amendment, and because the political challenge against the Court was voiced by a minority of states, while states continue to finance the Court's activities.[49]

Even though the reformed Court continues to execute its core functions – for which the old Court did not have a guarantee – strong resistance and protests by member states are not inconsequential. Short of tarnishing the Court's authority, such widespread negative feedback

44 Helfer and Voeten, "Walking Back Human Rights in Europe?," 797–827.

45 Ibid., 823.

46 Ibid.

47 Laurence R. Helfer and Erik Voeten, "Walking Back Dissents on the European Court of Human Rights: A Rejoinder to Alec Stone Sweet, Wayne Sandholtz and Mads Andenas," *European Journal of International Law* 32, no. 3 (2021): 911.

48 Alec Stone Sweet, Wayne Sandholtz, and Mads Andenas, "Dissenting Opinions and Rights Protection in the European Court: A Reply to Laurence Helfer and Erik Voeten," *European Journal of International Law* 32, no. 3 (2021): 897–906.

49 Sweet, Sandholtz, and Andenas, "The Failure to Destroy the Authority of the European Court of Human Rights," 41–42.

has the potential to influence the Court both directly and indirectly. First, pushback and criticism may eventually provoke formal changes. In fact, some of the core ideas expressed in High-Level Conferences have since been incorporated into the official protocols amending the Convention.[50] For example, Protocol 15, drafted after the Brighton Declaration, stipulates the inclusion of the principle of subsidiarity and margin of appreciation doctrine in the Preamble of the Convention.[51] Several civil society organizations have criticised this provision, as it would potentially curtail the Court's progressive spirit and represent a setback for human rights protection in Europe.[52] This reaction was warranted because preambles matter when it comes to the interpretation of a treaty text. Adding these two principles to the treaty text is likely to put extra pressure on the reformed Court to consider them.

Second, no matter how we identify it – backlash, political pushback, or widespread negative feedback – such strong signalling evokes some behavioural changes at the Court. Even if member state pushback does not openly and directly target the Court's authority, it indirectly influences the Court's behaviour, encouraging it to be selectively forbearing.[53] Member state calls for forbearance and negative feedback amounts to interference, which may not be direct or come in the form of an executive override. Nevertheless, the Court might nonetheless voluntarily relinquish some of its autonomy over its interpretive preferences in order to maintain its authority. As argued here, and as shown in the existing literature, international courts may seek to maintain their authority and support from member states by reacting to or pre-empting backlash.[54] Courtney Hillebrecht lists these strategies, which range from "dejudicialisation of

[50] The last two protocols are Protocol 15 and Protocol 16, which were opened for signature on June 24, 2013, and October 2, 2013, respectively.

[51] Protocol 16 came into force on August 1, 2018, for those states that have signed and ratified the protocol. Protocol 16 extends the jurisdiction of the Court to give advisory opinions to the highest courts and tribunals of the states upon their request – an idea that has been raised and reiterated in the Izmir and Brighton Declarations.

[52] Marisa Iglesias Vila, "Subsidiarity, Margin of Appreciation and International Adjudication within a Cooperative Conception of Human Rights," *International Journal of Constitutional Law* 15, no. 2 (2017): 393–413.

[53] The Courts often face tradeoffs between judicial independence, accountability, and transparency. For more, see Jeffrey L. Dunoff and Mark A. Pollack, "The Judicial Trilemma," *American Journal of International Law* 111, no. 2 (2017): 227.

[54] Richard H. Steinberg, "Judicial Lawmaking at the WTO: Discursive, Constitutional, and Political Constraints," *American Journal of International Law* 98, no. 2 (2004): 247–75; Daniel Abebe and Tom Ginsburg, "The Dejudicialization of International Politics?," *International Studies Quarterly* 63, no. 3 (2019): 521–30.

hot-button topics that could spark backlash to watering down judgments to induce compliance."[55] I add forbearance and selective forbearance to this list of backlash mitigation strategies, which I explain further in "Selective Forbearance: Argument and Findings."

Selective Forbearance: Argument and Findings

The new Court audaciously initiated a foundational change in the way the prohibition of torture and inhuman or degrading treatment is understood. The reformed Court, on the other hand, has been more reluctant to choose audacity over forbearance. This is predominantly because the political environment in which the reformed Court has to operate is different. This environment is coloured by widespread negative feedback, accompanied by member states' outcries over previous rulings that favoured politically unpopular groups.

Member states' call for forbearance has been stronger with respect to certain issue areas. The rights of immigrants and refugees have been one of them, for example. The clearest indication of such a call is the draft Copenhagen Declaration, where the Court was invited not to act "as an immigration appeals tribunal, but respect the domestic courts' assessment of evidence and interpretation and application of domestic legislation, unless arbitrary or manifestly unreasonable."[56] A look at the Court's recent jurisprudence indicates that the Court catered to state sensitivities about irregular migrants, asylum seekers, and refugees while also following a more progressive line with respect to other issue areas.

In Chapter 3, I explained that the reformed Court has a higher propensity to find a violation than the old Court and the new Court, which can be seen in Table 7.1. While the reformed Court's rate of finding a violation is 82%, the new Court's rate is 73%, and the old Court's rate is a meagre 30%. As explained there, when it comes to the propensity to find states in violation, the new Court makes the biggest jump with a 43-percentage-point increase, while the reformed Court only increases nine percentage points. In Figure 7.1, I present the results showing how the propensity to find a violation changed from the new Court era to the reformed Court era, broken down by issue area.

[55] Hillebrecht, *Saving the International Justice Regime*, 24.

[56] Danish and Chairmanship of the Committee of Ministers of the Council of Europe, "Draft Copenhagen Declaration," February 5, 2018, https://menneskeret.dk/sites/menneskeret.dk/files/media/dokumenter/nyheder/draft_copenhagen_declaration_05.02.18.pdf.

Table 7.1 *Propensity for finding a violation over time (duplicated)*

Era	Violation count	No violation count	Violation propensity	Difference in % points
Old Court	11	36	30%	–
New Court	893	325	73%	43%
Reformed Court	1,886	415	82%	9%

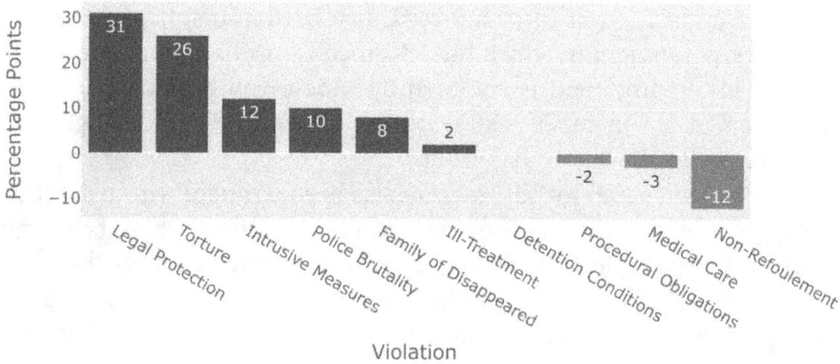

Figure 7.1 Change in propensity for finding a violation from the new Court to the reformed Court era (percentage points)

Looking at disaggregated scores across issue areas, we see that the reformed Court's propensity to find states in violation does not increase across the board. Rather, the reformed Court finds a violation less often than the new Court when it comes to cases about the *non-refoulement* principle (12-point decrease), the obligation to provide medical care (3-point decrease), and procedural obligations (2-point decrease). For the rest of the categories, the reformed Court either keeps up the practices of the new Court or shows an increase in propensity – with the highest increase of 31 percentage points concerning legal protection and 26 points concerning torture.

What explains this picture? The reformed Court's uneven support for progressive change *only* for certain obligations might not be fully explained only with reference to judges' changing profiles.[57] If the reason

[57] Stiansen and Voeten, "Backlash and Judicial Restraint"; Erik Voeten, "The Impartiality of International Judges: Evidence from the European Court of Human Rights," *American Political Science Review* 102, no. 4 (2008): 417–33.

was that more state-friendly judges have been sitting on the bench during the reformed Court period, then one would expect a downward trend for most if not all obligations concerned. Such a downward trend would include the obligation to provide legal protection or remedy, for example. This is an excellent example of a resource-intensive obligation that directs states to behave a certain way. It is also relatively less established (compared to the obligation to refrain from torturing individuals or the principle of the *non-refoulement*). However, we see that the reformed Court's propensity for finding a violation of this obligation increases more than any other for the period under study, with a 31-point increase.

The targeted increase and decrease of propensity in finding states in violation signals that there might be other explanations at play. In this chapter, I further explore what could explain the reformed Court's bifurcated approach toward different obligations under the norm against torture and inhuman or degrading treatment. In particular, I consider the influence of two factors: widespread *negative feedback* (voiced by mostly Western European states) and *issue characteristics* (whether the obligation concerned is a resource-intensive one). This study provides an ideal testing ground to compare the practices of the old Court, the new Court, and the reformed Court, and to trace how these factors may have informed their interpretive preferences.

I start with distinguishing the reformed Court's propensity scores across geographical regions (namely Western European and formerly communist countries) for cases about *non-refoulement* and medical care as they show the clearest difference.[58] The *non-refoulement* principle – states' obligation to refrain from expelling individuals, such as criminals or asylum seekers, to countries where they are likely to be tortured or subjected to inhuman or degrading treatment – was introduced by the old Court as early as 1989.[59] This was one of the few obligations that the old Court acknowledged, signalling that this issue was not as politically salient or contentious back then as it is today, as explained in Chapters 3 and 4. Table 7.2 displays how the old Court, the new Court, and the reformed Court treated claims concerning the *non-refoulement* principle.

[58] We also observe a slight (only two percentage points) decrease with respect to procedural obligations. However, here, the reformed Court's treatment of claims coming from Western and Eastern European countries is not sufficiently different. The reform Court keeps the new Court's propensity score of 93% for Western Europe and decreases two percentage points with respect to formerly communist countries, from 96% to 94%.

[59] Başak Çalı, Cathryn Costello, and Stewart Cunningham, "Hard Protection through Soft Courts? *Non-Refoulement* before the United Nations Treaty Bodies," *German Law Journal* 21, no. 3 (2020): 355–84.

Table 7.2 *Rate and number of violations of the* non-refoulement *principle across regions and different eras*

	Western	Formerly communist
Old Court	57% (4 out of 7)	–
New Court	67% (26 out of 39)	73% (8 out of 11)
Reformed Court	46% (52 out of 113)	75% (44 out of 59)

We see that the new Court had an increased propensity to find states in violation when reviewing claims concerning the *non-refoulement* principle for both Western and formerly communist Eastern European countries, while having a higher propensity for the latter – 67% and 73%, respectively. The reformed Court, on the other hand, remarkably decreased the rate at which it found Western countries in violation – a 21-point decrease. Furthermore, it slightly increased its propensity rate for finding the formerly communist countries in violation by two percentage points. This finding implies that the reformed Court has resorted to selective forbearance and showed more lenience toward the Western countries – a group that was also the most vocally opposed to rights for asylum seekers, refugees, and foreign criminals in and around the high-level meetings. It also demonstrates that the reformed Court can resort to selective forbearance even in the context of the prohibition of torture and inhuman or degrading treatment – an absolute prohibition that contains nonderogable rights.

I also analyzed the reasons why the reform Court did not find a violation and made a tally of the reasons provided, which is depicted in Table 7.3. We have learned (as shown in Table 7.2 above) that a clear majority of no-violation rulings are issued with respect to the Western European countries, as is the case for the violation rulings. The obligation to refrain from violating the *non-refoulement* principle is the only issue area where we observe more complaints brought before Western European states in the Article 3 jurisprudence. As we see in Table 7.3, while 70% of no-violation rulings issued against Western European countries are due to substantive reasons, 67% of no-violation rulings with respect to the formerly communist states are due to evidentiary reasons. This implies two things: First, it indicates that the evidentiary quality of cases brought against Western European and former communist countries might differ. Second, this difference affects the course of legal review. Due to the prior (evidentiary) issues, the reformed

Table 7.3 *Reasons for not finding a violation with respect to the* non-refoulement *principle across different regions (percentages and total numbers)*

	Western	Formerly communist
Substantive reasons	70% (43)	33% (5)
Evidentiary reasons	30% (18)	67% (10)
Total	100% (61)	100% (15)

Court cannot arrive at posterior (substantive) issues when reviewing cases brought against the formerly communist countries.

The finding concerning the reformed Court's treatment of claims related to the *non-refoulement* principle is consistent with what the existing literature observes as a more favourable treatment of cases concerning Western European countries.[60] This observation can also be traced qualitatively. For example, in *L. M. and Others* v. *Russia*, the Court found that the applicants' allegations were not "duly examined by the domestic authorities."[61] It then made its own assessment of whether the applicants would be subjected to torture and ill-treatment if they were to be returned to Syria, establishing that there is such a risk.[62] In *F. G.* v. *Sweden*, however, the Grand Chamber underlined that "in cases concerning the expulsion of asylum-seekers, the Court does not itself examine the actual asylum applications or verify how the States honour their obligations under the Geneva Convention relating to the status of refugees. Its main concern is whether effective guarantees exist that protect the applicant against arbitrary refoulement, be it direct or indirect, to the country from which he or she has fled."[63] In this case, the reformed Court agreed with the conclusions of the domestic authorities that the applicant's past political activities would not expose them to risk. Yet, the Court found Sweden in violation for not considering the impact of the applicant's conversion to Christianity as a factor – without establishing whether the applicant's conversion would increase the risk of ill-treatment that they may face upon their return to Iran. Even though the reformed Court found a violation in both of these cases, it treated them differently and assumed a larger role when reviewing a case against Russia

[60] Stiansen and Voeten, "Backlash and Judicial Restraint"; Çalı, "Coping with Crisis."
[61] *L. M. and Others* v. *Russia*, application no. 40081/14, 40088/14 and 40127/14, ECHR (October 15, 2015) §112.
[62] Ibid., §120–26.
[63] *F.G.* v. *Sweden*, application no. 43611/11, ECHR[GC] (March 23, 2016) §117.

Table 7.4 *Rate and number of violations regarding medical care across regions and different eras*

	Western	Formerly communist
Old Court	–	–
New Court	60% (15 out of 25)	80% (47 out of 59)
Reformed Court	74% (20 out of 27)	70% (89 out of 127)

and shied away from doing so when assessing the one against Sweden. This bifurcated approach explains, to a great extent, why we see a higher propensity to find a violation with respect to formerly communist countries in the most recent period.

We see a different trend for the cases concerning states' obligation to provide medical care in detention facilities, however. Table 7.4 shows that the rate of violation rulings increases for Western countries and decreases for formerly communist countries. This obligation was not recognised during the old Court, and the new Court had a higher propensity to find a violation for the formerly communist countries (80%) than for the Western European countries (60%). The reformed Court, however, had a slightly higher propensity to find a violation with respect to Western countries, amounting to only a four-percentage-point increase. Here, we observe a reverse pattern, with the reformed Court being more likely to find the Western European countries in violation.

Similar to the analysis of the cases related to the *non-refoulement* principle, I have looked at the reasons why the reformed Court issued no violation rulings, as shown in Table 7.5. I should note here that there are fewer cases under this category, which makes the analysis sensitive to smaller changes. Regardless, here we see that the reformed Court's treatment of Western and formerly communist countries differs from what we observed earlier. The reformed Court finds no violation due to substantive reasons in the majority of the cases – 86% and 92% of the cases brought against Western European and formerly communist countries, respectively. The no-violation rulings based on evidentiary reasons are in the minority, with 14% and 8% for Western and formerly communist countries, respectively.

Overall, in this example, we do not observe favourable treatment of Western European countries. I argue that the reformed Court turns to selective forbearance for different reasons here – reasons not fully investigated in the existing literature. What we see is not directly connected

Table 7.5 *Reasons for not finding a violation with respect to medical care across different regions (percentages and total numbers)*

	Western	Formerly communist
Substantive reasons	86% (6)	92% (35)
Evidentiary reasons	14% (1)	8% (3)
Total	100% (7)	100% (38)

to the reformed Court's specific response to (mostly) Western countries' criticism of the Court's previously progressive rulings with respect to asylum seekers, refugees, and foreign criminals. Hence, it is not a differential treatment motivated by the regime type of the responding states (i.e., established democracies vs. autocracies). Rather, the main concern is the issue characteristics and, more specifically, the reformed Court's unwillingness to put excessive burdens on states, which would result from strongly enforcing some resource-intensive positive obligations in resource-poor countries. The reformed Court resorts to selective forbearance, particularly when reviewing the applicants' request for release on health grounds. In such instances, the Court refrains from subjecting the decisions of the national authorities to a review and instead agrees with the solutions proposed at the national level. I argue that by avoiding burdensome rulings or an intrusive legal review, the reformed Court carefully pre-empts widespread negative feedback or backlash.

A qualitative reading of the no-violation rulings helps substantiate this claim. States' obligation to provide sufficient medical care to detainees and prisoners, as the name suggests, primarily corresponds to medical care offered to detainees and prisoners. A careful reading shows that the reformed Court was willing to apply the margin of appreciation doctrine to Western European and formerly communist countries alike, albeit without invoking this doctrine explicitly. For example, in *Goginashvili* v. *Georgia,* the reformed Court underlined that "[*s*]*tate's obligation to cure a seriously ill detainee is one of means, not of result*. Notably, the mere fact of a deterioration of the applicant's state of health, albeit capable of raising, at an initial stage, certain doubts concerning the adequacy of the treatment in prison, could not suffice, as such, for a finding of a violation of the State's positive obligations under Article 3 of the Convention."[64]

[64] *Goginashvili* v. *Georgia*, application no. 47729/08, ECHR (October 4, 2011), §71 (emphasis added).

In *Vasyukov* v. *Russia*, the reformed Court went even further, pronouncing that "while finding it particularly *disturbing* that *the applicant's infection with tuberculosis occurred in a penitentiary institution within the State's control*, the Court reiterates its constant approach that even if an applicant had contracted tuberculosis while in detention, this in itself would not imply a violation of Article 3, provided that he received treatment for it."[65] In this case, the reformed Court passed on the opportunity to find a state in violation for allowing the applicant to contract tuberculosis due to detainment conditions. It also forwent the occasion to pronounce that the responding states should take measures to prevent the spread of contractable diseases in detention facilities. Later in *Bagdonavičius* v. *Lithuania*, the reformed Court signalled that it is willing to consider the detention conditions' role on prisoners' health:

> The Court observes that in the cases concerning medical care in prison, it was most often faced with situations arising in connection with prisoners affected with severe to very severe ailments, such as to make their normal daily functioning very difficult. The present case differs from those cases in that the applicant's heart condition does not affect his everyday functioning in the same way as many serious illnesses do. That notwithstanding, the Court is ready to accept that as soon as he had his first myocardial infarction [heart attack], the applicant could have experienced considerable anxiety as to whether the medical care provided to him was adequate and whether it could be properly provided within the prison setting. At the same time, the Court is careful to note that although the applicant's heart illness was detected two years into his detention, nothing in the case file suggests that it came about his being imprisoned rather than by natural causes.[66]

The Court then agreed with the domestic courts' conclusions and refused to consider the applicant's release on the grounds of health conditions.[67] Indeed, such release requests often accompany the complaints related to insufficient medical care in detention facilities and prisons. When reviewing such claims, the European Court does not depart from the conclusions of the domestic authorities, arguing that "it cannot substitute its point of view for that of the domestic courts,"[68] and

[65] *Vasyukov* v. *Russia*, application no. 2974/05, ECHR (April 5, 2011), §66 (emphasis added).

[66] *Bagdonavičius* v. *Lithuania*, application no. 41252/12, ECHR (April 19, 2016) §77.

[67] Ibid., §85.

[68] *Hajoł* v. *Poland*, application no. 1127/06, ECHR (March 2, 2010) § 63. See also *Pakhomov* v. *Russia*, application no. 44917/08 ECHR (September 30, 2010), and *Bagdonavičius* v. *Lithuania*.

emphasizing that "Article 3 does not entitle a detainee to be released 'on compassionate grounds.'"[69]

The assessment of the no-violation rulings – the majority of which were issued against the formerly communist countries for the period under study – reveals that the reformed Court is willing to show deference to domestic authorities, not only in the Western European countries but also in countries such as Russia, Georgia, and Poland. Beyond a distinction between the West and the East, or consolidated or unconsolidated democracies, the Court's selective forbearance, in this instance, works with a different logic and serves two main purposes. First, it avoids financially burdening countries by requesting them to redirect more resources to their correctional facilities. Second, it carefully sidesteps the thorny issue of invalidating national legal review and asking domestic authorities to release prisoners on health grounds. This is despite the fact that stronger enforcement of Article 3 in this area would offer an extra layer of protection to prisoners and strengthen the right to health, which is not covered under the Convention.[70] However, issuing judgments with wider policy implications, such as requesting states to release prisoners on health grounds or asking especially resource-poor states to dedicate more resources to their prisons and detention centres, might provoke a political pushback, especially in the current environment. One can surmise that the reformed Court's cautious approach in this regard helps pre-empt further political pushback.

A Bifurcated Approach and Selective Forbearance through Landmark Rulings

Selective forbearance as a bifurcated approach has been the dominant mode of operation during the reformed Court era. It can be observed even in the reformed Court's treatment of the prohibition of torture and inhuman or degrading treatment, which is one of the – if not the – strongest prohibitions in the field of human rights. To illustrate how selective forbearance looks qualitatively, let us turn to two recent landmark Article 3 decisions: *Khlaifia and Others* v. *Italy [GC]* (2016),[71] and

[69] *Mozer* v. *the Republic of Moldova and Russia*, application no. 11138/10, ECHR[GC] (February 23, 2016) §178.

[70] Angus E. M. Wallace, "The European Court of Human Rights: A Tool for Improving Prison Health," *The Lancet Public Health* 5, no. 2 (2020): e78–79, https://doi.org/10.1016/S2468-2667(19)30258-0.

[71] *Khlaifia and Others* v. *Italy*, application no. 16483/12, ECHR[GC] (December 15, 2016).

Bouyid v. *Belgium[GC]* (2015).[72] These two rulings share some commonalities. They are both Grand Chamber judgments given in respect of the Western European countries around the same time – only one year apart. Yet, they have several differences. For example, they concern different types of complaints and obligations: The former concerns migrants' living conditions (a positive obligation), and the latter concerns police brutality (a negative obligation). In addition to these substantive differences, these two decisions also differ in terms of how the Grand Chamber dealt with them.

In *Khlaifia,* the Chamber had previously found that the conditions in which irregular migrants were held on the island of Lampedusa violated Article 3. It ruled that, although the exceptional wave of immigration was burdensome on the state, it did not exempt Italy from "its obligation to guarantee conditions that are compatible with respect for human dignity to all individuals."[73] This decision was in line with the Court's earlier jurisprudence with respect to the detention of irregular migrants, asylum seekers, and refugees. The new Court had already established state obligations to provide acceptable living conditions for irregular migrants in *Dougoz* v. *Greece* back in 2001.[74] In this audacious decision, the new Court characterised the suffering that migrants had to endure due to overcrowding and appalling living conditions as an Article 3 violation as discussed in Chapter 5.

Disagreeing with the Chamber ruling, the Italian government decided to request a referral to the Grand Chamber, and the Grand Chamber arrived at a different conclusion. More specifically, the Grand Chamber backed away from the Chamber's audacious approach and paid greater attention to the excessive burden that the Italian government bore.[75] It agreed that living conditions were "far from the ideal" and acknowledged the complaints about overcrowding and lack of hygiene, but did not consider them to be Article 3 violations.[76] None of the sitting judges issued a dissenting opinion on this ruling.

In *Bouyid,* the Grand Chamber issued an audacious ruling. The Chamber had earlier found that being slapped by a police officer, "though unacceptable," would not constitute "a sufficient degree of humiliation

[72] *Bouyid* v. *Belgium,* application no. 23380/09, ECHR[GC] (September 28, 2015).
[73] *Khlaifia and Others* v. *Italy,* application no. 16483/12, ECHR (September 1, 2015), §128.
[74] *Dougoz* v. *Greece,* application no. 40907/98, ECHR (March 6, 2001).
[75] *Khlaifia and Others* v. *Italy [GC],* §197.
[76] Ibid., §188.

or debasement" to be considered a violation of Article 3.[77] However, the Grand Chamber reversed this decision, arguing that a slap inflicted by police officers in a position of authority "may be perceived as humiliating" by the person receiving it.[78] Judges de Gaetano, Lemmens, and Mahoney (from Malta, Belgium, and the United Kingdom, respectively) dissented, arguing not only that the treatment does not constitute a violation but also that "it is not for the Court to impose general rules of conduct on law-enforcement officers."[79] Despite these dissenting opinions, *Bouyid* soon became the landmark decision lowering the threshold required for an act to qualify as police brutality.

These two cases accurately capture the conundrum that the reformed Court faces today. Should the Court draw stricter lines and forgo its audacity while its authority is challenged, or should it continue along the progressive trajectory that the new Court charted in the late 1990s? In the post-2010 period, the *de facto* Supreme Court of Europe faces a new reality: Widespread negative feedback is constraining not only in the abstract sense but also practically, as it can lead to formal changes that eventually may shrink the Court's discretionary space. The reformed Court has resorted to selective forbearance to counter the widespread negative feedback and the actual and potential loss of discretionary space. In other words, when under pressure, the reformed Court has eased its insistence on some of the more resource-intensive positive obligations, such as providing acceptable living conditions for irregular immigrants or refugees, while holding the line for other obligations, such as the obligation to refrain from using excessive force in law enforcement.

Due to persistent negative feedback, the reformed Court has not been able to take the overall audacious approach that the new Court could assume when launching the foundational change under the norm against torture and inhuman or degrading treatment in the late 1990s. The new Court revealed a different mindset when acknowledging Nahide's victimhood under Article 3, or irregular migrants' right to have acceptable living conditions in *Dougoz* v. *Greece*. In the post-2010 period, the reformed Court began to oscillate between audacity and forbearance at a higher rate and turned to selective forbearance at opportune times.

77 *Bouyid* v. *Belgium [GC]*, §56.
78 Ibid., §105–106.
79 *Bouyid* v. *Belgium [GC]*, Joint Partly Dissenting Opinion of Judges de Gaetano, Lemmens, and Mahoney.

On the one hand, the reformed Court has taken a step back from developing certain obligations, as we see in *Khlaifia*. It effectively took back some of the protections granted to irregular immigrants with the *Dougoz* decision. On the other hand, the reformed Court has continued to progressively sculpt other obligations, such as the obligation to refrain from engaging in police brutality, as we see in *Bouyid*. The difference between these two obligations is that while the former is a controversial resource-intensive positive obligation toward irregular immigrants and asylum seekers – one by which European states currently have no interest in being bound – the latter is a core negative obligation around which there is a general agreement.

This book's treatment of Article 3 cases substantiates what the resurgent literature theorises about current trends at the reformed Court. For example, Başak Çalı argues that the Court has been attentive to the changing attitudes of European states toward the European human rights system since the mid-to-late 2000s.[80] The Court has not spoken in a uniform voice, claims Çalı. Rather, the Court has developed a tendency to invoke the margin of appreciation for established democracies that it deems to be "good faith interpreters and thus guardians of the Convention" – particularly in response to the appeals led by the United Kingdom.[81] In parallel, the Court has developed bad faith jurisprudence concerning those that "show disrespect for the Convention values."[82] The second category is composed of the countries in Eastern Europe and the Caucasus, where democratic transitions are halted or reversed.

I find evidence for this argument, especially when it comes to the Court's treatment of the claims related to the *non-refoulement* principle under Article 3. However, my findings also show that issue characteristics matter a great deal. As discussed earlier, the reformed Court has been willing to afford a margin of appreciation even to countries such as Russia when reviewing claims about insufficient medical care in detention facilities.[83] Hence, the regime type of the responding state explains only some of the bifurcated behaviour. The issue characteristics, especially whether an obligation is resource-intensive or whether reviewing its implementation would require greater scrutiny of national decisions, are also important factors to consider.

[80] Çali, "Coping with Crisis," 269.
[81] Ibid., 243.
[82] Ibid.
[83] Ibid.

My analysis overall shows that the reformed Court has been operating in two different gears. This is most visibly shown in the comparative example of two recent Grand Chamber rulings concerning the living conditions of refugees and police brutality. While the Court has taken a step back concerning the obligation to provide acceptable living conditions for refugees, asylum seekers, and irregular migrants, it took a step forward with the obligation not to inflict excessive violence while enforcing the law. Both large-N analysis of the case law and select reading of the recent landmark rulings indicate that this bifurcated tendency is an outcome of institutional survival and resilience strategies that the reformed Court has been adapting in the face of potential and actual widespread negative feedback.

What Judges Think about Political Pushback and Future Directions of the Norm's Trajectory

Beyond a systematic and selective reading of the case law, the impact of the current political climate and widespread negative criticism can also be gleaned from the insights gathered in the context of my interviews in and around the Court in 2014 and 2015. Several of my interviewees at the Court directly talked about the impact of political pushback and backlash. One judge, in particular, laid out the scene as follows:

> We are living in a time when human rights are not so self-evident. We should not undermine the whole system of the European Convention by going too far. This is a risk for an international court. [We] think we can do more, but the backlash can be enormous. [We] have to be cautious. Sometimes the consequence would be taking a step back. You can still have dynamic interpretation, but the Court has to be cautious.[84]

Upon being asked when they thought this change occurred, they referred to 2010 and added: "the Court is conscious and avoids the impression that it is taking the role of the legislatures."[85] A former judge echoed this point, arguing that the risk of backlash has been high since 2010. He added: "the Court is losing its traditional friends like the United Kingdom, Switzerland, the Netherlands, and Denmark, and it is also losing Turkey."[86] A high-level Registry official told me that criticisms of the Court are also due to the nature of issues that the Court deals with: "The life of this institution

84 Interview 2.
85 Ibid.
86 Interview 17.

has always been a controversial one. Whenever the Court is perceived as touching on national interest, [the states] will scream. Objectively, there are cases the states do not like… cases that concern trade union rights or torture. This is not a feature that is going to go away."[87] The first judge cited above echoed this point when they told me that ethical issues, deportation, and asylum cases are politically sensitive cases and need to be treated with caution.[88]

Although it is impossible to make predictions about future trends, much can be inferred from the sentiments and opinions directly expressed by judges. When I asked fifteen Court judges about the future direction of the norm against torture and inhuman or degrading treatment, seven of them told me that the norm's expansion had reached its limits,[89] four claimed that there was still room for expansion,[90] and four abstained from directly answering.[91]

The seven who believed that the norm had reached its limit thought that the Court should be more cautious. Almost all judges in this camp – except one – are from Western European countries. One of them said that "there should be a line drawn… The Court should be aware of the implications the judgments are generating. Not everything can be inhuman or degrading. If everything is degrading, then nothing is. There is a difference between a fundamental right and a desired right. Fundamental rights should not be diluted."[92] Another judge with a similar background said: "The frontiers are well settled. We are perfectly aware of the language we use. We are not using the word 'torture' for everything. We should be absolutely precise and consistent with the case law. *Selmouni* was a deliberate step and such steps are not taken every day. We would lose our credibility if we change our approach every second year. We need to consistently follow our case law."[93] One other Western European judge said: "we probably reached a point where we have to maintain the standards."[94] Another echoed this sentiment and said that "[the standards] cannot get any lower than that," referring to the *Bouyid*.[95] Another judge who had previously

[87] Interview 20.
[88] Interview 2.
[89] Ibid.; Interview 3; Interview 4; Interview 6; Interview 8; Interview 9; Interview 15.
[90] Interview 1; Interview 7; Interview 10; Interview 14.
[91] Interview 5; Interview 11; Interview 12; Interview 13.
[92] Interview 3.
[93] Interview 8.
[94] Interview 9.
[95] Interview 15.

served at a constitutional court in a Western European country wanted the Court to maintain the standards and thought that this "requires constant balancing."[96] They added that when changing standards, "we need to consider what it costs to the state, what the civil society thinks, and what our role is."[97]

The four who believed that there is still room for norm expansion have mixed backgrounds – two from Eastern European countries and two from Western European countries. They also have a less uniform set of reasons for thinking the norm could be further expanded. For example, one judge from Eastern Europe stated firmly: "the new horizon is the metamorphosis of the inhuman treatment to torture."[98] They predicted that the issues categorised as inhuman treatment would slowly but surely be considered torture in the future. Another, with a similar background, argued that the Court should regulate the conduct of private parties.[99] Another added: "We need to be careful about new threats and be ready to expand this right to counter new challenges," such as the developments in cyberspace.[100] Finally, one judge from Western Europe disclosed that "the new frontier would be – but this perhaps is just wishful thinking on my part – to extend Article 3 to protect the unborn child, by dumping the Roman law concept of *persona*."[101]

Notably, interviewed judges from Western European countries call for caution or forbearance almost uniformly. Their vision dovetails with that of member states, as expressed in the final declarations of the High-Level Conferences. What member states and these judges have in common is their desire for a less interventionist supranational supervisory body that guards the existing principles without venturing into new understandings. In sum, the judges' views come down to two main arguments. First, they think that the Court has already acknowledged the lowest minimum thresholds to find a violation under this norm. If they raise the bar any higher, they might put the Court's credibility at risk. Second, they believe that the Court should instead spend its energy on safeguarding existing standards and winning state support for the achievements of the 1990s. One Western European judge identified this effort as "ensuring that the Convention remains a credible document."[102]

96 Interview 6.
97 Ibid.
98 Interview 1.
99 Interview 7.
100 Interview 14.
101 Interview 10.
102 Ibid.

These two reasons might be more connected than they first appear. The political climate in Europe calls for prudence. It requires the Court to put the brakes on issuing rights-expansive rulings and to concentrate its efforts on gaining state support and maintaining its legitimacy. This caution might appear even more warranted to the judges because the norm had already been substantially transformed in the late 1990s. However, it appears that these judges fear the repercussions, and that fear informs their opinions about whether to expand the norm further. Three of the seven judges who argued for halting the norm's expansion alluded to this connection.[103] Two of them, in particular, called for forbearance on the grounds that pushing for even more progressive standards would jeopardise the Court's credibility and the credibility of the standards it set.[104]

As for the group of judges who believe in the need for further expansion, they still appreciate a more proactive and instructive European Court. They explain how the norm can develop further in a way, for example, to cover the conduct of private actors or the challenges that new technologies bring. However, those who envision a more audacious role for the Court are in the minority, and they do not put forth a strong and unified vision about what remains to be done.

The judges' perspectives indicate that the current political climate is certainly not ripe for launching a new wave of progressive change. The prime reason is the aura of negative feedback alongside acts and threats of narrowing the Court's discretionary space. As I have argued, the permissive zone of discretion is the necessary condition for progressive change. On its own, it may not be enough, but it nevertheless remains a crucial factor. Without it, audacity becomes too costly, and the Court becomes too preoccupied with acquiring state support and respect for its decisions. Therefore, the Court leans toward selective forbearance, as we observe during the reformed Court period.

Moreover, direct and indirect state control over international courts has consequences. When international courts are under pressure, they are likely to prioritise securing resources for themselves, whether ideational (credibility, legitimacy) or material (funding). This is true even for human rights courts, which should be liberal-leaning under normal circumstances. Therefore, in times of backlash, the international courts' core function – the maintenance and refinement of norms – suffers. This is not simply a loss in the abstract but a loss in real terms; a loss that is most

103 Interview 3; Interview 6; Interview 8.

104 Interview 3; Interview 8.

felt by the victims who seek protection and who are left with no or limited recourse for remedy.[105]

The Backlash Debate

The overall approach adopted in this book can help show when progressive change is likely and when it is unlikely. It highlights the moments where we can expect stagnation or retraction of existing standards. When international courts' discretionary space is narrow – or there is a credible threat that this space will shrink – they face an increasing need to heed member state appeals or to pre-empt their reaction. International courts might not always favour progressive change that they had previously adhered to, as in the case of the treatment of irregular migrants, asylum seekers, and refugees in the post-2010 period. Their need for tactical balancing and desire to secure their authority and legitimacy may preclude the chances of progressive legal change on some matters, yet this does not mean that the shift is wholesale. As the *Boyuid* example shows, isolated instances of rights-expansive rulings may still appear. Rather, the essential finding is that the courts' need for institutional survival and resilience comes before any other agenda. Therefore, while there are sporadic progressive change episodes in the current period, the expansive interpretation is not evenly applied – this is the case even when one restricts the analysis to a single norm, as I do here.

My findings reveal that the reformed Court has reserved its audacious rulings only for select obligations under Article 3. This uneven application of audacity (and forbearance) indicates that judges' changing profiles – with more state-friendly judges being elected – may not fully explain the current trends at the Court. Rather, they point us to the institutional strategies fashioned to mitigate and prevent political pushback and uphold the authority of the Court. They also show the importance of issue characteristics and the targeted criticism voiced by certain member states in shaping these strategies. These findings, thus, contribute to the burgeoning debate on the sources and the consequences of the backlash against the European Court in particular and liberal institutions in general. They also help one contextualise and historicise the costs and consequences of member state attempts to influence the Court's interpretive preferences through formal and informal means. My analysis of how member states

[105] Hillebrecht, *Saving the International Justice Regime*, 31.

employed these means to influence the way the Court carried out the judicial review over five decades complements this debate, which predominantly assesses the situation with today's optics. An important lesson to draw from this analysis is that the backlash is neither new nor unique to today's political climate. The Court has seen different episodes of backlash, and in return, it has relied on its inbuilt resilience strategy – general or selective forbearance – to fend off political pushback.[106] As a matter of fact, the Court's unvarying progressive track in the late 1990s is the exception rather than the rule, an exception that was conditioned upon several factors described in Chapter 5.

Conclusion

This chapter has discussed the current trends at the reformed Court against the backdrop of the recent reform initiatives and the general atmosphere of widespread negative feedback and backlash since the 2010s. To do so, it has relied on the results of the content analysis carried out on the case law between 1967 and 2016, a close reading of some of the recent landmark judgments, as well as the insights gathered from elite interviews conducted with current and former judges. I have assessed the extent to which the reformed Court resorts to selective forbearance, which spurs stagnation or even regression of the rights-expansive trends *only* with respect to certain obligations. I have found that the reformed Court, challenged by widespread negative feedback, selectively pays heed to member states' concerns, and I have explained how this bifurcated approach manifests itself.

The reformed Court continues a progressive line of reasoning when it comes to certain core obligations, such as the obligation to refrain from using excessive force during law enforcement operations (i.e., police brutality) or the provision of legal remedy. Yet, it adopts a more forbearing attitude toward certain other obligations, such as the obligation to uphold the *non-refoulement* principle or the provision of sufficient medical care in detention centres. Looking at the Court's recent decisions concerning the rights of irregular immigrants, refugees, and asylum seekers under Article 3, I have shown that the Court began to backtrack on its progressive

[106] For an analysis of the Court's resilience strategies, see Mikael Rask Madsen, "The Narrowing of the European Court of Human Rights? Legal Diplomacy, Situational Self-Restraint, and the New Vision for the Court," *European Convention on Human Rights Law Review* 2, no. 2 (2021): 180–208.

tendencies in the late 1990s and early 2000s. This evokes the memories of the old Court that had to prioritise member states' interests and could only enact change when it was absolutely safe to do so. I have concluded by exploring the future trajectory of the norm against torture and inhuman or degrading treatment, as the ECHR judges see it, and by discussing how these findings contribute to the debate on the backlash against international courts and liberal institutions.

8

Conclusion

International courts are important global actors of a complex nature. Unlike domestic courts, international courts do not represent government power, nor do they command unconditional or consistent state or public support. Nevertheless, continuous support from states is precisely what they need. The importance of states is the Achilles' heel for international courts. They need states to enforce their decisions and uphold their legitimacy. They also depend on states for funding, resources, and personnel. Therefore, courts need to maintain and, occasionally, cultivate state support. They do so by offering trade-offs or resorting to avoidance.[1] They allow states some leeway by either not finding them in violation or by passing on opportunities to recognise new individual rights and state obligations. To complicate matters, member states are not the only audiences that the international courts care about. Courts are also interested in obtaining and maintaining a good image in the eyes of the legal community, civil society, and academia. Such an objective requires completely different behaviour, such as issuing progressive landmark rulings or positively contributing to the development of International Law. We can, therefore, imagine international courts being pulled in opposite directions by these completely different motivations: keeping states content while upholding a good reputation in the eyes of the (legal) community.

This book presents theoretical insights into international courts' need for tactical balancing and how their relationship with states may shape their interpretive preferences by relying on the case of the European Court of Human Rights. I argue that courts like the European Court engage in resilience strategies necessary for their institutional survival – that is, maintaining their institution's image while also ensuring their continued access to resources and support. I identify two main resilience strategies: *forbearance*,

[1] Miles Jackson, "Judicial Avoidance at the European Court of Human Rights: Institutional Authority, the Procedural Turn, and Docket Control," *International Journal of Constitutional Law* 20, no. 1 (2022): 3.

which refers to the underutilization of one's institutional power;[2] and *audacity*, which describes an institution's use of its authority to the maximum. "Maximum" here means that an institution behaves legally and does not imply that it has crossed into abuse of power (i.e., excess). Forbearance, in turn, does not imply that an institution would refuse to undertake the functions for which it was created (i.e., dereliction). Rather, it means that they will exert the minimum effort without taking on the challenge of being actors of (progressive) change.

I argue that when forbearing, courts are less willing to recognise new rights and obligations, and they have an overall lower propensity for finding states in violation. On the contrary, when audacious, courts have more willingness to acknowledge new rights and obligations, and they have a higher propensity for finding states in violation. Forbearance and audacity have different implications. While forbearance signals that courts can operate at a lower sovereignty cost to member states, audacity sets them as authoritative voices of international legal development. Forbearance helps win over state support, while audacity replenishes courts' reputational credit in the eyes of the international legal community. They also produce different outcomes, especially in the field of international human rights governance. While audacity expands the protections offered to the victims, forbearance leads to retractive rulings reversing this expansion or upholding the *status quo* in favour of member states.

Theoretical Framework and Methods

International courts serve crucial functions such as dispute resolution, treaty application, or provision of legal advice. But, every one of them comes with sovereignty costs.[3] This means international courts are costly to states for a variety of reasons: First, international courts undertake functions that are normally state functions, such as interpreting treaties or completing incomplete contracts.[4] Hence, by delegating to courts, states

[2] Alisha Holland, *Forbearance as Redistribution: The Politics of Informal Welfare in Latin America* (Cambridge: Cambridge University Press, 2017); Alisha C. Holland, "Forbearance," *American Political Science Review* 110, no. 2 (2016): 232–46.

[3] Emilie M. Hafner-Burton, Edward D. Mansfield, and Jon C. W. Pevehouse, "Human Rights Institutions, Sovereignty Costs and Democratization," *British Journal of Political Science* 45, no. 1 (2015): 1–27.

[4] Clifford J. Carrubba and Matthew Gabel, "International Courts: A Theoretical Assessment," *Annual Review of Political Science* 20, no. 1 (2017): 55–73; Gillian K. Hadfield, "Judicial Competence and the Interpretation of Incomplete Contracts," *Journal of Legal Studies* 23, no. 1 (1994): 159-84.

lose some degree of control. Second, international courts exert a degree of authority over states. Courts like the European Court are mandated to review complaints brought by private individuals against states and ask them to pay compensation when found in violation. These are all costly for states, not only in the financial sense but also in a political and symbolic sense. International courts are also known to issue rulings with wider policy implications. For example, the European Court asked Austria to allow same-sex couples to adopt each other's children.[5] It requested Switzerland not to ban begging on the streets[6] and that Bulgaria improve the conditions of psychiatric institutions and social care homes.[7]

Relying on the existing literature, I argue that states may attempt to influence courts and reduce the sovereignty costs in two main ways: First, they may do so formally by limiting courts' discretionary space. Discretionary space refers to the room for manoeuvre that courts enjoy when undertaking their mandates. When this discretionary space is wide, they can carry out their functions in line with their own preferences without fearing repercussions from member states.[8] When it is narrow, then courts have limited discretion and are more likely to be deferent. Second, states may also seek to affect courts informally by resorting to negative feedback, which can come in different intensities ranging from criticism, political pushback, or full-on backlash.[9] When such feedback is sparse, it may not affect courts much. However, when it is widespread and shared by states which normally constitute the courts' support base, such negative feedback may influence the courts and their interpretive choices to a great extent.[10]

[5] *X. and Others* v. *Austria*, application no. 19010/07, ECHR[GC] (February 19, 2013). Only five months after this ruling, Austria amended its civil code to allow unmarried same-sex couples to adopt children. For more, ILGA Europe, "Austria becomes the 14th European country to allow same-sex second-parent adoption" (August 1, 2013) available at www.ilga-europe.org/resources/news/latest-news/austria-becomes-14th-european-country-allow-same-sex-second-parent.

[6] *Lăcătuş* v. *Switzerland*, application no. 14065/15, ECHR (January 19, 2021).

[7] *Stanev* v. *Bulgaria*, application no. 36760/06, ECHR[GC] (January 17, 2012).

[8] Alec Stone Sweet and Thomas Brunell, "Trustee Courts and the Judicialization of International Regimes: The Politics of Majoritarian Activism in the ECHR, the EU, and the WTO," *Journal of Law and Courts* 1, no. 1 (2013).

[9] Daniel Abebe and Tom Ginsburg, "The Dejudicialization of International Politics?," *International Studies Quarterly* 63, no. 3 (2019): 521–30; Richard H. Steinberg, "Judicial Lawmaking at the WTO: Discursive, Constitutional, and Political Constraints," *American Journal of International Law* 98, no. 2 (2004): 247–75.

[10] Alec Stone Sweet, Wayne Sandholtz, and Mads Andenas, "Dissenting Opinions and Rights Protection in the European Court: A Reply to Laurence Helfer and Erik Voeten,"

Drawing from the rich literature on international courts and judicial behaviour, as well as the insights gathered from expert interviews with judges and other legal professionals, I have created a theoretical framework. As explained in the Introduction and Chapter 1, one would expect that when courts have *narrow discretionary space* and *receive widespread negative feedback*, there will be less space for audacity, and they will lean toward forbearance. When courts have *narrow discretionary space* but are spared from *widespread negative feedback*, they can be selectively audacious – especially when the stakes are low or when dealing with politically less contentious issues. When courts have *wide discretionary space* and *no widespread negative feedback*, they will be overall audacious. When courts have *wide discretionary space* and *receive widespread negative feedback*, they will be selectively forbearing. While being overall audacious, they will act forbearingly when it comes to contentious issues. That is to say, their forbearance will be tailored to actual or potential criticism. The breadth of discretionary space determines the overall tendency; the existence of widespread negative feedback indicates whether a given court will resort to selective forbearance or not.

This theory works on the assumption that left to their own devices, courts like the European Court – whose mandate dictates that they protect and safeguard human rights – would be overall audacious. Nevertheless, formal constraints and widespread negative feedback from member states might compel the courts to consider forbearance or selective forbearance. Even a mere threat, when widespread, may influence the courts.

The theoretical framework operates on the meso-level and views these strategies to be decided collectively by the Court as an institution. While not counting out the importance of the input from individual judges, the theory views their influence to be diffuse. Judges elected for limited terms are not really the agents that store the Court's institutional memory and guard its culture. This is a task carried out by the long-term staff, or the Court's bureaucracy, so to speak, such as the members of the Registry and law clerks. In addition, the Court's long-term, yet not elected, staff also undertake or contribute to some of the core functions, such as admissibility decisions or legal review, and they help set the Court's institutional priorities.[11] They, therefore, also join in the efforts to strategically adjust the

European Journal of International Law 32, no. 3 (2021): 897–906; Laurence R. Helfer and Erik Voeten, "Walking Back Human Rights in Europe?" *European Journal of International Law* 31, no. 3 (2020): 797–827.

[11] For a great analysis of the international courts' bureaucracies, see Tommaso Soave, *The Everyday Makers of International Law: From Great Halls to Back Rooms*, Cambridge

Court's interpretive preferences. Underlining the role of the elected judges and non-elected Court bureaucracy, the book advances an institutional explanation as to why and how the Court adjusts its interpretive preferences. In so doing, it complements the existing approaches that explain judicial strategies based on judges' profiles,[12] or the presence of a coalition of subnational supporters (or compliance constituencies) that cultivate judicial lawmaking by facilitating the implementation of court rulings.[13]

The framework also considers additional sociopolitical and legal factors. It expects that the courts' audacious tendencies increase when change attempts are in line with (1) widespread societal needs, (2) well-established legal principles and precedents developed by other courts and institutions, and (3) civil society campaigns. Hence, these factors are important in cultivating progressive tendencies in international courts. However, they might not be sufficient on their own. I argue that courts cannot prioritise these external factors above state interests unless they enjoy a wide discretionary space. My findings support this expectation and underline the importance of these additional factors. Yet, they also show that, in the case of the European Court, the Court's relationship with states is the most influential factor, as is the degree to which states constrain the Court with direct and indirect control mechanisms.

The case of the European Court of Human Rights has provided a fruitful testing ground to observe how states' control mechanisms may influence international courts' behaviour and interpretive preferences. I have analyzed when and how much the European Court has been progressive by looking at its treatment of the prohibition of torture and inhuman or degrading

Studies in International and Comparative Law (Cambridge: Cambridge University Press, 2022); Tommaso Pavone, *The Ghostwriters: Lawyers and the Politics behind the Judicial Construction of Europe*, New edition (Cambridge and New York: Cambridge University Press, 2022).

12 Erik Voeten, "The Impartiality of International Judges: Evidence from the European Court of Human Rights," *American Political Science Review* 102, no. 4 (2008): 417–33; Erik Voeten, "The Politics of International Judicial Appointments: Evidence from the European Court of Human Rights," *International Organization* 61, no. 4 (2007): 669–701; Mikael Rask Madsen, "The Legitimization Strategies of International Judges: The Case of the European Court of Human Rights," in *Selecting Europe's Judges: A Critical Review of the Appointment Procedures to the European Courts*, ed. Michal Bobek (Oxford: Oxford University Press, 2015), 259–76.

13 See, for example, Karen J. Alter and Laurence R. Helfer, "Nature or Nurture?" Judicial Lawmaking in the European Court of Justice and the Andean Tribunal of Justice," *International Organization* 64, no. 4 (2010): 563–92; Øyvind Stiansen, "Directing Compliance? Remedial Approach and Compliance with European Court of Human Rights Judgments," *British Journal of Political Science* 51, no. 2 (2021): 899–907.

treatment between 1967 and 2016. Adopting a mixed-method approach, I have combined a range of social science methods with legal analysis. In particular, I have carried out content analysis of 2,294 rulings related to this prohibition to map out the Court's anti-torture jurisprudence. This large-scale analysis helped me identify when the Court acknowledged new obligations and when its propensity to find violations increased or decreased. I have supported these findings with legal analysis of landmark rulings and elite interviews conducted with experts both in and around the Court. More specifically, I interviewed current and former judges, law clerks working for the Court's Registry, representatives of civil society groups, and lawyers who brought cases before the Court. I have used these findings and insights to refine my key concepts and test my expectations.

The European Court is a fitting case to better understand how these expectations work in practice. Although the European Court might appear to be a single case, it is, in fact, three cases because the Court went through a significant institutional transformation in the course of its lifetime. Some of these transformations left a mark on its institutional structure, as well as its behaviour patterns. As explained in greater detail in Chapter 2, looking at the characteristics of the Court as an institution, one can confidently divide its history into three stages: the old Court, the new Court, and the reformed Court.

The Old Court (1959–1998)

The old Court is the earliest version of the Court. In this incarnation, the Court worked part-time and operated alongside the European Commission of Human Rights – a defunct institution that was in charge of filtering the applications brought by individuals and referring cases to the European Court. At this stage, the Court did not have full control of its docket. More importantly, the Court did not have compulsory jurisdiction. Initially, only a few states conditionally accepted the Court's jurisdiction, and their acceptance came with a time limit, two-to-five-year renewable terms. In other words, delegation to the Court was not automatic but optional. Similarly, not all the members accepted the right of individual petitions. They simply did not allow their citizens to bring a complaint before the European Court. This meant that the Court did not have a docket with a lifeline. Due to these structural constraints, it was not always clear that it would be able to carry out the functions for which it was created. The Court could enjoy only a narrow discretionary space, like a *tree in a box* with little space to grow.

The New Court (1998–2010)

The structure of the Court changed substantially in 1998 with Protocol 11. The Court became a permanent, full-time institution with compulsory jurisdiction. The European Commission which was formerly in charge of filtering applications was abolished. Therefore, individuals had direct access to the Court. Protocol 11 brought along two significant changes: First, all the member states of the Council of Europe had to recognise the Court's jurisdiction. This effectively meant that delegation to the Court became automatic. Second, all individuals residing in or complaining against any Council of Europe member state could bring their complaints before the Court without any exceptions. With these structural changes, the new Court could have a docket with a lifeline that the Court itself could control. This meant that the new Court began its life as an institution with a wide discretionary space. With its formal constraints removed, the Court finally had a space to grow and take root. It was finally taken out of its box and planted in the ground.

The Reformed Court (2010–Present)

This story had another twist, however. The Court's progressive rulings, especially about the rights of immigrants and states' duties to provide legal protection to vulnerable groups, caught political attention and became targets of political campaigns of mostly right-wing groups.[14] As a result, the Court entered a new phase in the 2010s. Member states attempted to take back some control and reduce their sovereignty costs. They effectively wanted to prune the growing tree that the Court became and to direct it as to where *not* to expand.

They did this in two ways: First, member states resorted to voicing public criticism at a greater rate, and as a result, negative feedback became more commonplace. Criticism came not only from countries like Russia and Turkey but from the United Kingdom, Switzerland, and Denmark.[15] It was troublesome to hear criticism coming from Western

[14] Erik Voeten, "Populism and Backlashes against International Courts," *Perspectives on Politics* 18, no. 2 (2020): 407–22; Mikael Rask Madsen, "Two-Level Politics and the Backlash against International Courts: Evidence from the Politicisation of the European Court of Human Rights," *The British Journal of Politics and International Relations* 22, no. 4 (2020): 728–38.

[15] Isabela Garbin Ramanzini and Ezgi Yildiz, 'Revamping to Remain Relevant: How Do the European and the Inter-American Human Rights Systems Adapt to Challenges?', *Journal of Human Rights Practice* 12, no. 3 (2020): 768–80.

democracies that normally constitute the Court's support base. Losing the support of its traditional allies would be more costly to the Court. Second, member states initiated a reform process to discuss the future of the Court with a series of High-Level Conferences held in Switzerland, Turkey, the United Kingdom, Belgium, and Denmark between 2010 and 2018. Meetings were concluded with declarations that served as road maps to improve the European human rights regime. States also used this opportunity to express their visions for the Court, criticizing some of its progressive tendencies, especially concerning the rights of immigrants.

These structural and contextual differences imply that the European Court can be considered as three distinct case studies. I have applied the theoretical framework, developed on the basis of secondary sources and expert interviews, to assess the degree to which the old Court, the new Court, and the reformed Court have been forbearing or audacious. To this end, I have used a large-N study of the case law on the prohibition of torture and inhuman or degrading treatment under the European Convention on Human Rights.

Findings

My analysis shows that the changing structural constraints and varying intensities of negative feedback informed the Court's operation and interpretive preferences and shaped the dominant judicial strategies at the Court. Table 8.1 situates the different incarnations of the Court and identifies their dominant judicial strategies with an increasing audacity scale in ascending order from (1) general forbearance, (2) selective audacity, and (3) selective forbearance to (4) general audacity.

While at no point did the Court have general forbearance as the overarching strategy (1), the old Court favoured selective audacity (2), alongside a tendency toward forbearance. The new Court could afford to adopt audacity as its main judicial strategy to a great extent (3), whereas the reformed Court resorted instead to selective forbearance (4) in order to mitigate the relentless negative feedback and the political pushback it received.

In addition to pointing out the overall tendencies of the Court – different versions of it, to be exact – Table 8.1 helps contextualise the Court's varying attitudes toward the prohibition of torture and inhuman or degrading treatment. The expectations presented in the table guide the identification of the three most important turning points in the Court's anti-torture jurisprudence.

Table 8.1 *Judicial strategies of the Court in its different incarnations*

		Widespread negative feedback	
		Yes	No
Discretionary space	Narrow	*General forbearance* (1)	*Selective audacity* (2) *Old Court
	Wide	*Selective forbearance* (3) *Reformed Court	*General audacity* (4) *New Court

First, the old Court showed an overall forbearing tendency with select audacious rulings concerning politically low-stake issues. Primarily, the old Court was hesitant to override states' national security concerns, yet it could make great strides when the stakes were low, most visibly observed in the case of judicial corporal punishment – a judicial practice that was not employed much in Europe except in the United Kingdom, as described in Chapter 4.

Second, the new Court exhibited an overall audacious tendency, as explained in Chapters 5 and 6. My analysis of the Court's jurisprudence over five decades confirms this and shows that the most significant transformation took place under the new Court's watch: The emergence of positive obligations transpired in the late 1990s in rapid succession and with virtually no opposition. This was also due to the favourable sociopolitical context, which allowed the new Court to audaciously effectuate change without prioritizing state interests. Despite their late appearance and resource-intensive nature, positive obligations constitute an important segment of the Court's jurisprudence on Article 3 – making up 62% of the jurisprudence between 1967 and 2016.

Finally, the reformed Court acted selectively forbearing. While it continued to audaciously develop certain obligations, such as refraining from inflicting police brutality, it shied away from doing so when it came to certain other obligations. This was most remarkable in its treatment of claims touching upon sensitive state interests, such as the rights of immigrants, asylum seekers, and refugees, or the state obligation to provide sufficient medical care in detention centres. The reformed Court turned to selective forbearance when treating these claims in order to mitigate and preempt widespread negative feedback and political pushback, as discussed in Chapter 7. Overlapping grievances expressed by the Court's long-time allies such as the United Kingdom, Denmark, and Switzerland (as well as by newcomers like Russia) compelled the Court to resort to forbearance in the 2010s, especially in cases related to the *non-refoulement* principle under Article 3. Yet, the reformed Court has kept up with a progressive record when it comes to other obligations, such as the provision of legal remedy or the obligation to curb excessive force during law enforcement operations.

The analysis of the reformed Court's bifurcated approach presents us with interesting results, some confirming and some deviating from the existing literature. First, the reformed Court's selective forbearance, especially concerning the *non-refoulement* principle, indicates that the driver behind the current trends at the Court might not be the changing profile of judges.[16] As explained in Chapter 7, a more state-friendly cohort of judges would have a lower propensity to find states in violation concerning most other less-established and resource-intensive obligations, such as the provision of legal protection and remedy. However, we observe exactly the opposite. The reformed Court increased its propensity to find a violation of the obligation to provide legal protection more than any other obligation. At the same time, it decreased its propensity to find a violation of the *non-refoulement* obligation more than any other obligation. The treatment of these two obligations could not be more different.

Second, looking at the reformed Court's treatment of the claims concerning the *non-refoulement* principle, I also observe a favourable treatment of Western European countries that are known to be "good faith interpreters" – similar to what is argued in the literature.[17] Third, an assessment of the reformed Court's approach to claims concerning medical care at detention facilities demonstrates the importance of issue characteristics, which has not been fully explored in the literature. In this case, we see that the reformed Court's selective forbearance is not limited to Western European countries. On the contrary, the reformed Court shows a good amount of deference to formerly communist countries, particularly when reviewing the quality of medical care offered and the applicants' request for release on health grounds. I argue that this is most likely because the reformed Court is hesitant to strongly enforce a resource-intensive

[16] The judges' changing profile has been presented as a potential explanation in Øyvind Stiansen and Erik Voeten, "Backlash and Judicial Restraint: Evidence from the European Court of Human Rights," *International Studies Quarterly* 64, no. 4 (2020): 770–84; Helfer and Voeten, "Walking Back Human Rights in Europe?"

[17] Başak Çalı, "Coping with Crisis: Whither the Variable Geomety in the Jurisprudence of the European Court of Human Rights," *Wisconsin International Law Journal* 35, no. 2 (2018): 237–76.

obligation in resource-poor countries and to overrule the decisions of the national authorities.

Perhaps the most vivid illustration of the reformed Court's bifurcated approach is the comparison of the recent landmark rulings on the living conditions of refugees and irregular migrants and the obligation not to inflict excessive violence during law enforcement operations. This comparative assessment reveals that while the reformed Court took a step back concerning the former, it took a step forward with respect to the latter. This finding reminds us that progress might not always be wholesale, and that progressive achievements might be more fragile than we realise; hard-earned rights, which we greatly enjoy today, might be chipped away or even unavailable tomorrow.

Contributions

Between Forbearance and Audacity demonstrates how norms are entangled with power. Sometimes norms constrain power, and sometimes they are constrained by power. The transformation of the norm against torture and inhuman or degrading treatment within the European human rights regime reflects this delicate balance. State control over the definition of norms may go beyond their role in drafting treaties. This is especially the case when they attempt to be back-seat drivers instead of yielding control to specialised authorities like international courts.[18] As for international courts, they are reliable checks on the excess of state power. Nevertheless, they may have their own drive for power, especially when they fall into an "authority trap," trading their progressive instincts for ideational and material resources.[19] Laws and norms that improve the lives of victims like Nahide develop in between these tactical moves against and for power. Yet, such victims are also the ones that bear the brunt of the Court's choice of forbearance over audacity. The degree of protection that these norms offer is not a given, nor is it always on the rise. This is most clearly seen in the case of the reformed Court's forbearing treatment of the claims concerning the *non-refoulement* principle and the rights of detained migrants.[20]

The theory and analysis presented here explain how such episodes of forbearance and audacity have left their mark on the norm against torture

[18] Ezgi Yildiz and Nico Krisch, "Authority Matters: Structures of Norm Change in International Politics," *Unpublished Manuscript*, 2022

[19] Sarah S. Stroup and Wendy H. Wong, *The Authority Trap: Strategic Choices of International NGOs* (Ithaca: Cornell University Press, 2017).

[20] Helfer and Voeten, "Walking Back Human Rights in Europe?"

and inhuman or degrading treatment. In so doing, they offer several contributions to the broader literature on international norms, international courts, and institutions. While some of these contributions are specific to the case of the European Court and its anti-torture jurisprudence, some prove themselves to be generalizable to understand the trends at other courts and institutions that work with delegated authority.

First, the empirical analysis helps trace the European Court's jurisprudential trends and explain why and when the Court has been progressive, as well as how norms change over time. The findings also document the contents of the norm against torture and inhuman or degrading treatment, showing that 62% of the claims under this norm pertain to positive obligations that only appeared on the radar in the late 1990s. This counterintuitive finding and contextualised analysis shed light on the European Court and the transformation of the norm against torture and inhuman or degrading treatment under the European Convention. Although the findings are specific to the case of Article 3, this approach identifies the conditions for transformative legal change and offers insights into how similar analyses can be conducted on other international courts or concerning other norms.

Second, the book also presents empirical evidence of how direct and indirect state control over courts may look. States can abolish courts or make them dysfunctional.[21] However, this is only in extreme cases. The more mundane and common effect that states often seek is influencing courts' interpretive choices, as we see here. This finding has implications for the recent debates on the backlash against international courts and liberal institutions. Beyond its normative impact, this recent wave of backlash has practical negative repercussions for the protection of vulnerable groups such as migrants and refugees in Europe and beyond. Because when states influence the courts' interpretive choices through negative feedback, it often comes at the expense of such vulnerable groups. My analysis shows that granting courts and institutions a wide zone of discretion will reduce the need for forbearance to cater to state interests (i.e., prioritizing state interests over their core objectives). It also points out the fact that states' expressed preferences for forbearance might have a long-term influence on judicial practices and human rights enforcement. Forbearing tendencies may have an enduring legacy, as we see in the case of

[21] See, for example, Mark A. Pollack, "International Court Curbing in Geneva: Lessons from the Paralysis of the WTO Appellate Body," *Governance*, accessed June 5, 2022, https://doi.org/10.1111/gove.12686.

the *Ireland* v. *the United Kingdom* ruling discussed in the Introduction.[22] Countering such tendencies with judicial courage and audacity requires a structurally favourable institutional setup and supportive discursive environment. Such concerns should be reflected in the institutional design decisions when creating and reforming international courts and court-like bodies.

Third, *Between Forbearance and Audacity* provides insights into the inner working of international courts. Courts and court-like institutions may not be only inclined to push the boundaries of their mandates.[23] On the contrary, they may occasionally choose to underutilise their privileges and power so they can cultivate state support – one can expect to see this pattern at other courts and institutions working with delegated authority. The framework and the key concepts, *audacity* and *forbearance*, promise to explain this dynamic elsewhere, such as in the International Court of Justice and the Court of Justice of the European Union. They can also explain some of the tendencies we observe in other institutions with delegated authority, such as the World Health Organization or the World Trade Organization. My findings here call for reflecting on state influence on other institutions with public policy impact, and for carrying out comparative studies on how they navigate their political environment and widespread negative feedback.

Taking Stock and Going Forward: Legal Change Elsewhere

International courts have always played an important role by updating treaties and completing incomplete contracts. Today, there is even an increased need for these functions. With the decline of multilateral treaty-making,[24] international courts are often called upon to offer governance solutions in areas where there is no clear international agreement, such as the environment or climate change.[25] Therefore, courts are likely to play

22 *Ireland* v. *the United Kingdom*, application no. 5310/71, ECHR (January 18, 1978).

23 Michael N. Barnett and Martha Finnemore, "The Politics, Power, and Pathologies of International Organizations," *International Organization* 53, no. 4 (1999): 699–732.

24 Joost Pauwelyn, Ramses A. Wessel, and Jan Wouters, "When Structures Become Shackles: Stagnation and Dynamics in International Lawmaking," *European Journal of International Law* 25, no. 3 (2014): 733–63; Nico Krisch, "The Decay of Consent: International Law in an Age of Global Public Goods," *American Journal of International Law* 108, no. 1 (2014): 1–40.

25 Helen Keller and Corina Heri, "The Future Is Now: Climate Cases before the ECtHR," *Nordic Journal of Human Rights* 40, no. 1 (2022): 153–174, https://doi.org/10.1080/18918131.2022.2064074.

even more important roles in the future. It is crucial to understand what motivates courts to adopt progressive agendas or back away from doing so.

Beyond the example of the transformation of the norm against torture and inhuman or degrading treatment, the analytical approach and the findings presented here offer a way to study legal change to better understand when international courts are likely to serve as change agents. This is a phenomenon that has so far received limited attention in the International Relations literature on international norms and legal change.[26] The role of international courts does not take up an important place in analyses of how norms are created or how they change over time.[27] Treaty negotiations, where the parties come up with definitions and standards that are most favourable to them, are considered the decisive political interactions. However, as we have seen, lawmaking continues beyond this moment of origin. The extralegal concerns, especially the role of power, that are at the forefront during treaty negotiations do not suddenly disappear when the treaties are concluded. Instead, they retreat to the background, informing the way in which international courts and tribunals apply those treaties. This book has brought these concerns to light, in particular, the role of structural constraints and powerful criticism on the international courts' likelihood to initiate progressive legal change.

Another important novelty that the book has advocated for is disaggregating abstract norms into tangible obligations. Doing so means taking obligations as a reference point to study norm change. Focusing on obligations helps trace not only how norms change over time, but also how norms are contested and why certain norms are not fully internalised. First, it is possible to contest a portion of a norm rather than contesting it in its entirety. Contestation might be directed at some of the obligations contained within the norm. For example, state contestation about their obligation to provide ideal living conditions to irregular migrants and refugees does not necessarily imply the contestation of the norm against torture and inhuman or degrading treatment in its entirety. European states

[26] There are, of course, notable exceptions. See, for example, Laurence R. Helfer and Erik Voeten, "International Courts as Agents of Legal Change: Evidence from LGBT Rights in Europe," *International Organization* 68, no. 1 (2014): 77–110; Ingo Venzke, *How Interpretation Makes International Law: On Semantic Change and Normative Twists* (Oxford and New York: Oxford University Press, 2012).

[27] For exceptions, see Druscilla Scribner and Tracy Slagter, "Recursive Norm Development: The Role of Supranational Courts," *Global Policy* 8, no. 3 (2017): 322–32; Zoltán I Búzás and Erin R Graham, "Emergent Flexibility in Institutional Development: How International Rules Really Change," *International Studies Quarterly* 64, no. 4 (2020): 821–33.

may continue to comply with the rest of the obligations that the norm entails, only objecting to that specific portion.

Second, the norm's transformation might make it difficult for states to comply.[28] As legal standards of accountability increase over time, states have to continuously adapt their practices to remain in compliance with the norm. This requires states to be more actively engaged if they intend to keep up with changing standards. For example, after Nahide's case, where the Court formally acknowledged states' obligation to protect domestic violence victims under Article 3, Turkey and other European countries had to readjust their own national policies and legal practices in order to remain compliant. Norm compliance, therefore, is not a one-time effort that can only be measured by taking state ratification of relevant international treaties as a reference.[29] Rather, it is an ongoing iterative exercise that requires states to follow decisions of international courts and institutions concerning what a given norm entails.

Moreover, the theoretical framework, key concepts, and methodological approach adopted here open up new avenues for research on international courts and norm development. Similar studies can be conducted with respect to other legal norms in the European Convention. The proposed framework and methodology also display strong potential for uncovering the behavior of a range of judicial and quasi-judicial interpretative bodies – such as the Inter-American Court of Human Rights, the Court of Justice of the European Union, the International Court of Justice, the International Criminal Court, the International Criminal Tribunals for Rwanda and Yugoslavia, or relevant UN treaty bodies. The framework and associated concepts could also be used in a comparative fashion to probe the extent to which international courts tend to serve as actors of change. An analysis of how tribunals with roughly similar zones of discretion effect (or fail to effect) change would serve as a good basis to better understand international courts' behavior.[30]

[28] What I refer to here is norm compliance rather than compliance with court judgments.

[29] Emilie M. Hafner-Burton and Kiyoteru Tsutsui, "Human Rights in a Globalizing World: The Paradox of Empty Promises," *American Journal of Sociology* 110, no. 5 (2005): 1373–1411; Steven C. Poe, "The Decision to Repress: An Integrative Theoretical Approach to the Research on Human Rights and Repression," in *Understanding Human Rights Violations*, ed. Sabine C. Carey and Steven C. Poe (Burlington: Ashgate, 2004), 16–38.

[30] For some recent examples of such comparative analyses, see Jillienne Haglund, *Regional Courts, Domestic Politics, and the Struggle for Human Rights* (Cambridge: Cambridge University Press, 2020); Courtney Hillebrecht, *Saving the International Justice Regime: Beyond Backlash against International Courts* (Cambridge and New York: Cambridge University Press, 2021).

The re-application of the framework introduced here requires calibrating the concepts and the scope conditions, however. The importance of the zone of discretion would still apply in general, but its determinants should be established in a particular context and for a given court. As explained in the Introduction and Chapter 1, an international court's discretionary space enlarges and shrinks as a function of its autonomy or authority. A court's autonomy is measured in reference to its independence from the member states that fall under a given court's jurisdiction. A court's authority emanates from its reputation not only in the eyes of states but also among the broader international community. For some courts and quasi-judicial bodies, authority can be boosted by the support of national judiciaries or civil society groups in the absence of strong political support.[31]

For example, the Inter-American Court of Human Rights is a very different institution, structurally and culturally.[32] Unlike the European Court, it has diversified its source of support and funding.[33] It has successfully built an alternative support group that includes diverse actors, such as civil society organizations, international organizations, and European governments.[34] This has reduced the Inter-American Court's dependency on member states and created the space for the Inter-American Court to refine its trademark as a progressive human rights court, which is the key to retaining and enlarging its alternative support group. The existence of such alternative supporters would ideally weaken the influence of some negative feedback effect, for example. Thus, the framework should be adjusted in light of such particular features when applied to other courts and contexts.

Such comparative assessments and sophisticated studies that look into the political dynamics of court practices are more necessary than

[31] Alexandra Huneeus, Javier Couso, and Rachel Sieder, "Introduction," in *Cultures of Legality: Judicialization and Political Activism in Latin America*, ed. Javier Couso, Alexandra Huneeus, and Rachel Sieder (Cambridge University Press, 2010), 3; Alexandra Huneeus, "Constitutional Lawyers and the Inter-American Court's Varied Authority," *Law and Contemporary Problems* 79, no. 1 (2016): 183.

[32] Ezgi Yildiz, "Enduring Practices in Changing Circumstances: A Comparison of the European Court of Human Rights and the Inter-American Court of Human Rights," *Temple International and Comparative Law Journal* 34, no. 2 (2020): 309–38.

[33] Silvia Steininger, "Creating Loyalty: Communication Practices in the European and Inter-American Human Rights Regimes," *Global Constitutionalism* 11, no. 2 (2022): 161-196.

[34] Heidi Nichols Haddad, *The Hidden Hands of Justice: NGOs, Human Rights, and International Courts* (New York: Cambridge University Press, 2018); Heidi Nichols Haddad, "Judicial Institution Builders: NGOs and International Human Rights Courts," *Journal of Human Rights* 11, no. 1 (2012): 126–49.

ever.[35] Growth in the emergence and use of international courts is a distinctive feature of the post-Cold War period. This is not likely to go away. What is new in this picture is the varying degree of political push-back and backlash against these courts. The strategies of such attacks may vary, yet their overall purpose is to subdue these institutions. This is why it is imperative to study how courts and court-like bodies work under ideal circumstances, as well as how they operate under pressure. Such analyses are vital to reveal the causes of jurisprudential trends that expand or restrict rights. They also demonstrate how power operates behind the scenes to choose which victims deserve protection and how much protection they deserve. Through such analyses, we also get to learn more about how norms shape power and how legal refinement touches the lives of victims we encountered in this book, such as Nahide. While they remain the real protagonists of legal change, their impact is filtered through various institutional concerns and the changing winds of power.

[35] Roger P. Alford, "The Proliferation of International Courts and Tribunals: International Adjudication in Ascendance," *Proceedings of the ASIL Annual Meeting* 94 (2000): 160–65; Thomas Buergenthal, "Proliferation of International Courts and Tribunals: Is It Good or Bad?," *Leiden Journal of International Law* 14, no. 2 (2001): 267–75.

BIBLIOGRAPHY

Abbott, Kenneth W., Robert O. Keohane, Andrew Moravcsik, Anne-Marie Slaughter, and Duncan Snidal. "The Concept of Legalization." *International Organization* 54, no. 3 (2000): 401–19. https://doi.org/10.1162/002081800551271.

Abbott, Kenneth W., and Duncan Snidal. "Hard and Soft Law in International Governance." *International Organization* 54, no. 3 (2000): 421–56. https://doi.org/10.1162/002081800551280.

Abbott, Kenneth W., and Duncan Snidal. "Why States Act through Formal International Organizations." *Journal of Conflict Resolution* 42, no. 1 (1998): 3–32.

Abebe, Daniel, and Tom Ginsburg. "The Dejudicialization of International Politics?" *International Studies Quarterly* 63, no. 3 (2019): 521–30. https://doi.org/10.1093/isq/sqz032.

Acharya, Amitav. "How Ideas Spread: Whose Norms Matter? Norm Localization and Institutional Change in Asian Regionalism." *International Organization* 58, no. 2 (2004): 239–75.

Addo, Michael K., and Nicholas Grief. "Does Article 3 of the European Convention on Human Rights Enshrine Absolute Rights?" *European Journal of International Law* 9, no. 3 (1998): 510–24. https://doi.org/10.1093/ejil/9.3.510.

Aksenova, Marina, and Iryna Marchuk. "Reinventing or Rediscovering International Law? The Russian Constitutional Court's Uneasy Dialogue with the European Court of Human Rights." *International Journal of Constitutional Law* 16, no. 4 (2018): 1322–46. https://doi.org/10.1093/icon/moy088.

Alford, Roger P. "The Proliferation of International Courts and Tribunals: International Adjudication in Ascendance." *Proceedings of the ASIL Annual Meeting* 94 (2000): 160–65. https://doi.org/10.1017/S027250370005549X.

Allhoff, Fritz. *Terrorism, Ticking Time-Bombs, and Torture*. Chicago: The University of Chicago Press, 2012.

Alston, Philip, and Gerard Quinn. "The Nature and Scope of States Parties' Obligations under the International Covenant on Economic, Social and Cultural Rights." *Human Rights Quarterly* 9, no. 2 (1987): 156–229. https://doi.org/10.2307/762295.

Alter, Karen J. "Agents or Trustees? International Courts in Their Political Context." *European Journal of International Relations* 14, no. 1 (2008): 33–63. https://doi.org/10.1177/1354066107087769.

Alter, Karen J. "'Delegating to International Courts: Self-Binding vs. Other-Binding Del' by Karen J. Alter." *Law and Contemporary Problems* 71, no. 1 (2008).

Alter, Karen J. "The Evolution of International Law and Courts." *The Oxford Handbook of Historical Institutionalism*, March 17, 2016. https://doi.org/10.1093/oxfordhb/9780199662814.013.35.

Alter, Karen J. *The New Terrain of International Law: Courts, Politics, Rights.* Princeton and Oxford: Princeton University Press, 2014.

Alter, Karen J., and Laurence R. Helfer. "Nature or Nurture? Judicial Lawmaking in the European Court of Justice and the Andean Tribunal of Justice." *International Organization* 64, no. 4 (2010): 563–92. https://doi.org/10.1017/S0020818310000238.

Alter, Karen J., James T. Gathii, and Laurence R. Helfer. "Backlash against International Courts in West, East and Southern Africa: Causes and Consequences." *European Journal of International Law* 27, no. 2 (2016): 293–328. https://doi.org/10.1093/ejil/chw019.

Alter, Karen J., Laurence R. Helfer, and Mikael Madsen. "How Context Shapes the Authority of International Courts." *Law and Contemporary Problems* 79, no. 1 (2016): 1–36.

Altwicker, Tilmann. "Switzerland: The Substitute Constitution in Times of Popular Dissent." In *Criticism of the European Court of Human Rights: Shifting the Convention System: Counter-Dynamics at the National and EU Level*, edited by Patricia Popelier, Koen Lemmens, and Sarah Lambrecht, 385–411. Cambridge: Intersentia, 2016.

Anagnostou, Dia. "The Strasbourg Court, Democracy and the Protection of Marginalised Individuals and Minorities." In *The European Court of Human Rights and the Rights of Marginalised Individuals and Minorities in National Context*, edited by Dia Anagnostou and Evangelia Psychogiopoulou, 1–26. Leiden and Boston: Brill Nijhoff, 2010.

Arendt, Hannah. *Eichmann in Jerusalem: A Report on the Banality of Evil*, 1st edition. New York: Penguin Classics, 2006.

Arnardóttir, Oddný Mjöll. "The Brighton Aftermath and the Changing Role of the European Court of Human Rights." *Journal of International Dispute Settlement* 9, no. 2 (2018), 223–39. https://doi.org/10.1093/jnlids/idx002.

Arold, Nina-Louisa. *The Legal Culture of the European Court of Human Rights.* Leiden and Boston: Brill Nijhoff, 2007.

Association for the Prevention of Torture. "The Definition of Torture: Proceedings of an Expert Seminar." Geneva, November 10, 2001.

Aubrey, Stefan M. *The New Dimension of International Terrorism.* Zurich: VDF Hochschulverlag AG, 2004.

Aydinli, Ersel. "Between Security and Liberalization: Decoding Turkey's Struggle with the PKK." *Security Dialogue* 33, no. 2 (2002): 209–25.

Baer, Madeline. *Stemming the Tide: Human Rights and Water Policy in a Neoliberal World.* New York: Oxford University Press, 2017.

Bantekas, Ilias, and Lutz Oette. *International Human Rights Law and Practice*. New York: Cambridge University Press, 2013.

Barber, Catherine Corey. "Tackling the Evaluation Challenge in Human Rights: Assessing the Impact of Strategic Litigation Organisations." *The International Journal of Human Rights* 16, no. 3 (2012): 411–35.

Barnett, Michael, and Liv Coleman. "Designing Police: Interpol and the Study of Change in International Organizations." *International Studies Quarterly* 49, no. 4 (2005): 593–619.

Barnett, Michael N., and Martha Finnemore. "The Politics, Power, and Pathologies of International Organizations." *International Organization* 53, no. 4 (1999): 699–732.

Basoğlu, Metin, ed. *Torture and Its Definition in International Law: An Interdisciplinary Approach*. New York: Oxford University Press, 2017.

Bates, Ed. "The Birth of the European Convention on Human Rights – and the European Court of Human Rights." In *The European Court of Human Rights between Law and Politics*, edited by Jonas Christoffersen and Mikael Rask Madsen, 17–42. New York: Oxford University Press, 2011.

Bates, Ed. *The Evolution of the European Convention on Human Rights: From Its Inception to the Creation of a Permanent Court of Human Rights*. Oxford and New York: Oxford University Press, 2010.

Baumgärtel, Moritz. *Demanding Rights: Europe's Supranational Courts and the Dilemma of Migrant Vulnerability*. Cambridge: Cambridge University Press, 2019.

Baumgärtel, Moritz. "Facing the Challenge of Migratory Vulnerability in the European Court of Human Rights." *Netherlands Quarterly of Human Rights* 38, no. 1 (2020): 12–29. https://doi.org/10.1177/0924051919898127.

Baxter, Richard Reeve "International Law in 'Her Infinite Variety.'" *International and Comparative Law Quarterly* 29, no. 4 (1980): 549–66.

Becket, James. "The Greek Case before the European Human Rights Commission." *Human Rights* 1, no. 1 (1970): 91–117.

Ben-Josef Hirsch, Michal, and Jennifer M. Dixon. "Conceptualizing and Assessing Norm Strength in International Relations." *European Journal of International Relations* 27 no. 2 (2021): 521–547. https://doi.org/10.1177/1354066120949628.

Berger, Tobias. *Global Norms and Local Courts: Translating the Rule of Law in Bangladesh*. Oxford and New York: Oxford University Press, 2017.

Beyer, Jessica L., and Stephanie C. Hofmann. "Varieties of Neutrality: Norm Revision and Decline." *Cooperation and Conflict* 46, no. 3 (2011): 285–311. https://doi.org/10.1177/0010836711416956.

Bogdandy, Armin von, and Ingo Venzke. "In Whose Name? An Investigation of International Courts' Public Authority and Its Democratic Justification." *European Journal of International Law* 23, no. 1 (2012): 7–41. https://doi.org/10.1093/ejil/chr106.

Bothe, Michael. "Legal and Non-Legal Norms – a Meaningful Distinction in International Relations?" *Netherlands Yearbook of International Law* 11 (1980): 65–95. https://doi.org/10.1017/S0167676800002725.

Boucher, David. *The Limits of Ethics in International Relations: Natural Law, Natural Rights, and Human Rights in Transition*. Oxford and New York: Oxford University Press, 2009.

Bradley, Curtis, and Judith Kelley. "The Concept of International Delegation." *Law and Contemporary Problems* 71, no. 1 (2008): 1–36.

Brems, Eva. "Positive Subsidiarity and Its Implications for the Margin of Appreciation Doctrine." *Netherlands Quarterly of Human Rights* 37, no. 3 (2019): 201-27. https://doi.org/10.1177/0924051919861798.

Brems, Eva, and Janneke Gerards, eds. *Shaping Rights in the ECHR: The Role of the European Court of Human Rights in Determining the Scope of Human Rights*. Cambridge: Cambridge University Press, 2014.

Brems, Eva, and Laurens Lavrysen. "Procedural Justice in Human Rights Adjudication: The European Court of Human Rights." *Human Rights Quarterly* 35, no. 1 (2013): 176–200.

Breyer, Stephen. "Judicial Activism: Power without Responsibility?" In *Judicial Activism: Power without Responsibility?*, edited by Benjamin Kiely, 71–86. Melbourne: The University of Melbourne, 2006.

Brunnée, Jutta, and Stephen J. Toope. *Legitimacy and Legality in International Law: An Interactional Account*. Cambridge: Cambridge University Press, 2010.

Bryman, Alan. *Social Research Methods*, 4th edition. Oxford and New York: Oxford University Press, 2012.

Brysk, Alison, and Michael Stohl. *Contesting Human Rights: Norms, Institutions and Practice*. Cheltenham: Edward Elgar Publishing, 2019.

Buergenthal, Thomas. "Proliferation of International Courts and Tribunals: Is It Good or Bad?" *Leiden Journal of International Law* 14, no. 2 (2001): 267–75. https://doi.org/10.1017/S0922156501000139.

Burai, Erna. "Parody as Norm Contestation: Russian Normative Justifications in Georgia and Ukraine and Their Implications for Global Norms." *Global Society* 30, no. 1 (2016): 67–77. https://doi.org/10.1080/13600826.2015.1092424.

Búzás, Zoltán I, and Erin R Graham. "Emergent Flexibility in Institutional Development: How International Rules Really Change." *International Studies Quarterly* 64, no. 4 (2020): 821–33. https://doi.org/10.1093/isq/sqaa049.

Byron, Christine. "A Blurring of the Boundaries: The Application of International Humanitarian Law by Human Rights Bodies." *Virginia Journal of International Law* 47, no. 4 (2007): 839–96.

Cakal, Ergun. "Assessing (and Making Sense of) Severity: Conceptualising and Contextualising Torture's Core." *Nordic Journal of International Law* 91, no. 2 (2022): 284–309. https://doi.org/10.1163/15718107-91020003.

Çalı, Başak. "Autocratic Strategies and the European Court of Human Rights." *European Convention on Human Rights Law Review* 2, no. 1 (2021): 11–19. https://doi.org/10.1163/26663236-bja10015.

Çalı, Başak. "Coping with Crisis: Whither the Variable Geometry in the Jurisprudence of the European Court of Human Rights." *Wisconsin International Law Journal* 35, no. 2 (2018): 237–76.

Çalı, Başak, Cathryn Costello, and Stewart Cunningham. "Hard Protection through Soft Courts? Non-Refoulement before the United Nations Treaty Bodies." *German Law Journal* 21, no. 3 (April 2020): 355–84. https://doi.org/10.1017/glj.2020.28.

Çalı, Basak, Anne Koch, and Nicola Bruch. "The Legitimacy of Human Rights Courts: A Grounded Interpretivist Analysis of the European Court of Human Rights." *Human Rights Quarterly* 35, no. 4 (2013): 955–84.

Capoccia, Giovanni. "When Do Institutions 'Bite'? Historical Institutionalism and the Politics of Institutional Change." *Comparative Political Studies* 49, no. 8 (2016): 1095–1127. https://doi.org/10.1177/0010414015626449.

Capoccia, Giovanni, and R. Daniel Kelemen. "The Study of Critical Junctures: Theory, Narrative, and Counterfactuals in Historical Institutionalism." *World Politics* 59, no. 3 (2007): 341–69.

Caron, David D. "Towards a Political Theory of International Courts and Tribunals." *Berkeley Journal of International Law* 24, no. 2 (2006): 401–22.

Carrubba, Clifford J., and Matthew Gabel. "International Courts: A Theoretical Assessment." *Annual Review of Political Science* 20, no. 1 (2017): 55–73. https://doi.org/10.1146/annurev-polisci-051215-022917.

Cassese, Antonio. "The Prohibition on Torture and Inhuman or Degrading Treatment or Punishment." In *Human Dimension of International Law: Selected Papers of Antoine Cassese*, edited by Paola Gaeta and Salvatore Zappala, 295–331. New York: Oxford University Press, 2008.

Cerna, Christina M. "The Inter-American System for the Protection of Human Rights." *Florida Journal of International Law* 16, no. 1 (2004): 195–211.

Chandler, David. "The Ideological (Mis)Use of Human Rights." In *Human Rights: Politics and Practice*, edited by Michael Goodhart, 189–212. Oxford: Oxford University Press, 2009.

Christoffersen, Jonas, and Mikael Rask Madsen. "Introduction: The European Court of Human Rights between Law and Politics." In *The European Court of Human Rights between Law and Politics*, edited by Jonas Christoffersen and Mikael Rask Madsen, 1–14. New York: Oxford University Press, 2011.

Cichowski, Rachel A. "Civil Society and the European Court of Human Rights – Oxford Scholarship." In *The European Court of Human Rights between Law and Politics*, edited by Jonas Christoffersen and Mikael Rask Madsen, 77–97. Oxford: Oxford University Press, 2011.

Clark, Robert P. "Patterns of ETA Violence, 1968–1980." In *Political Violence and Terror: Motifs and Motivations*, edited by Peter H. Merkl, 283–311. Berkeley: University of California Press, 1986.

Clifford, Bob. "Introduction: Fighting for New Rights." In *The International Struggle for New Human Rights*, edited by Bob Clifford, 1–13. Philadelphia: University of Pennsylvania Press, 2011.

Cohen, Harlan. "Theorizing Precedent in International Law." In *Interpretation in International Law*, edited by Andrea Bianchi, Daniel Behn, and Matthew Windsor, 268–89. Oxford: Oxford University Press, 2015.

Cohen, Harlan Grant, Nienke Grossman, Andreas Follesdal, and Geir Ulfstein, eds., *Legitimacy and International Courts*. Cambridge: Cambridge University Press, 2018.

Colter, Lucy, and Can Yeginsu. "Inquests and the 'Detachable' Article 2 Obligation: In Re McCaughey." *Judicial Review* 16, no. 3 (2011): 290–96. https://doi.org/10.5235/108546811797434110.

Cooley, Alexander. "Authoritarianism Goes Global: Countering Democratic Norms." *Journal of Democracy* 26, no. 3 (2015): 49–63. https://doi.org/10.1353/jod.2015.0049.

Coolsaet, Rik. "EU Counterterrorism Strategy: Value Added or Chimera?" *International Affairs* 86, no. 4 (2010): 857–73.

Cooper, Sarah Lucy. "Marriage, Family, Discrimination & Contradiction: An Evaluation of the Legacy and Future of the European Court of Human Rights' Jurisprudence on LGBT Rights." *German Law Journal* 12, no. 10 (2011): 1746–63. https://doi.org/10.1017/S2071832200017545.

Cornell, Svante E. "The Kurdish Question in Turkish Politics." In *Dangerous Neighborhood: Contemporary Issues in Turkey's Foreign Relations*, edited by Michael Radu, 123–42. New Brunswick and London: Transaction Publishers, 2003.

Council of Europe. "Preparatory Work on Article 3 of the European Convention of Human Rights." DH (56) 5. Strasbourg, May 22, 1956.

Council of Europe. "Vienna Declaration," October 9, 1993. https://search.coe.int/cm/Pages/result_details.aspx?ObjectId=0900001680536c83.

Creamer, Cosette D., and Zuzanna Godzimirska. "Trust in the Court: The Role of the Registry of the European Court of Human Rights." *European Journal of International Law* 30, no. 2 (2019): 665–87. https://doi.org/10.1093/ejil/chz035.

Cross, Frank B., and Stefanie A. Lindquist. "The Scientific Study of Judicial Activism." *Minnesota Law Review* 91, no. 6 (2007): 1752–84.

Danish and Chairmanship of the Committee of Ministers of the Council of Europe. "Draft Copenhagen Declaration," February 5, 2018. https://menneskeret.dk/sites/menneskeret.dk/files/media/dokumenter/nyheder/draft_copenhagen_declaration_05.02.18.pdf.

Deitelhoff, Nicole, and Lisbeth Zimmermann. "Norms under Challenge: Unpacking the Dynamics of Norm Robustness." *Journal of Global Security Studies* 4, no. 1 (2019): 2–17. https://doi.org/10.1093/jogss/ogy041.

Deitelhoff, Nicole, and Lisbeth Zimmermann. "Things We Lost in the Fire: How Different Types of Contestation Affect the Robustness of International Norms." *International Studies Review* 22, no. 1 (2020): 51–76. https://doi.org/10.1093/isr/viy080.

Diehl, Paul F., and Charlotte Ku. *The Dynamics of International Law*. Cambridge: Cambridge University Press, 2010.

Dignan, James. *Understanding Victims and Restorative Justice*. New York: Open University Press, 2005.

Donahue, Deirdre. "Human Rights in Northern Ireland: Ireland v. the United Kingdom." *Boston College International and Comparative Law Review* 3, no. 2 (1980): 377–432.

Donald, Alice, and Philip Leach. "A Wolf in Sheep's Clothing: Why the Draft Copenhagen Declaration Must Be Rewritten." *EJIL: Talk!* (blog), February 21, 2018. www.ejiltalk.org/a-wolf-in-sheeps-clothing-why-the-draft-copenhagen-declaration-must-be-rewritten/.

Donnelly, Jack. "Normative versus Taxonomic Humanity: Varieties of Human Dignity in the Western Tradition." *Journal of Human Rights* 14, no. 1 (2015): 1–22.

Donnelly, Jack. *Universal Human Rights in Theory and Practice*. Ithaca: Cornell University Press, 2013.

Dothan, Shai. "Judicial Tactics in the European Court of Human Rights." *Chicago Journal of International Law* 12, no. 1 (2011). https://chicagounbound.uchicago.edu/cjil/vol12/iss1/6.

Dothan, Shai. *Reputation and Judicial Tactics: A Theory of National and International Courts*. Cambridge: Cambridge University Press, 2014.

Dunne, Tim, and Marianne Hanson. "Human Rights in International Relations." In *Human Rights: Politics and Practice*, 3rd edition, edited by Michael Goodhart, 61–76. Oxford: Oxford University Press, 2016.

Dunoff, Jeffrey L., and Mark A. Pollack. "International Judicial Practices: Opening the Black Box of International Courts." *Michigan Journal of International Law* 40, no. 1 (2018): 47–114.

Dunoff, Jeffrey L., and Mark A. Pollack. "The Judicial Trilemma." *American Journal of International Law* 111, no. 2 (2017): 225–76. https://doi.org/10.1017/ajil.2017.23.

Duranti, Marco. *The Conservative Human Rights Revolution: European Identity, Transnational Politics, and the Origins of the European Convention*. Oxford and New York: Oxford University Press, 2017.

Dzehtsiarou, Kanstantsin. *Can the European Court of Human Rights Shape European Public Order?* Cambridge: Cambridge University Press, 2021.

Dzehtsiarou, Kanstantsin. "European Consensus and the Evolutive Interpretation of the European Convention on Human Rights." *German Law Journal* 12, no. 10 (2011): 1731–45.

Dzehtsiarou, Kanstantsin. *European Consensus and the Legitimacy of the European Court of Human Rights*. Cambridge: Cambridge University Press, 2015.

Dzehtsiarou, Kanstantsin, and Alan Greene. "Legitimacy and the Future of the European Court of Human Rights: Critical Perspectives from Academia and Practitioners." *German Law Journal*. 12, no. 10 (2011): 1707–15.

Dzehtsiarou, Kanstantsin, and Conor O'Mahony. "Evolutive Interpretation of Rights Provisions: A Comparison of the European Court of Human Rights and the U.S. Supreme Court." *Columbia Human Rights Law Review* 44, no. 2 (2013): 309–66.

Ebobrah, Solomon T. "International Human Rights Courts." In *The Oxford Handbook of International Adjudication*, edited by Cesare Romano, Yuval Shany, and Karen J. Alter, 225–49. Oxford and New York: Oxford University Press, 2014.

Elsig, Manfred, and Mark A. Pollack. "Agents, Trustees, and International Courts: The Politics of Judicial Appointment at the World Trade Organization." *European Journal of International Relations* 20, no. 2 (2014): 391–415. https://doi.org/10.1177/1354066112448201.

European Court of Human Rights. "Annual Report 2011." Strasbourg: Registry of the European Court, 2012.

European Court of Human Rights. "ECHR Registry." Accessed September 10, 2019. www.echr.coe.int/Pages/home.aspx?p=court/howitworks&c=.

European Court of Human Rights. "Practical Guide on Admissibility Criteria," January 1, 2014. Available at www.echr.coe.int/Documents/Admissibility_guide_ENG.pdf.

European Court of Human Rights. "Reform of the Court: Filtering of Cases Successful in Reducing Backlog." *Press Release, ECHR 312 (2013)*, October 24, 2013.

European Court of Human Rights. Rules of the Court (2014). www.echr.coe.int/Documents/Rules_Court_ENG.pdf.

Fariss, Christopher J. "The Changing Standard of Accountability and the Positive Relationship between Human Rights Treaty Ratification and Compliance." *British Journal of Political Science* 48, no. 1 (2018): 239–71. https://doi.org/10.1017/S000712341500054X.

Fariss, Christopher J. "Respect for Human Rights Has Improved over Time: Modeling the Changing Standard of Accountability." *American Political Science Review* 108, no. 2 (2014): 297–318.

Fariss, Christopher J., and Geoff Dancy. "Measuring the Impact of Human Rights: Conceptual and Methodological Debates." *Annual Review of Law and Social Science* 13, no. 1 (2017): 273–94. https://doi.org/10.1146/annurev-lawsocsci-110316-113333.

Fenwick, Helen. "Enhanced Subsidiarity and a Dialogic Approach – Or Appeasement in Recen Cases on Criminal Justice, Public Order and Counter-Terrorism at Strasbourg against the UK?" In *The UK and European Human Rights: A Strained Relationship?*, edited by Katja S. Ziegler, Elizabeth Wicks, and Loveday Hodson, 193–214. Oxford and Portland: Bloomsbury Publishing, 2015.

Ferrer Mac-Gregor, Eduardo. "The Right to the Truth as an Autonomous Right under the Inter-American Human Rights System." *Mexican Law Review* 9, no. 1 (2016): 121–39. https://doi.org/10.1016/j.mexlaw.2016.09.007.

Finnemore, Martha, and Kathryn Sikkink. "International Norm Dynamics and Political Change." *International Organization* 52, no. 4 (1998): 887–917.

Fioretos, Orfeo. "Historical Institutionalism in International Relations." *International Organization* 65, no. 2 (2011): 367–99.

Fleischer, Julia, and Nina Reiners. "Connecting International Relations and Public Administration: Toward a Joint Research Agenda for the Study of International Bureaucracy." *International Studies Review* 23, no. 4 (2021): 1230–47. https://doi.org/10.1093/isr/viaa097.

Føllesdal, Andreas. "Subsidiarity and International Human-Rights Courts: Respecting Self-Governance and Protecting Human Rights – Or Neither?" *Law and Contemporary Problems* 79, no. 2 (2016): 147–63.

Follesdal, Andreas. "Survey Article: The Legitimacy of International Courts." *Journal of Political Philosophy* 28, no. 4 (2020): 476–99. https://doi.org/10.1111/jopp.12213.

Follesdal, Andreas, Johan Karlsson Schaffer, and Geir Ulfstein. "International Human Rights and the Challenge of Legitimacy." In *The Legitimacy of International Human Rights Regimes: Legal, Political and Philosophical Perspectives*, edited by Andreas Føllesdal, Johan Karlsson Schaffer, and Geir Ulfstein, 1–31. Cambridge: Cambridge University Press, 2013.

Forowicz, Magdalena. *The Reception of International Law in the European Court of Human Rights*. International Courts and Tribunals Series. Oxford and New York: Oxford University Press, 2010.

Forsythe, David P. *Human Rights in International Relations*. New York: Cambridge University Press, 2006.

Fredman FBA, Sandra. *Human Rights Transformed: Positive Rights and Positive Duties*. Oxford: Oxford University Press, 2008. https://doi.org/10.1093/acprof:oso/9780199272761.001.0001.

Freitas, Tiago Fidalgo de. "Theories of Judicial Behavior and the Law: Taking Stock and Looking Ahead." In *Judicial Activism: An Interdisciplinary Approach to the American and European Experiences*, edited by Luís Pereira Coutinho, Massimo La Torre, and Steven D. Smith, 105–17. Cham and New York: Springer, 2015.

García-Montoya, Laura, and James Mahoney. "Critical Event Analysis in Case Study Research." *Sociological Methods & Research*, July 8, 2020, 0049124120926201. https://doi.org/10.1177/0049124120926201.

Garoupa, Nuno, and Tom Ginsburg. *Judicial Reputation: A Comparative Theory*. Chicago: University of Chicago Press, 2015.

Gerards, Janneke. "Inadmissibility Decisions of the European Court of Human Rights: A Critique of the Lack of Reasoning." *Human Rights Law Review* 14, no. 1 (2014): 148–58. https://doi.org/10.1093/hrlr/ngt044.

Gerards, Janneke. "Margin of Appreciation and Incrementalism in the Case Law of the European Court of Human Rights." *Human Rights Law Review* 18, no. 3 (2018): 495–515. https://doi.org/10.1093/hrlr/ngy017.

Ginsburg, Tom. "Bounded Discretion in International Judicial Lawmaking." *Virginia Journal of International Law* 45, no. 3 (2005): 631–73.

Gismondi, Giovanna. "Denial of Justice: The Latest Indigenous Land Disputes before the European Court of Human Rights and the Need for an Expansive Interpretation of Protocol 1." *Yale Human Rights and Development Law Journal* 18 (2016): 1–55.

Glas, Lize R. "From Interlaken to Copenhagen: What Has Become of the Proposals Aiming to Reform the Functioning of the European Court of Human Rights?" *Human Rights Law Review* 20, no. 1 (2020): 121–51. https://doi.org/10.1093/hrlr/ngaa001.

Goldhaber, Michael. *A People's History of the European Court of Human Rights: A People's History of the European Court of Human Rights.* New Brunswick: Rutgers University Press, 2008.

Goldston, James A. "Public Interest Litigation in Central and Eastern Europe: Roots, Prospects, and Challenges." *Human Rights Quarterly 28*, no. 2 (2006): 492–527.

Goldston, James A. "The Struggle for Roma Rights: Arguments That Have Worked." *Human Rights Quarterly* 32, no. 2 (2010): 311–25.

Gordon, Rebecca. *Mainstreaming Torture: Ethical Approaches in the Post-9/11 United States.* Oxford and New York: Oxford University Press, 2014.

Gourgourinis, Anastasios. "The Distinction between Interpretation and Application of Norms in International Adjudication." *Journal of International Dispute Settlement* 2, no. 1 (2011): 31–57. https://doi.org/10.1093/jnlids/idq022.

Greenberg, Karen J., ed. *The Torture Debate in America.* Cambridge and New York: Cambridge University Press, 2005.

Greenberg, Karen J., and Joshua L. Dratel, eds. *The Torture Papers: The Road to Abu Ghraib*, 1st edition. New York: Cambridge University Press, 2005.

Greer, Steven. "Is the Prohibition against Torture, Cruel, Inhuman and Degrading Treatment Really 'Absolute' in International Human Rights Law?" *Human Rights Law Review* 15, no. 1 (2015): 101–37. https://doi.org/10.1093/hrlr/ngu035.

Greer, Steven. "The Interpretation of the European Convention on Human Rights: Universal Principle or Margin of Appreciation?" *UCL Human Rights Review* 3 (2010): 1–14.

Greer, Steven. "Should Police Threats to Torture Suspects Always Be Severely Punished? Reflections on the Gäfgen Case." *Human Rights Law Review* 11, no. 1 (2011): 67–89. https://doi.org/10.1093/hrlr/ngr001.

Greer, Steven C. *The Margin of Appreciation: Interpretation and Discretion under the European Convention on Human Rights.* Strasbourg: Council of Europe, 2000.

Greer, Steven, and Luzius Wildhaber. "Revisiting the Debate about 'Constitutionalising' the European Court of Human Rights." *Human Rights Law Review* 12, no. 4 (2012): 655–87.

Gregg, Benjamin. *Human Rights as Social Construction*. New York: Cambridge University Press, 2011.

Guelke, Adrian. "Loyalist and Republican Perceptions of the Northern Ireland Conflict: The UDA and Provisional IRA." In *Political Violence and Terror: Motifs and Motivations*, edited by Peter H. Merkl, 91–122. Berkeley: University of California Press, 1986.

Haddad, Heidi Nichols. *The Hidden Hands of Justice: NGOs, Human Rights, and International Courts*. New York: Cambridge University Press, 2018. https://doi.org/10.1017/9781108557313.

Haddad, Heidi Nichols. "Judicial Institution Builders: NGOs and International Human Rights Courts." *Journal of Human Rights* 11, no. 1 (2012): 126–49. https://doi.org/10.1080/14754835.2012.648154.

Hadfield, Gillian K. "Judicial Competence and the Interpretation of Incomplete Contracts." *Journal of Legal Studies* 23, no. 1 (1994): 159–84. https://doi.org/10.1086/467919.

Hafner-Burton, Emilie M., Edward D. Mansfield, and Jon C. W. Pevehouse. "Human Rights Institutions, Sovereignty Costs and Democratization." *British Journal of Political Science* 45, no. 1 (2015): 1–27. https://doi.org/10.1017/S0007123413000240.

Hafner-Burton, Emilie M., and Kiyoteru Tsutsui. "Human Rights in a Globalizing World: The Paradox of Empty Promises." *American Journal of Sociology* 110, no. 5 (2005): 1373–1411. https://doi.org/10.1086/428442.

Haglund, Jillienne. *Regional Courts, Domestic Politics, and the Struggle for Human Rights*. Cambridge: Cambridge University Press, 2020. https://doi.org/10.1017/9781108776561.

Hajjar Lisa, *Torture: A Sociology of Violence and Human Rights*. New York; London: Routledge, 2013.

Harmsen, Robert. "The European Convention on Human Rights after Enlargement." *The International Journal of Human Rights* 5, no. 4 (2010): 18–43.

Hartmann, Jacques. "A Danish Crusade for the Reform of the European Court of Human Rights." *EJIL: Talk!* (blog), November 14, 2017. www.ejiltalk.org/a-danish-crusade-for-the-reform-of-the-european-court-of-human-rights/.

Haslam, S. Alexander, and Stephen Reicher. "Beyond the Banality of Evil: Three Dynamics of an Interactionist Social Psychology of Tyranny." *Personality and Social Psychology Bulletin* 33, no. 5 (2007): 615–22.

Hawkins, Darren G., David A. Lake, Daniel L. Nielson, and Michael J. Tierney, eds. *Delegation and Agency in International Organizations*. Cambridge: Cambridge University Press, 2006.

Hawkins, Darren, and Wade Jacoby. "Agent Permeability, Principal Delegation and the European Court of Human Rights." *The Review of International Organizations* 3, no. 1 (2008): 1–28. https://doi.org/10.1007/s11558-007-9014-1.

Helfer, Laurence R. "The Burdens and Benefits of Brighton." *ESIL Reflections* 1, no. 1 (2012): 1–6.

Helfer, Laurence R., and Karen J. Alter. "Legitimacy and Lawmaking: A Tale of Three International Courts." *Theoretical Inquiries in Law* 14, no. 2 (2013): 479–504. https://doi.org/10.1515/til-2013-024.

Helfer, Laurence R. "Redesigning the European Court of Human Rights: Embeddedness as a Deep Structural Principle of the European Human Rights Regime." *European Journal of International Law* 19, no. 1 (2008): 125–59.

Helfer, Laurence R., and Clare Ryan. "LGBT Rights as Mega-Politics: Litigating before the ECtHR," Duke Law School Public Law & Legal Theory Series No. 2021-32, January 15, 2022. https://doi.org/10.2139/ssrn.3867604.

Helfer, Laurence R., and Anne-Marie Slaughter. "Why States Create International Tribunals: A Response to Professors Posner and Yoo." *California Law Review* 93, no. 3 (2005): 899–956.

Helfer, Laurence R., and Erik Voeten. "International Courts as Agents of Legal Change: Evidence from LGBT Rights in Europe." *International Organization* 68, no. 1 (2014): 77–110. https://doi.org/10.1017/S0020818313000398.

Helfer, Laurence R, and Erik Voeten. "Walking Back Dissents on the European Court of Human Rights: A Rejoinder to Alec Stone Sweet, Wayne Sandholtz and Mads Andenas." *European Journal of International Law* 32, no. 3 (2021): 907–14. https://doi.org/10.1093/ejil/chab058.

Helfer, Laurence R, and Erik Voeten. "Walking Back Human Rights in Europe?" *European Journal of International Law* 31, no. 3 (2020): 797–827. https://doi .org/10.1093/ejil/chaa071.

Heri, Corina. *Responsive Human Rights: Vulnerability, Ill-Treatment and the ECtHR*. Gordonsville: Hart Publishing, 2021.

Heri, Corina. "The ECtHR's Pending Climate Change Case: What's Ill-Treatment Got to Do with It?" *EJIL: Talk!* (blog), December 22, 2020. www.ejiltalk.org/the-ecthrs-pending-climate-change-case-whats-ill-treatment-got-to-do-with-it/.

High-Level Conference on the Future of the European Court of Human Rights. Brighton Declaration (19–20 April). www.echr.coe.int/Documents/Brussels_Declaration_ENG.pdf.

High-Level Conference on the Future of the European Court of Human Rights. Brussels Declaration (2015). www.echr.coe.int/Documents/Brussels_Declaration_ENG.pdf.

High-Level Conference on the Future of the European Court of Human Rights. Copenhagen Declaration (2018). www.echr.coe.int/Documents/Copenhagen_Declaration_ENG.pdf.

High-Level Conference on the Future of the European Court of Human Rights. Interlaken Declaration (2010). www.echr.coe.int/Documents/2010_Interlaken_FinalDeclaration_ENG.pdf.

High-Level Conference on the Future of the European Court of Human Rights. Izmir Declaration (2011). www.echr.coe.int/Documents/2011_Izmir_FinalDeclaration_ENG.pdf.

Hillebrecht, Courtney. *Saving the International Justice Regime: Beyond Backlash against International Courts*. Cambridge and New York: Cambridge University Press, 2021.

Hodson, Loveday. "Activating the Law: Exploring the Legal Responses of NGOs to Gross Rights Violations." In *Making Human Rights Intelligible: Towards a Sociology of Human Rights*, edited by Mikael Rask Madsen and Gert Verschraegen, 267–82. Oxford and Portland: Hart Publishing, 2013.

Hodson, Loveday. *NGOs and the Struggle for Human Rights in Europe*. Oxford and Portland: Hart Publishing, 2011.

Hofmann, Stephanie C., and Andrew I. Yeo. "Business as Usual: The Role of Norms in Alliance Management." *European Journal of International Relations* 21, no. 2 (2015): 377–401. https://doi.org/10.1177/1354066114533978.

Holland, Alisha. *Forbearance as Redistribution: The Politics of Informal Welfare in Latin America*. New York: Cambridge University Press, 2017.

Holland, Alisha C. "Forbearance." *American Political Science Review* 110, no. 2 (2016): 232–46. https://doi.org/10.1017/S0003055416000083.

Huneeus, Alexandra. "Constitutional Lawyers and the Inter-American Court's Varied Authority." *Law and Contemporary Problems* 79, no. 1 (2016): 179–207.

Huneeus, Alexandra, Javier Couso, and Rachel Sieder. "Introduction." In *Cultures of Legality: Judicialization and Political Activism in Latin America*, edited by Javier Couso, Alexandra Huneeus, and Rachel Sieder, 3–22. Cambridge: Cambridge University Press, 2010.

Ikenberry, G. John. *After Victory: Institutions, Strategic Restraint, and the Rebuilding of Order after Major Wars*. Princeton: Princeton University Press, 2001.

Jackson, Miles. "Judicial Avoidance at the European Court of Human Rights: Institutional Authority, the Procedural Turn, and Docket Control." *International Journal of Constitutional Law* 20, no. 3 (2022): 112–*140*.

Jacobs, Alan M. "Social Policy Dynamics." In *The Oxford Handbook of Historical Institutionalism*, edited by Orfeo Fioretos, Tulia G. Falleti, and Adam Sheingate, 340–54. New York: Oxford University Press, 2016.

Johns, Leslie. *Strengthening International Courts: The Hidden Costs of Legalization*. Ann Arbor: University of Michigan Press, 2015.

Johnson, Douglas A., Alberto Mora, and Averell Schmidt. "The Strategic Costs of Torture." *Foreign Affairs*, January 26, 2017. www.foreignaffairs.com/articles/united-states/strategic-costs-torture.

Johnson, Paul James, and Silvia Falcetta. "Sexual Orientation Discrimination and Article 3 of the European Convention on Human Rights: Developing the Protection of Sexual Minorities." *European Law Review*, April 2018, 167–85.

Johnstone, Ian. *The Power of Deliberation: International Law, Politics and Organizations*. Oxford and New York: Oxford University Press, 2011.

Joint Committee on Human Rights (House of Lords, House of Commons). "Counter-Terrorism Policy and Human Rights (Seventeenth Report): Bringing Human

Rights Back In – Human Rights Joint Committee." London, March 25, 2010. https://publications.parliament.uk/pa/jt200910/jtselect/jtrights/86/8607.htm.

Jurkovich, Michelle. "What Isn't a Norm? Redefining the Conceptual Boundaries of 'Norms' in the Human Rights Literature." *International Studies Review* 22, no. 3 (2020): 693–711. https://doi.org/10.1093/isr/viz040.

Kahn, Paul W. *Sacred Violence: Torture, Terror, and Sovereignty*. Ann Arbor: University of Michigan Press, 2009.

Kälin, Walter. "The Struggle against Torture." *International Review of the Red Cross* 12, no. 324 (1998): 433–44.

Kamminga, M. T. "The Thematic Procedures of the UN Commission on Human Rights." *Netherlands International Law Review* 34, no. 3 (1987): 299–323. https://doi.org/10.1017/S0165070X00010342.

Kapardis, Andreas. *Psychology and Law: A Critical Introduction*. New York: Cambridge University Press, 2010.

Kapiszewski, Diana. "Tactical Balancing: High Court Decision Making on Politically Crucial Cases." *Law and Society Review* 45, no. 2 (2011): 471–506. https://doi.org/10.1111/j.1540-5893.2011.00437.x.

Kapotas, Panos, and Vassilis P. Tzevelekos. *Building Consensus on European Consensus: Judicial Interpretation of Human Rights in Europe and Beyond*. Cambridge: Cambridge University Press, 2019.

Kassimeris, Christos, and Lina Tsoumpanou. "The Impact of the European Convention on the Protection of Human Rights and Fundamental Freedoms on Turkey's EU Candidacy." *The International Journal of Human Rights* 12, no. 3 (2008): 329–45.

Keck, Margaret E., and Kathryn Sikkink. *Activists Beyond Borders: Advocacy Networks in International Politics*. Ithaca; London: Cornell University Press, 1998.

Keller, Helen, and Corina Heri. "Deliberation and Drafting: European Court of Human Rights (ECtHR)." In *Max Planck Encyclopedia of International Procedural Law (EiPro)*. Oxford Public International Law, May 2018. https://opil.ouplaw.com/view/10.1093/law-mpeipro/e3210.013.3210/law-mpeipro-e3210.

Keller, Helen, and Corina Heri. "The Future Is Now: Climate Cases before the ECtHR." *Nordic Journal of Human Rights* 40, no. 10 (2022): 153–174. https://doi.org/10.1080/18918131.2022.2064074.

Keller, Helen, and Alec Stone Sweet. "Introduction: The Reception of the ECHR in National Legal Order." In *A Europe of Rights: The Impact of the ECHR on National Legal Systems*, edited by Helen Keller and Alec Stone Sweet, 3–26. Oxford, New York: Oxford University Press, 2008.

Kelly, Tobias. *This Side of Silence: Human Rights, Torture, and the Recognition of Cruelty*. Philadelphia: University of Pennsylvania Press, 2012.

Knox, John H., and Ramin Pejan, eds. *The Human Right to a Healthy Environment*. Cambridge: Cambridge University Press, 2018.

Koch, Ida Elisabeth. *Human Rights As Indivisible Rights: The Protection of Socio-Economic Demands under the European Convention on Human Rights*. Leiden, Boston: Martinus Nijhoff Publishers, 2009.

Krahenmann, Sandra. "Positive Obligations in Human Rights Treaties." Graduate Institute of International and Development Studies, 2012.

Krippendorff, Klaus. *Content Analysis: An Introduction to Its Methodology*. Thousand Oaks: SAGE Publications, 2018.

Krisch, Nico. "The Decay of Consent: International Law in an Age of Global Public Goods." *American Journal of International Law* 108, no. 1 (2014): 1–40. https://doi.org/10.5305/amerjintelaw.108.1.0001.

Krisch, Nico. "Liquid Authority in Global Governance." *International Theory* 9, no. 2 (July 2017): 237–60. https://doi.org/10.1017/S1752971916000269.

Krisch, Nico, and Ezgi Yildiz. "The Many Paths of Change in International Law: A Frame" in *The Many Paths of Change in International Law*, edited by Nico Krisch and Ezgi Yildiz, Oxford and New York: Oxford University Press, 2023.

Krook, Mona Lena, and Jacqui True. "Rethinking the Life Cycles of International Norms: The United Nations and the Global Promotion of Gender Equality." *European Journal of International Relations* 18, no. 1 (2012): 103–27. https://doi.org/10.1177/1354066110380963.

Kurban, Dilek. *Limits of Supranational Justice: The European Court of Human Rights and Turkey's Kurdish Conflict*. Cambridge and New York: Cambridge University Press, 2020.

Kurban, Dilek. "Protecting Marginalised Individuals and Minorities in the ECtHR: Litigation and Jurisprudence in Turkey." In *The European Court of Human Rights and the Rights of Marginalised Individuals and Minorities in National Context*, edited by Dia Anagnostou and Evangelia Psychogiopoulou, 159–82. Boston and Leiden: Martinus Nijhoff, 2010.

LaFleur, Vinca. "A View from America: Tactical Unity, Strategic Divide." In *Europe Confronts Terrorism*, edited by Karin Von Hippel, 191–207. Basingstoke and New York: Palgrave Macmillan, 2005.

Langford, Malcolm, and Daniel Behn. "Managing Backlash: The Evolving Investment Treaty Arbitrator?" *European Journal of International Law* 29, no. 2 (2018): 551–80. https://doi.org/10.1093/ejil/chy030.

Lantis, Jeffrey S. "Theories of International Norm Contestation: Structure and Outcomes." *Oxford Research Encyclopedia of Politics*, June 28, 2017. https://doi.org/10.1093/acrefore/9780190228637.013.590.

Larkins, Christopher M. "Judicial Independence and Democratization: A Theoretical and Conceptual Analysis." *American Journal of Comparative Law* 44, no. 4 (1996): 605–26. https://doi.org/10.2307/840623.

Latour, Bruno. *The Making of Law: An Ethnography of the Conseil d'Etat*. Cambridge and UK: Polity Press, 2010.

Lauren, Paul Gordon. *The Evolution of International Human Rights: Visions Seen*, 3rd edition. Philadelphia: University of Pennsylvania Press, 2011.

Lauritzen, Paul. *The Ethics of Interrogation: Professional Responsibility in an Age of Terror*. Washington, DC: Georgetown University Press, 2013.

Lauterpacht, H., J. Harcourt Barrington, Norman Bentwich, W. Harvey Moore, Patrick Spens, and Mr. Barrington. "The Proposed European Court of Human Rights." *Transactions of the Grotius Society* 35 (1949): 25–47.

Lauterpacht, Hersch. *An International Bill of the Rights of Man*. New York: Columbia University Press, 1945.

Lavrysen, Laurens. *Human Rights in a Positive State: Rethinking the Relationship between Positive and Negative Obligations under the European Convention on Human Rights*, 1st edition. Cambridge and Antwerp and Portland: Intersentia, 2016.

Lavrysen, Laurens, and Natasa Mavronicola. *Coercive Human Rights: Positive Duties to Mobilise the Criminal Law under the ECHR*. Oxford: Hart Publishing, 2020.

Leach, Philip. *Taking a Case to the European Court of Human Rights*, 3rd edition. Oxford and New York: Oxford University Press, 2011.

Letsas, George. "The ECHR as a Living Instrument: Its Meaning and Legitimacy." In *Constituting Europe: The European Court of Human Rights in a National, European and Global Context*, edited by Andreas Føllesdal, Birgit Peters, and Geir Ulfstein, 106–41. New York: Cambridge University Press, 2013.

Letsas, George. "Strasbourg's Interpretive Ethic: Lessons for the International Lawyer." *European Journal of International Law* 21, no. 3 (2010): 509–41.

Letsas, George. *A Theory of Interpretation of the European Convention on Human Rights*. Oxford: Oxford University Press, 2007.

Levitsky, Steven, and Daniel Ziblatt. *How Democracies Die*. New York: Crown, 2018.

Liese, Andrea. "Exceptional Necessity – How Liberal Democracies Contest the Prohibition of Torture and Ill-Treatment When Countering Terrorism." *Journal of International Law and International Relations* 5, no. 1 (2009): 17–48.

Lindquist, Stefanie A, and Frank B. Cross. *Measuring Judicial Activism*. Oxford: Oxford University Press, 2009.

Lixinski, Lucas. "The Consensus Method of Interpretation by the Inter-American Court of Human Rights." *Canadian Journal of Comparative and Contemporary Law* 3, no. 1 (2017): 65–95.

Madsen, Mikael Rask. "The Challenging Authority of the European Court of Human Rights: From Cold War Legal Diplomacy to the Brighton Declaration and Backlash." *Law and Contemporary Problems* 79, no. 1 (2016).

Madsen, Mikael Rask. "From Cold War Instrument to Supreme European Court: The European Court of Human Rights at the Crossroads of International and National Law and Politics." *Law and Social Inquiry* 32, no. 1 (2007): 137–59.

Madsen, Mikael Rask. "International Human Rights and the Transformation of European Society: From 'Free Europe' to the Europe of Human Rights." In *Law and the Formation of Modern Europe: Perspectives from the Historical Sociology of Law*, edited by Mikael Rask Madsen and Chris Thornhill, 245–74. Cambridge: Cambridge University Press, 2014.

Madsen, Mikael Rask. "The Legitimization Strategies of International Judges: The Case of the European Court of Human Rights." In *Selecting Europe's Judges: A Critical Review of the Appointment Procedures to the European Courts*, edited by Michal Bobek, 259–76. Oxford: Oxford University Press, 2015.

Madsen, Mikael Rask. "The Narrowing of the European Court of Human Rights? Legal Diplomacy, Situational Self-Restraint, and the New Vision for the Court." *European Convention on Human Rights Law Review* 2, no. 2 (2021): 180–208. https://doi.org/10.1163/26663236-bja10023.

Madsen, Mikael Rask. "Protracted Institutionalization of the Strasbourg Court: From Legal Diplomacy to Integrationist Jurisprudence." In *The European Court of Human Rights between Law and Politics*, edited by Jonas Christoffersen and Mikael Rask Madsen, 43–61. New York: Oxford University Press, 2011.

Madsen, Mikael Rask. "Rebalancing European Human Rights: Has the Brighton Declaration Engendered a New Deal on Human Rights in Europe?" *Journal of International Dispute Settlement* 9, no. 2 (2018): 199–222.

Madsen, Mikael Rask. "Two-Level Politics and the Backlash against International Courts: Evidence from the Politicisation of the European Court of Human Rights." *The British Journal of Politics and International Relations* 22, no. 4 (2020): 728–38. https://doi.org/10.1177/1369148120948180.

Madsen, Mikael Rask, Pola Cebulak, and Micha Wiebusch. "Backlash against International Courts: Explaining the Forms and Patterns of Resistance to International Courts." *International Journal of Law in Context* 14, no. 2 (2018): 197–220. https://doi.org/10.1017/S1744552318000034.

Mahoney, James, and Kathleen Thelen. "A Theory of Gradual Institutional Change." In *Explaining Institutional Change: Ambiguity, Agency, and Power*, edited by James Mahoney and Kathleen Thelen, 1–37. New York: Cambridge University Press, 2010.

Mandaville, Peter. "Muslim Transnational Identity and State Responses in Europe and the UK after 9/11: Political Community, Ideology and Authority." *Journal of Ethnic and Migration Studies* 35, no. 3 (2009): 491–506.

Marchuk, Iryna, and Marina Aksenova. "The Tale of Yukos and of the Russian Constitutional Court's Rebellion against the European Court of Human Right." *Osservatorio Costituzionale, Associazione Italiana Dei Costituzionalisti (AIC)*, 2017. www.osservatorioaic.it/the-tale-of-yukos-and-of-the-russian-constitutional-court-s-rebellion-against-the-european-court-of-human-rights.html.

Marks, Susan. "Yes, Virginia, Extradition May Breach the European Convention of Human Rights." *The Cambridge Law Journal* 49, no. 2 (1990): 194–97.

Matta, Aaron, and Armen Mazmanyan. "Russia: In Quest for a European Identity." In *Criticism of the European Court of Human Rights: Shifting the*

Convention System: Counter-Dynamics at the National and EU Level, edited by Patricia Popelier, Sarah Lambrecht, and Koen Lemmens, 481–502. Cambridge: Intersentia, 2016.

Mavronicola, Natasa. "Is the Prohibition against Torture and Cruel, Inhuman and Degrading Treatment Absolute in International Human Rights Law? A Reply to Steven Greer." *Human Rights Law Review* 17, no. 3 (2017): 479–98.

Mavronicola, Natasa. *Torture, Inhumanity and Degradation under Article 3 of the ECHR: Absolute Rights and Absolute Wrongs*. Oxford and New York: Hart Publishing, 2021.

Mayer, Jane. "Outsourcing Torture: The Secret History of America's 'Extraordinary Rendition' Program." In *The United States and Torture: Interrogation, Incarceration, and Abuse*, edited by Marjorie Cohn, 137–160. New York and London: New York University Press, 2011.

McCoy, Alfred W. *Torture and Impunity: The U.S. Doctrine of Coercive Interrogation*. Madison, Wisconsin: The University of Wisconsin Press, 2012.

Méndez, Juan E., and Marjory Wentworth. *Taking a Stand: The Evolution of Human Rights*. New York: Palgrave Macmillan, 2011.

Merrills, John. "International Adjudication and Autonomy." In *International Organizations and the Idea of Autonomy: Institutional Independence in the International Legal Order* edited by Richard Collins and Nigel D. White, 160–177. New York: Routledge, 2011.

Mirabella, Daniel. "The Death and Resurrection of Natural Law." *The Western Australian Jurist* 2, no. 1 (2011): 251–60.

Moeckli, Daniel. *Human Rights and Non-Discrimination in the "War on Terror."* Oxford and New York: Oxford University Press, 2008.

Monar, Jörg. "Common Threat and Common Response? The European Union's Counter-Terrorism Strategy and Its Problems." *Government and Opposition* 42, no. 3 (2007): 292–313.

Moral, Ignacio de la Rasilla del. "The Increasingly Marginal Appreciation of the Margin-of-Appreciation Doctrine." *German Law Journal* 7, no. 6 (2006): 611–23. https://doi.org/10.1017/S2071832200004892.

Moravcsik, Andrew. "The Origins of Human Rights Regimes: Democratic Delegation in Postwar Europe." *International Organization* 54, no. 2 (2000): 217–52.

Moses, Lyria Bennett. "Understanding Legal Responses to Technological Change of in Vitro Fertilization." *Minnesota Journal of Law, Science and Technology* 6, no. 2 (2005): 505–618.

Mowbray, Alastair. *The Development of Positive Obligations under the European Convention on Human Rights by the European Court of Human Rights*. Oxford and Portland: Hart Publishing, 2004.

Mowbray, Alastair. "Subsidiarity and the European Convention on Human Rights." *Human Rights Law Review* 15, no. 2 (2015): 313–41.

Moyn, Samuel. *Christian Human Rights*. Philadelphia : University of Pennsylvania Press, 2015.

Moyn, Samuel. *The Last Utopia*. Cambridge, MA: Harvard University Press, 2010.

Müller, Harald, and Carmen Wunderlich. *Norm Dynamics in Multilateral Arms Control: Interests, Conflicts, and Justice*. Athens, and London: University of Georgia Press, 2013.

Neal, Andrew W. "Securitization and Risk at the EU Border: The Origins of FRONTEX." *JCMS: Journal of Common Market Studies* 47, no. 2 (2009): 333–56.

Neier, Aryeh. *The International Human Rights Movement: A History*. Princeton: Princeton University Press, 2012.

Nowak, Manfred, and Elizabeth McArthur. "The Distinction between Torture and Cruel, Inhuman and Degrading Treatment." *Torture* 16, no. 3 (2006): 147–51.

O'Boyle, Michael. "The Imperiled Success of the European Court of Human Rights." In *Trente Ans de Droit Européen Des Droits de l'Homme. Études à La Mémoire de Wolfgang Strasser*, edited by Hanno Hartig, 251–64. Brussels: Nemesis/Bruylant, 2007.

O'Boyle, Michael. "Torture and Emergency Powers under the European Convention on Human Rights: Ireland v. the United Kingdom." *American Journal of International Law* 71, no. 4 (1977): 674–706.

Oette, Lutz. "The Prohibition of Torture and Persons Living in Poverty: From the Margins to the Centre." *International and Comparative Law Quarterly* 70, no. 2 (2021): 307–41. https://doi.org/10.1017/S0020589321000038.

O'Mara, Shane. *Why Torture Doesn't Work: The Neuroscience of Interrogation*. Cambridge, MA: Harvard University Press, 2015.

Onuf, Nicholas. *International Legal Theory: Essays and Engagements, 1966–2006*, 1st edition. New York: Routledge-Cavendish, 2008.

Orakhelashvili, Alexander. "Restrictive Interpretation of Human Rights Treaties in the Recent Jurisprudence of the European Court of Human Rights." *European Journal of International Law* 14, no. 3 (2003): 529–68. https://doi.org/10.1093/ejil/14.3.529.

Pallitto, Robert M. *Torture and State Violence in the United States: A Short Documentary History*, 1st edition. Baltimore: Johns Hopkins University Press, 2011.

Parliamentary Assembly. Procedure for Electing Judges to the European Court of Human Rights, AS/Cdh/Inf (2015) 02 Rev 1 § (2015).

Parry, John T. *Understanding Torture: Law, Violence, and Political Identity*. Ann Arbor: University of Michigan Press, 2010.

Pasnau, Robert. *Thomas Aquinas on Human Nature: A Philosophical Study of Summa Theologiae*. New York: Cambridge University Press, 2002.

Paulo, Norbert. *The Confluence of Philosophy and Law in Applied Ethics*. London: Palgrave Macmillan, 2016.

Pauwelyn, Joost. "Is It International Law or Not, and Does It Even Matter?" In *Is It International Law or Not, and Does It Even Matter?*, edited by Joost Pauwelyn, Ramses A. Wessel, and Jan Wouters, 125–61. Oxford University Press, 2012.

Pauwelyn, Joost, and Manfred Elsig. "The Politics of Treaty Interpretation: Variations and Explanations across International Tribunals." In *Interdisciplinary*

Perspectives on International Law and International Relations: The State of the Art, edited by Jeffrey L. Dunoff and Mark A. Pollack, 445–74. Cambridge: Cambridge University Press, 2012.

Pauwelyn, Joost, Ramses A. Wessel, and Jan Wouters. "When Structures Become Shackles: Stagnation and Dynamics in International Lawmaking." *European Journal of International Law* 25, no. 3 (2014): 733–63. https://doi.org/10.1093/ejil/chu051.

Pavone, Tommaso. *The Ghostwriters: Lawyers and the Politics behind the Judicial Construction of Europe*. Cambridge and New York: Cambridge University Press, 2022.

Phillips, Barry. "The Case for Corporal Punishment in the United Kingdom. Beaten into Submission in Europe?" *International and Comparative Law Quarterly* 43, no. 1 (1994): 153–63. https://doi.org/10.1093/iclqaj/43.1.153.

Poe, Steven C. "The Decision to Repress: An Integrative Theoretical Approach to the Research on Human Rights and Repression." In *Understanding Human Rights Violations: New Systematic Studies*, Sabine C. Carey and Steven C. Poe, 16–38. Burlington: Ashgate, 2004.

Pollack, Mark. "Learning from the Americanists (Again): Theory and Method in the Study of Delegation." *West European Politics* 25, no. 1 (2002): 200–219. https://doi.org/10.1080/713869589.

Pollack, Mark A. "Delegation, Agency, and Agenda Setting in the European Community." *International Organization* 51, no. 1 (1997): 99–134.

Pollack, Mark A. *The Engines of European Integration: Delegation, Agency, and Agenda Setting in the EU*. Oxford: Oxford University Press, 2003.

Pollack, Mark A. "International Court Curbing in Geneva: Lessons from the Paralysis of the WTO Appellate Body." *Governance*. 20 March 2022. https://doi.org/10.1111/gove.12686.

Raffaele, Sabato. "Judicial Dialogue: The Experience of Italy." In *Judicial Dialogue and Human Rights*, edited by Amrei Müller and Hege Elisabeth Kjos, 267–84. New York: Cambridge University Press, 2017.

Ramanzini, Isabela Garbin, and Ezgi Yildiz. "Revamping to Remain Relevant: How Do the European and the Inter-American Human Rights Systems Adapt to Challenges?" *Journal of Human Rights Practice* 12, no. 3 (2020): 768–80. https://doi.org/10.1093/jhuman/huaa038.

Reidy, Aisling. "The Prohibition of Torture: A Guide to the Implementation of Article 3 of the European Convention on Human Rights." Human Rights Handbooks, No.6. Strasbourg: Council of Europe, 2003.

Reidy, Aisling, et al. "Gross Violations of Human Rights: Invoking the European Convention on Human Rights in the Case of Turkey." *Netherlands Quarterly of Human Rights* 15, no. 1 (1997): 161–75.

Reiners, Nina. *Transnational Lawmaking Coalitions for Human Rights*. Cambridge and New York: Cambridge University Press, 2021.

Rejali, Darius. *Torture and Democracy*. Princeton: Princeton University Press, 2009.

Robinson, Oliver C. "Sampling in Interview-Based Qualitative Research: A Theoretical and Practical Guide." *Qualitative Research in Psychology* 11, no. 1 (2014): 25–41. https://doi.org/10.1080/14780887.2013.801543.

Rodley, Nigel, and Matt Pollard. *The Treatment of Prisoners under International Law*. New York: Oxford University Press, 2009.

Ronen, Yael, and Yale Naggan. "Third Parties." In *The Oxford Handbook of International Adjudication*, edited by Cesare P. R. Romano, Karen J. Alter, and Yuval Shany, 806-27. Oxford and New York: Oxford University Press, 2013.

Sahin, Selver B. "Combatting Violence against Women in Turkey: Structural Obstacles." *Contemporary Politics* 28, no. 2 (2022): 204–24. https://doi.org/10.1080/13569775.2021.1992131.

Sandholtz, Wayne. "Dynamics of International Norm Change: Rules against Wartime Plunder." *European Journal of International Relations* 14, no. 1 (2008): 101–31. https://doi.org/10.1177/1354066107087766.

Sandholtz, Wayne. "International Norm Change." *Oxford Research Encyclopedia of Politics*, June 28, 2017. https://doi.org/10.1093/acrefore/9780190228637.013.588.

Sandholtz, Wayne, and Kendall W. Stiles. *International Norms and Cycles of Change*. Oxford and New York: Oxford University Press, 2008.

Scharf, Michael P. "Seizing the 'Grotian Moment': Accelerated Formation of Customary International Law in Times of Fundamental Change." *Cornell International Law Journal* 43, no. 3 (2010): 439–69.

Schiemann, John W. *Does Torture Work?* Oxford and New York: Oxford University Press, 2018.

Schlüter, Karen. "The Council of Europe, the Standard Setter." In *Human Rights in Europe: A Fragmented Regime?* edited by Malte Brosig, 30–56. Frankfurt am Main: Peter Lang AG, 2006.

Schmidt, Averell, and Kathryn Sikkink. "Breaking the Ban? The Heterogeneous Impact of US Contestation of the Torture Norm." *Journal of Global Security Studies* 4, no. 1 (2019): 105–22. https://doi.org/10.1093/jogss/ogy036.

Scribner, Druscilla, and Tracy Slagter. "Recursive Norm Development: The Role of Supranational Courts." *Global Policy* 8, no. 3 (2017): 322–32. https://doi.org/10.1111/1758-5899.12453.

Seawright, Jason, and John Gerring. "Case Selection Techniques in Case Study Research: A Menu of Qualitative and Quantitative Options." *Political Research Quarterly* 61, no. 2 (2008): 294–308. https://doi.org/10.1177/1065912907313077.

Senate Select Committee on Intelligence, Search, and Dianne Feinstein. *The Senate Intelligence Committee Report on Torture: Committee Study of the Central Intelligence Agency's Detention and Interrogation Program*. Brooklyn: Melville House, 2014.

Shapiro, Martin. *Courts: A Comparative and Political Analysis*. Chicago: University of Chicago Press, 1986.

Shapiro, Martin, and Alec Stone Sweet. *On Law, Politics, and Judicialization*, 1st edition. Oxford and New York: Oxford University Press, 2002.

Shue, Henry. *Basic Rights: Subsistence, Affluence, and U.S. Foreign Policy*. Princeton: Princeton University Press, 1996.

Sikkink, Kathryn. *Evidence for Hope: Making Human Rights Work in the 21st Century*. Princeton: Princeton University Press, 2017.

Smet, Stijn. "Conflicts between Absolute Rights: A Reply to Steven Greer." *Human Rights Law Review* 13, no. 3 (2013): 469–98.

Snyder, Sarah B. *Human Rights Activism and the End of the Cold War: A Transnational History of the Helsinki Network*. Cambridge: Cambridge University Press, 2011.

Soave, Tommaso. *The Everyday Makers of International Law: From Great Halls to Back Rooms*. Cambridge: Cambridge University Press, 2022.

Soley, Ximena, and Silvia Steininger. "Parting Ways or Lashing Back? Withdrawals, Backlash and the Inter-American Court of Human Rights." *International Journal of Law in Context* 14, no. 2 (2018): 237–57. https://doi.org/10.1017/S1744552318000058.

Spano, Robert. "The Future of the European Court of Human Rights – Subsidiarity, Process-Based Review and the Rule of Law." *Human Rights Law Review* 18, no. 3 (2018): 473–94.

Spano, Robert. "Universality or Diversity of Human Rights? Strasbourg in the Age of Subsidiarity." *Human Rights Law Review* 14, no. 3 (2014): 487–502.

Spier, Jaap. "'There Is No Future without Addressing Climate Change.'" *Journal of Energy and Natural Resources Law* 37, no. 2 (2019): 181–204. https://doi.org/10.1080/02646811.2019.1565197.

Sprinzak, Ehud. "Right-wing Terrorism in a Comparative Perspective: The Case of Split Delegitimization." *Terrorism and Political Violence* 7, no. 1 (1995): 17–43.

Staunton, Eglantine, and Jason Ralph. "The Responsibility to Protect Norm Cluster and the Challenge of Atrocity Prevention: An Analysis of the European Union's Strategy in Myanmar." *European Journal of International Relations* 26, no. 3 (,2020): 660–86. https://doi.org/10.1177/1354066119883001.

Steinberg, Richard H. "The Decline of Global Trade Negotiations – and the Rise of Judicial and Regional Alternatives." *Journal of Scholarly Perspectives* 5, no. 01 (2009). https://escholarship.org/uc/item/3q08n2vf.

Steinberg, Richard H. "Judicial Lawmaking at the WTO: Discursive, Constitutional, and Political Constraints." *American Journal of International Law* 98, no. 2 (2004): 247–75. https://doi.org/10.2307/3176728.

Steininger, Silvia. "Creating Loyalty: Communication Practices in the European and Inter-American Human Rights Regimes." *Global Constitutionalism* 11, no. 2 (2022): 161-196. https://doi.org/10.1017/S2045381721000241.

Stiansen, Øyvind. "Directing Compliance? Remedial Approach and Compliance with European Court of Human Rights Judgments." *British Journal of Political Science* 51, no. 2 (2021): 899–907. https://doi.org/10.1017/S0007123419000292.

Stiansen, Øyvind, and Erik Voeten. "Backlash and Judicial Restraint: Evidence from the European Court of Human Rights." *International Studies Quarterly* 64, no. 4 (2020): 770–84. https://doi.org/10.1093/isq/sqaa047.

Stimmer, Anette. "Beyond Internalization: Alternate Endings of the Norm Life Cycle." *International Studies Quarterly* 63, no. 2 (2019): 270–80. https://doi.org/10.1093/isq/sqz001.

Stone, Geoffrey R. "Selective Judicial Activism." *Texas Law Review* 89, no. 6 (2011): 1423–32.

Stone Sweet, Alec. "The European Court of Justice and the Judicialization of EU Governance." *Living Reviews in European Governance* 5, no. 2 (2010): 1–50.

Stone Sweet, Alec, and Thomas L. Brunell. "Trustee Courts and the Judicialization of International Regimes: The Politics of Majoritarian Activism in the European Convention on Human Rights, the European Union, and the World Trade Organization." *Journal of Law and Courts* 1, no. 1 (2013): 61–88.

Stone Sweet, Alec, Wayne Sandholtz, and Mads Andenas. "Dissenting Opinions and Rights Protection in the European Court: A Reply to Laurence Helfer and Erik Voeten." *European Journal of International Law* 32, no. 3 (2021): 897–906. https://doi.org/10.1093/ejil/chab057.

Stone Sweet, Alec, Wayne Sandholtz, and Mads Andenas. "The Failure to Destroy the Authority of the European Court of Human Rights: 2010–2018," *The Law and Practice of International Courts and Tribunals* 21, no. 2 (2022): 244–77.

Stoyanova, Vladislava. "Fault, Knowledge and Risk within the Framework of Positive Obligations under the European Convention on Human Rights." *Leiden Journal of International Law* 33, no. 3 (2020): 601–20. https://doi.org/10.1017/S0922156520000163.

Streeck, Wolfgang, and Kathleen Thelen, eds. *Beyond Continuity: Institutional Change in Advanced Political Economies*. Oxford and New York: Oxford University Press, 2005.

Streeck, Wolfgang, and Kathleen Thelen, "Introduction: Institutional Change in Advanced Political Economies." In *Beyond Continuity: Institutional Change in Advanced Political Economies*, edited by Wolfgang Streeck and Kathleen Thelen, 1–39. Oxford: Oxford University Press, 2005.

Stroup, Sarah S., and Wendy H. Wong. *The Authority Trap: Strategic Choices of International NGOs*. Ithaca: Cornell University Press, 2017.

Tallberg, Jonas. "The Anatomy of Autonomy: An Institutional Account of Variation in Supranational Influence." *JCMS: Journal of Common Market Studies* 38, no. 5 (2000): 843–64. https://doi.org/10.1111/1468-5965.00267.

Tallberg, Jonas. "Delegation to Supranational Institutions: Why, How, and with What Consequences?" *West European Politics* 25, no. 1 (2002): 23–46. https://doi.org/10.1080/713601584.

Tapp, June Louin. "Psychology and the Law: An Overture." *Annual Review of Psychology* 27, no. 1 (1976): 359–404.

Thatcher, Mark, and Alec Stone Sweet. "Theory and Practice of Delegation to Non-Majoritarian Institutions." *West European Politics* 25, no. 1 (2002): 1–22. https://doi.org/10.1080/713601583.

Theilen, Jens T. *European Consensus between Strategy and Principle*. Baden-Baden: Nomos Publishers, 2021.

Thomas, Daniel C. *The Helsinki Effect: International Norms, Human Rights, and the Demise of Communism*. Princeton: Princeton University Press, 2001.

Torres, Felix E. "Reparations: To What End? Developing the State's Positive Duties to Address Socio-Economic Harms in Post-Conflict Settings through the European Court of Human Rights." *European Journal of International Law* 32, no. 3 (2021): 807–34.

UN General Assembly. Basic Principles and Guidelines on the Right to a Remedy and Reparation for Victims of Gross Violations of International Human Rights Law and Serious Violations of International Humanitarian Law, Resolution 60/147 Resolution 60/147 § (2005). www.ohchr.org/EN/ProfessionalInterest/Pages/RemedyAndReparation.aspx.

UN General Assembly. Convention against Torture and Other Cruel, Inhuman or Degrading Treatment or Punishment, United Nations, Treaty Series, 1465, p. 85, § (1987).

UN Human Rights Committee (HRC). General comment no. 31 [80], The nature of the general legal obligation imposed on States Parties to the Covenant, CCPR/C/21/Rev.1/Add.13 § (2004).

UN Voluntary Fund for Victims of Torture. "Interpretation of Torture in the Light of the Practice and Jurisprudence of International Bodies," 2011. www.ohchr.org/Documents/Issues/Torture/UNVFVT/Interpretation_torture_2011_EN.pdf.

Van den Eynde, Laura. "An Empirical Look at the Amicus Curiae Practice of Human Rights NGOs before the European Court of Human Rights." *Netherlands Quarterly of Human Rights* 31, no. 3 (2013): 271–313.

Venzke, Ingo. "Between Power and Persuasion: On International Institutions' Authority in Making Law." *Transnational Legal Theory* 4, no. 3 (2013): 354–73. https://doi.org/10.5235/20414005.4.3.354.

Venzke, Ingo. *How Interpretation Makes International Law: On Semantic Change and Normative Twists*. Oxford and New York: Oxford University Press, 2012.

Venzke, Ingo. "Understanding the Authority of International Courts and Tribunals: On Delegation and Discursive Construction." *Theoretical Inquiries in Law* 14, no. 2 (2013): 381–410. https://doi.org/10.1515/til-2013-020.

Vet, Freek van der. "Seeking Life, Finding Justice: Russian NGO Litigation and Chechen Disappearances before the European Court of Human Rights." *Human Rights Review* 13, no. 3 (2012): 303–25. https://doi.org/10.1007/s12142-012-0226-2.

Vila, Marisa Iglesias. "Subsidiarity, Margin of Appreciation and International Adjudication within a Cooperative Conception of Human Rights." *International Journal of Constitutional Law* 15, no. 2 (2017): 393–413. https://doi.org/10.1093/icon/mox035.

Vincent, Andrew. *The Politics of Human Rights*. Oxford and New York: Oxford University Press, 2010.

Voeten, Erik. "The Impartiality of International Judges: Evidence from the European Court of Human Rights." *American Political Science Review* 102, no. 4 (2008): 417–33. https://doi.org/10.1017/S0003055408080398.

Voeten, Erik. "Making Sense of the Design of International Institutions." *Annual Review of Political Science* 22, no. 1 (2019): 147–63. https://doi.org/10.1146/annurev-polisci-041916-021108.

Voeten, Erik. "The Politics of International Judicial Appointments: Evidence from the European Court of Human Rights." *International Organization* 61, no. 4 (2007): 669–701. https://doi.org/10.1017/S0020818307070233.

Voeten, Erik. "Populism and Backlashes against International Courts." *Perspectives on Politics* 18, no. 2 (2020): 407–22. https://doi.org/10.1017/S1537592719000975.

Von Hippel, Karin. "Introduction: Europe Confronts Terrorism." In *Europe Confronts Terrorism*, edited by Karin Von Hippel, 1–14. Basingstoke and New York: Palgrave Macmillan, 2005.

Walklate, Sandra. *Imagining The Victim Of Crime*. Maidenhead: Open University Press, 2007.

Wallace, Angus EM. "The European Court of Human Rights: A Tool for Improving Prison Health." *The Lancet Public Health* 5, no. 2 (2020): e78–79. https://doi.org/10.1016/S2468-2667(19)30258-0.

Wallace, J. Clifford. "Jurisprudence of Judicial Restraint: A Return to the Moorings." *George Washington Law Review* 50, no. 1 (1981): 1–16.

Warbrick, Colin. "The European Response to Terrorism in an Age of Human Rights." *European Journal of International Law* 15, no. 5 (2004): 989–1018.

Webster, Elaine. *Dignity, Degrading Treatment and Torture in Human Rights Law: The Ends of Article 3 of the European Convention on Human Rights*. London: Routledge, 2018.

Weissbrodt, David. "The Role of the Human Rights Committee in Interpreting and Developing Humanitarian Law." *University of Pennsylvania Journal of International Law 31*, no. 4 (2010): 1185–1238.

Wiener, Antje. *Contestation and Constitution of Norms in Global International Relations*. Cambridge: Cambridge University Press, 2018.

Wildhaber, Luzius. "'Rethinking the European Court of Human Rights'." In *The European Court of Human Rights between Law and Politics*, edited by Jonas Christoffersen and Mikael Rask Madsen, 204–30. New York: Oxford University Press, 2011.

Williams, Andrew. *EU Human Rights Policies: A Study in Irony*. Oxford, New York: Oxford University Press, 2004.

Winston, Carla. "Norm Structure, Diffusion, and Evolution: A Conceptual Approach." *European Journal of International Relations* 24, no. 3 (2018): 638–61. https://doi.org/10.1177/1354066117720794.

Xenos, Dimitris. *The Positive Obligations of the State under the European Convention of Human Rights*. London and New York: Routledge, 2012.

Yildiz, Ezgi. "A Court with Many Faces: Judicial Characters and Modes of Norm Development in the European Court of Human Rights." *European Journal of International Law* 31, no. 1 (2020): 73–99. https://doi.org/10.1093/ejil/chaa014.

Yildiz, Ezgi. "Enduring Practices in Changing Circumstances: A Comparison of the European Court of Human Rights and the Inter-American Court of Human Rights." *Temple International & Comparative Law Journal* 34, no. 2 (2020): 309–38.

Yildiz, Ezgi. "Extraterritoriality Reconsidered: Functional Boundaries as Repositories of Jurisdiction." In *The Extraterritoriality of Law: History, Theory, Politics*, edited by Daniel S. Margolies, Umut Özsu, Maïa Pal, and Ntina Tzouvala, 215–27. Oxon and New York: Routledge, 2019.

Yildiz, Ezgi. "Judicial Creativity in the Making: The Pilot Judgment Procedure a Decade after Its Inception." *Interdisciplinary Journal of Human Rights Law* 8, no. 1 (2015): 81–102.

Yildiz, Ezgi, "Interpretative Evolution of the Norm Prohibiting Torture and Inhuman or Degrading Treatment under the European Convention" in *Language and Legal Interpretation in International Law*, edited by Anne Lise Kjær and Joanna Lam, 295-314. New York: Oxford University Press, 2022.

Yildiz, Ezgi, and Umut Yüksel. "Understanding the Limitations of Behavioralism: Lessons from the Field of Maritime Delimitation." *German Law Journal* 23, no. 3 (2022): 413–30. https://doi.org/10.1017/glj.2022.24.

Yildiz, Ezgi, Umut Yüksel, Chanya Punyakumpol, and Carlos Carrillo. "New Norms in Old Regimes: Judicial Strategies for Importing Environmental Norms." *Unpublished Manuscript*, 2022.

Zarbiyev, Fuad. "Judicial Activism." In *Max Planck Encyclopedia of International Procedural Law (EiPro)*. Oxford: Oxford University Press, 2018. https://opil.ouplaw.com/view/10.1093/law-mpeipro/e2864.013.2864/law-mpeipro-e2864?rskey=BMfOnJ&result=1&prd=MPIL

Zarbiyev, Fuad. "Judicial Activism in International Law – A Conceptual Framework for Analysis." *Journal of International Dispute Settlement* 3, no. 2 (2012): 247–78. https://doi.org/10.1093/jnlids/ids005.

Zarbiyev, Fuad. "Saying Credibly What the Law Is: On Marks of Authority in International Law." *Journal of International Dispute Settlement* 9, no. 2 (2018): 291–314. https://doi.org/10.1093/jnlids/idy004.

Zimmermann, Doron. "The European Union and Post-9/11 Counterterrorism: A Reappraisal." *Studies in Conflict & Terrorism* 29, no. 2 (2006): 123–45.

Zwingel, Susanne. "How Do Norms Travel? Theorizing International Women's Rights in Transnational Perspective." *International Studies Quarterly* 56, no. 1 (2012): 115–29. https://doi.org/10.1111/j.1468-2478.2011.00701.x.

INDEX

For EU product safety concerns, contact us at Calle de José Abascal, 56–1°,
28003 Madrid, Spain or eugpsr@cambridge.org.

www.ingramcontent.com/pod-product-compliance
Lightning Source LLC
Chambersburg PA
CBHW050454270525
27275CB00004B/215

* 9 7 8 1 0 0 9 1 0 0 0 4 5 *